GLOBAL ACADEME

Global Academe
Engaging Intellectual Discourse

Edited by

Silvia Nagy-Zekmi and Karyn Hollis

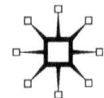

GLOBAL ACADEME
Copyright © Silvia Nagy-Zekmi and Karyn Hollis, 2012

All rights reserved.

First published in 2012 by
PALGRAVE MACMILLAN®
in the United States—a division of St. Martin's Press LLC,
175 Fifth Avenue, New York, NY 10010.

Where this book is distributed in the UK, Europe and the rest of the
World, this is by Palgrave Macmillan, a division of Macmillan Publishers
Limited, registered in England, company number 785998, of
Houndmills, Basingstoke, Hampshire RG21 6XS.

Palgrave Macmillan is the global academic imprint of the above
companies and has companies and representatives throught the world.

Palgrave® and Macmillan® are registered trademarks in the United
States, the United Kingdom, Europe and other countries.

ISBN 978-1-349-29819-8   ISBN 978-1-137-01493-1 (eBook)
DOI 10.1057/9781137014931
Library of Congress Cataloging-in-Publication Data

Global academe : engaging intellectual discourse / edited by
  Silvia Nagy-Zekmi and Karyn Hollis.
    p. cm.
  Includes bibliographical references.
  1. Intellectuals—United States. 2. College teachers—United States.
  I. Nagy, Silvia, 1953– II. Hollis, Karyn L., 1948–
  HM728.G56 2011
  305.5'5201—dc23   2011023388

A catalogue record of the book is available from the British Library.

Design by Integra Software Services

First edition: January 2012

Contents

Figures	vii
Acknowledgments	ix
Contributors	xi
Introduction: The Location of Public Intellectual Discourse *Silvia Nagy-Zekmi and Karyn Hollis*	1

Part I Homo Academicus: Making the Case

1. In the Marketplace of Illusion: The Public Intellectual in a Landscape of Mediated Humanness — 15
   Joseph Robertson

2. From Rational to Relevant: What Counts as "Public" Knowledge? — 39
   J. Scott Andrews

3. From the Organic through the Specific to the Accidental: Cultural Studies and the (Potential) Proliferation of Contemporary Categories of the Academic as Public Intellectual — 51
   Handel K. Wright

4. Beyond the Specialist/Generalist Framework: Reflections on Three Decades of the Comparative History of Intellectuals Discourse — 61
   Kjetil Ansgar Jakobsen

5. Homo Academicus, Quo Vadis? — 85
   Jan Servaes

6. The Enemy Within?: Intellectuals, Violence, and the "Postmodern Condition" — 99
   Matteo Stocchetti

7 Far Out! Exile, Hipsterism, and the Existential
   Situation of the African American Public Intellectual   121
   Adebe DeRango-Adem

8 Language and Limitations: Toward a New Praxis of
   Public Intellectualism   135
   Kathryn Comer and Tim Jensen

Part II Case Studies

9 Should Philosophers Become Public Intellectuals?   151
   Samuel C. Rickless

10 The Ethics of Public Intellectual Work   163
   David Beard

11 Multilingual Academics in a Global World and the
   Burden of Responsibility   179
   Lahcen E. Ezzaher

12 International Perspectives on Speaking Truth to Power   189
   D. Ray Heisey and Ehsan Shaghasemi

13 Imagined Community Service: Queering Narratives of
   Place and Time in Service Learning   199
   Amin Emika

Figures

8.1 Frequency of use of "public intellectual" in print
media, 1980–2005, "Major Papers," Nexis Database   138

Acknowledgments

The idea for *Global Academe* came from the numerous discussions we, the editors, had with one another and with others (colleagues, friends) about the role of intellectuals in society, a topic we already explored in *Truth to Power: Public Intellectuals In and Out of Academe*, published in 2010. Since we observed that discourses of academics and the so-called public intellectuals are sometimes at odds with each other, we wanted to get to the bottom of this (pseudo?) dichotomy to find out where the fault lines were and to discover how such a complex topic might be tackled. After much debate, we approached the issue with a deconstructivist spirit.

The authors in this volume—scholars in different phases of their careers, with diverse interests and trajectories who contributed to their own field of study (Philosophy, Rhetoric, and Communication, for example), and/or to interdisciplinary fields, such as cultural studies—enriched the debate by entrusting their articles to us, for which we are grateful.

We are indebted to John Pugh for offering us the image of his mural, "An Academe," for the cover of this book. Both his art and his generous gesture are much appreciated.

With regard to the production of the manuscript, our special recognition goes to graduate assistant Paula Plastic, who helped us with the first revision and formatting. Burke Gerstenschlager, editor, and Kaylan Connally, editorial assistant at Palgrave MacMillan, have been exceptionally professional, helpful, and easy to work with; our sincere thanks go to them as well.

Both of us are faculty members at Villanova University in different departments. We owe thanks to our department chairs, Mercedes Juliá of the Department of Romance Languages and Literatures and Evan Radcliffe of the Department of English, for their unwavering support of this project.

This list would not be complete without mentioning our respective husbands, Nadir and Paul, whose encouragement and support were vital for the fruition of this book.

Silvia Nagy-Zekmi and Karyn Hollis

Contributors

J. Scott Andrews is a Ph.D. candidate in Communication at the Pennsylvania State University whose research explores the intersections of rhetoric, philosophy, and the humanities. His dissertation, "Troping Democracy: Synecdoche and Whitman's New Constitution," considers the rhetorical function of synecdoche in Whitman's complex reconstitution of the *pluribus* and the *unum* toward a "United States" in "Democratic Vistas" as a species of the more general capacity of language and rhetoric to constitute the parts and wholes of "the world" as we know it. His work has been presented at the National Communication Association and Rhetoric Society of America, among other conferences, and a forthcoming issue of *Speaker & Gavel* will feature his "Objectivity in Rhetorical Criticism: Husserl's Late Phenomenology." For more information: http://rhetoricjsa.yolasite.com/resources/Curriculum%20Vitae.pdf.

David Beard, Ph.D., is an associate professor of Rhetoric in the Department of Writing Studies at the University of Minnesota Duluth. He researches the history, theory, and pedagogy of rhetoric as an interdisciplinary formation. He has published in journals such as the *International Journal of Listening, Archival Science, Philosophy and Rhetoric, Southern Journal of Communication, and Enculturation,* among other venues. Additionally, he has placed essays in *What We Are Becoming: Developments in Undergraduate Writing Majors* (USUP), *Engaging Audience: Writing in an Age of New Literacies* (NCTE), *Coming of Age: The Advanced Writing Curriculum* (Boynton/Cook), and the *SAGE Handbook of Rhetorical Studies.* With Richard Enos, he edited *Advances in the History of Rhetoric* (2007). For more information: http://umn-d.academia.edu/DavidBeard/.

Kathryn Comer, Ph.D., is an assistant professor of English at Barry University in Miami Shores, Florida. She earned her Ph.D. in Rhetoric, Composition, and Literacy Studies at the Ohio State University, where she cofounded the digital journal, *Harlot: A Revealing*

Look at the Arts of Persuasion (www.harlotofthearts.org/). Her current research revolves around multimodal narrative design, composition pedagogy, and public-oriented rhetoric. For more information: http://kathrynbcomer.net/Professional/Home.html.

Adebe DeRango-Adem is a recent MA graduate in English/Cultural Studies affiliated with the New York Research Center who writes on issues related to race and social justice. Her research interests include racial passing, critical race theory, and the politics of interraciality. She is also a writer for ColorLines (Applied Research Center), Editor of the *Race-Talk blog* (Kirwan Institute), and author of a chapbook entitled *Sea Change* (2007). Her debut full-length poetry collection, *Ex Nihilo*, was published by Frontenac House in 2010. For more information: http://www.adebe.wordpress.com.

Amin Emika is a graduate student at West Virginia University where he teaches composition and professional writing courses. He currently works at the Center for Literary Computing and has worked as a Graduate Student Administrator at the WVU Writing Center. His current research interests include service learning, narrative theory and identity construction, and the relationship between professional writing courses and workplace writing.

Lahcen E. Ezzaher, Ph.D., is a professor of English at the University of Northern Colorado. He has published a book titled *Writing and Cultural Influence: Studies in Rhetorical History, Orientalist Discourse, and Post-Colonial Criticism* (2003). His most recent publications include an English translation of Alfarabi's commentary on Aristotle's *Rhetoric* (Rhetorica, 2008), an English translation of Avicenna's commentary on Aristotle's *Rhetoric* (*Advances in the History of Rhetoric*, 2011), and articles on issues of language and multiculturalism. He is currently working on a book manuscript titled *Three Arabic Treatises in Rhetoric: The Commentaries of Alfarabi, Avicenna, and Averroes on Aristotle's Rhetoric*, to be published by Southern Illinois University Press. For more information: http://www.unco.edu/english/facstaff/ezzaher.html.

D. Ray Heisey, Ph.D., was a professor emeritus of Communication at Kent State University and past president of the International Association for Intercultural Communication (2001-2003). He passed away in 2011. He worked extensively on comparative intercultural communication, particularly on the cultural exchanges between the Far and Middle East and the United States. His publications include *Chinese Perspectives in Rhetoric and Communication* (2000), and "Global Communication and Human Understanding" (2000). For more information: http://dept.kent.edu/comm/HTML/heisey.htm.

Karyn Hollis, Ph.D., is an associate professor in the English Department at Villanova University where she directs the Concentration in Writing and Rhetoric Program and is associate director of the Cultural Studies Program. Her research projects examine self-representation and gender on Facebook, the relationship between new forms of media and social activism, and the history of gendered discursive practice. She has published *Liberating Voices: Writing at the Bryn Mawr Summer School for Women Workers* (2004), which was supported by a year-long research grant from the National Endowment for the Humanities. She also teaches in Villanova's Latin American Studies Program and has published *Poesía del Pueblo para el Pueblo: Talleres Nicaragüenses de Poesía* on the poetry workshop movement in Nicaragua (1991). She has articles in several anthologies and in journals such as *Women's Studies Quarterly, Studies in Latin American Popular Culture, College Composition and Communication, Journal of Advanced Composition,* and *The Writing Instructor.* For more information: http://www19.homepage.villanova.edu/karyn.hollis/.

Kjetil Ansgar Jakobsen, Ph.D., is the Henrik Steffens professor of Northern European studies at the Humboldt University in Berlin. He has published a large number of essays and articles on problems of cultural history and theory. In the late 1990s he was a visiting scholar at the Centre européen de sociologie in Paris, and contributed to two special issues on the comparative history of intellectuals in the journal *Liber,* edited by Pierre Bourdieu. In his doctoral thesis Jakobsen compared Niklas Luhmann's approach to aesthetic autonomy with that of Bourdieu (*Kritikk av den reine autonomi: Ibsen, verden og de norske intellektuelle* (A critique of pure autonomy: Ibsen, the world and the Norwegian intellectual 2006). The first of two volumes on the history of cosmopolitan thought edited by Jakobsen appeared in 2010. His most recent book tells the story of *Les Archives de la planète* (The archive of the planet) and of Albert Kahn's Scandinavian expedition in 1910, *Norge i farger 1910. Bilder fra Albert Kahns verdensarkiv.*

Tim Jensen is a Ph.D. candidate in the Rhetoric, Composition, and Literacy Studies Program at the Ohio State University, where he researches social movement rhetoric, collective emotion, and affect theory. His interest in nonrational rhetorics is grounded in the stark fact that an economic system based on perpetual growth is neither sustainable nor sane. His recent work is found in *The Megarhetorics of Globalized Development* (with Wendy Hesford) and *The Journal of Aesthetics & Protest*. For more information: http://english.osu.edu/people/person.cfm?ID= 2517.

Silvia Nagy-Zekmi, Ph.D., is a professor of Hispanic and Cultural Studies, and director of the Cultural Studies Program, and the Graduate Program in Hispanic Studies at Villanova University. Her latest publications include *Perennial Empire* (2011) and *Colonization or Globalization? Postcolonial Exploration of Imperial Expansion* (2009, both with Chantal Zabus), *Truth to Power; Public Intellectuals In and Out of Academe* (2010, with Karyn Hollis), *Moros en la costa: Orientalismo en América Latina* (2008), *Paradoxical Citizenship: Edward Said* (2006, 2008); *Democracy in Chile: The Legacy of September 11, 1973* (with Fernando Leiva, 2005), *Le Maghreb Postcolonial* (2003), among others. She writes about postcolonial and cultural theories, Latin American and Francophone Arab literature, and is part of the editorial board of journals, such as the *Journal of Empire Studies*, the *Revista Iberoamericana* and reviews articles for *Postcolonial Text, Journal of Material Culture,* and *Journal of Arabic Literature*. For more information: http://www19.homepage.villanova.edu/silvia.nagyzekmi/.

John Pugh (cover artist) is an award-wining muralist painter. He has completed over 250 murals, and his work has appeared in articles/media worldwide, including *Time, Artweek, LA Times, New York Times, USA Today, Good Morning America, London Sun, Tokyo Mainichi*, BBC World News, *Art Business News, Public Art Review, Southwest Art,* and *San Francisco Examiner*. He is the author of a book *The Murals of John Pugh; Beyond Trompe L'oeil*. For more information: www.artofjohnpugh.com.

Samuel C. Rickless, Ph.D., is a professor of Philosophy at the University of California, San Diego. His areas of research include ancient philosophy (particularly Plato), early modern philosophy (particularly John Locke and George Berkeley), ethics, and constitutional law. Among his recent publications, "The Moral Status of Enabling Harm" (2011), "Plato's Definition(s) of Sophistry" (2010), "The Right to Privacy Unveiled" (2007), and *Plato's Forms in Transition: A Reading of the Parmenides* (2007). He is currently working on a book on Locke for Wiley-Blackwell's *Great Minds* series, a book on Berkeley's argument for idealism, an article on Hume's theory of the passions, and an article (coauthored with Dana K. Nelkin) on the doctrine of double effect. For more information: http://philosophyfaculty.ucsd.edu/faculty/rickless/Rickless/Home.html.

Joseph Robertson is visiting instructor of Spanish language and Humanities at Villanova University. He is the coeditor of the literary journal *Naufragios,* www.RevistaNaufragios.com, has published three volumes of poetry in Spanish, and is a member of the Spanish-language literary workshop "Pinzón 9." He is the founder and director of the publishing project Casavaria and the creator of The Hot Spring Network (www.TheHotSpring.net), a social networking project designed to bring researchers, inventors, and laypeople together to accelerate the pace of paradigm-shift innovations across diverse disciplines. In September, he published the report *Building a Green Economy: The Economics of Carbon Pricing and the Transition to Clean, Renewable Fuels.* At Villanova, he also launched and moderates the ClimateTalks roundtables series www.ClimateTalks.info. For more information: http://www06.homepage.villanova.edu/joseph.robertson/.

Jan Servaes, Ph.D., is professor and chair of the Department of Communication at the University of Massachusetts in Amherst. Recently he has been appointed UNESCO Chair in Communication for Sustainable Social Change. His most recent edited books are *Moving Targets, Mapping the Paths between Communication, Technology and Social Change in Communities* (2007) and *Communication for Development and Social Change* (2007). For more information: http://www.umass.edu/communication/faculty_staff/servaes.shtml.

Ehsan Shaghasemi is a Ph.D. candidate in Communication at the University of Tehran and a member of the International Academy of Intercultural Research. Along with D. Ray Heisey he worked on several joint projects including "The Cross-Cultural Schemata Iranian–American People have toward Each Other," in addition to "A comparative Rhetorical Analysis of the 14th Dalai Lama Tenzin Gyatso," and "Iranians and Americans: Beyond the Media Construct." For more information: http://tehran.academia.edu/EhsanShaghasemi/CurriculumVitae.

Matteo Stocchetti, Ph.D., is director of the Graduate Program in Media Management and Senior Lecturer at Arcada University of Applied Sciences in Helsinki, where he teaches Critical Media Analysis. Among his recent publications, (with Johanna Sumiala-Seppanen) are *Images and Communities: The Visual Construction of the Social* (2007), and "War Is Love: Gender and War Narrative in

Transnational Broadcasting" (2009). His current research interests include issues of power associated with the media and visual communication in particular, the political role of organized violence, and the terms of intellectual criticism in the conditions of late modern societies. For more information: http://networkcultures.org/wpmu/netporn/speakers/matteo-stocchetti/.

Handel K. Wright, Ph.D., is a professor and director of the Centre for Culture, Identity and Education, University of British Columbia (http://www.ccie.educ.ubc.ca/). He is coeditor of the book series African and Diasporic Cultural Studies (University of Ottawa) and serves on the editorial board of several cultural studies and education journals including the *International Journal of Cultural Studies,* the *European Journal of Cultural Studies,* the *Canadian Journal of Education,* and *Postcolonial Studies in Education.* He has published widely on critical multiculturalism and antiracism, Africana cultural studies, cultural studies of education, qualitative research, and postreconceptualization curriculum theorizing. Most recently he has coedited (with Meaghan Morris) a special issue of *Cultural Studies* on "Transnationalism and Cultural Studies" (2011) and a book (with Keyan Tomaselli) *Africa, Cultural Studies and Difference* (2011). For more information: http://ccie.educ.ubc.ca/people.html.

Introduction

The Location of Public Intellectual Discourse

Silvia Nagy-Zekmi and Karyn Hollis

With the evolution of the modes and ways of communication that made it possible, globalization seems to have challenged and ultimately destabilized many established social norms and forms of identity, especially those associated with the nation-state. Within the context of modernity in which the nation-state must be understood, identity is thought of as fixed and immutable. One of the consequences of globalization (i.e., global thinking) is the disruption of the notion that a culture is equivalent or at the very least that it corresponds to a specific geographical space (a country). The disjuncture between a nation-state and the location of (its) culture is displayed not only in forms of cultural resistance, but by the presence of specific countercultural elements; to understand this disjuncture requires a deeper scrutiny of the interaction between culture and nation, that is to say, the role of nation in shaping the culture and the role of culture in sustaining the nation-state. This relationship is not "natural"; it is historically produced and traceable in cultural practices. Therefore, to pay attention to discourse is essential because the nation-state and the colonial order it generated are maintained largely by discourse in the Foucauldian sense, though imperial relations have been initiated chiefly by wars. Current tendencies of globalization are viewed by many (Giddens, Robertson, albeit with very different views on the meaning of globalization) as the continuation of the "outward expansion of Europe[1]" (Held et al. 289) by both economic treaties and wars. Mirroring (or generating?) economic trends, the nation constructed by discursive notions of binary opposites—such as purity, civilization, and modernity on the one hand, and half-breed, uncivilized non-white on the other—is based on the corresponding territorial and identitary dichotomy of center-periphery, self-other, and so on. Pierre Bourdieu, among many others, suggested that neoliberalism, that is, the current dismantling of the great achievements of the welfare state (in health, education, labor, social security), has adopted the discourses of the nation-state (with its nationalistic overtones and hierarchically prescribed power positions) and those of globalization reflecting a transnational and borderless world. This "paradoxical *doxa*," as Bourdieu puts it,

> is conservative but presents itself as progressive; it seeks the restoration of the past order in some of its most archaic aspects (especially as regards economic relations), yet it passes regressions, reversals, and surrenders off as forward looking reforms or revolutions leading to a whole new age of abundance and liberty (as with the language of the so-called new economy and the celebratory discourse around "network firms" and the Internet).
>
> (64–65)

Decolonization of vast regions of the world, interglobal and instantaneous communication, diasporic migrations, and permeable borders have created flexible, hybrid, and performative identities in the current era, thus challenging the notion of identity as it is represented by the metanarratives of modernity. According to these "master narratives"—to use Lyotard's expression—identity functions within the concept of the sovereignty of a homogeneous nation whose origins are linked to colonial regimes that can be traced back to the rise of European capitalism. It may be suggested that globalization theories would benefit from dialogue and the cross-fertilization of ideas (cf. Krishnaswamy and Hawley 15) provided by the framework of postcolonial theories. The "civilizing mission" of the colonial enterprise has, indeed, been replaced by (often violent) "efforts of democratization" (in Iraq, for example), that is to say, by exporting, yet again, Western models of governance and economic systems that will likely benefit their initiator, rather than those on the receiving end. As Nobel laureate Amartya Sen points out, "Just because the poor have made some gains as a consequence of globalization does not mean that it promotes a fair and equitable system." However, Sen warns against equating globalization with Westernization, for it would

distract attention from the many potential benefits of global integration....
The central issue of contention is not globalization itself, nor is it the use of
the market as an institution, but the inequity in the overall balance of *institutional arrangements* which produces *very unequal sharing of the benefits* of
globalization.

(added emphasis 14)

Globalization touches not only the economic structures, of which
technological advances are vital parts, but also the realm of the cultural, of which the changes in the mode of transmitting information
are crucial.

The representation of the economic, political, cultural, and, more
importantly, global interrelations between agents involved in the process of intellectual activity is at the core of the inquiry in this volume
that scrutinizes a distinct transformation occurring in the modalities of intellectual production also detectable in the changing role of
academics themselves. These changes affect the ability of academics
to contribute to public discourse, due to the increasing corporatization of institutions of higher education, which is documented
and examined not only from an objectivist, historical standpoint,
but also through imaginative theoretical constructs based on cultural relativism. Examples of past and current attitudes of intellectuals
regarding their role in society are thus analyzed from a transnational
perspective by focusing on the exchange of ideologies, the influences
of state power, democracy, and lack thereof within and beyond the
increasingly translucent walls of academe. The wide-ranging yet ideologically rather homogeneous coverage of global or local events in the
"mainstream" media[2] illustrates the undeniable fact that academic and
mediatic discourses are sometimes at odds with each other. Furthermore, the economically supported power structures find expression in
academic and also public discussions that aim to delineate and limit
the function of the intellectual in a society.

The notion that public intellectuals are in decline has again become
fashionable in the United States, and they are often portrayed as
trapped between academe and the "real" world, or between the private and the public sphere (Nagy-Zekmi-Hollis xv). In our transitional
era, due to a worldwide political and economic crisis since 2008, world
powers are slowly shifting into different positions of authority, making
the debate concerning intellectual contributions to public discourse
timelier than ever. Scholars, especially those in humanities and the
social sciences, often (but not often enough) try to influence public
discourse on economic, political, and societal issues; however, their

ability to do so is curtailed by the shifting priorities of academic institutions evidenced in the hiring of more "developers" (fundraisers) and fewer faculty, especially those on tenure track. Questions related to this predicament are examined in depth by the contributors to this volume not only through discourses within academe, but also by taking on the larger question, namely, how can the voices of scholars and erudite thinkers penetrate the hegemonic discourses of the globalized, corporate-owned media? And how do the media receive and represent the contribution of intellectuals to the academic and public spheres? Moreover, what is the role played by the emerging noncorporate media (blogs, electronic journals, and e-publications) in the production of public discourse? As Benjamin Lee states in an article that links the nation and academic disciplinarity, conceptions of democracy presuppose notions of "collective interest" and "popular sovereignty," which, in turn, depend on forms of public subjectivity such as "the voice of the people" and "public opinion" (241).

This collection of essays is a response to the noticeable scarcity of books about intellectuals and their various societal roles, particularly those that include the treatment of academics in the discussion of the intellectual realm. Richard Posner's *Public Intellectuals: A Study of Decline* (2001) is a prime example serving the neoliberal agenda, for the author recognizes as notable American intellectuals only those with a very specific political bent, so much so that he produces a list (!) of names that he considers to belong in this category. Paul Johnson's *Intellectuals: From Marx and Tolstoy to Sartre and Chomsky* (2007) gives a historical, diachronic account of the decisive role certain intellectuals played over time in the history of the United States, and so does the edited volume by Melzer et al., *The Public Intellectual: Between Philosophy and Politics*. None of these books includes a theoretically driven analysis of the discourses that articulated, defended, or repudiated certain intellectual positions. Similarly, Hollinger and Capper's *The American Intellectual Tradition* constructs a historical review of the American intellectual tradition, in the widest sense, but it too lacks the systemic underpinnings of the production of intellectual discourse regulated by power, rather than the "course of history." The collection of articles by Helen Small is most thought-provoking if somewhat eclectic, with its focus on intellectual activity at large that does not address Academy as a locus of intellectual production. The goal of the present volume is to direct attention to the controversy surrounding academics and their engagement in public intellectual discourse, particularly when their contribution reflects a specific social or political agenda.

INTRODUCTION 5

The articles collected here present new scholarship on the definition of intellectuals and their contribution to public discourse generated both within and outside of academe. Indeed, intellectuals have been fulfilling the role of the Foucauldian *parrhesiastes* (mentioned in the articles by Matteo Stocchetti and David Beard), negotiating access to public discourse for centuries, but their opinions may have never been more crucial to the public good. Edward Said, admittedly following Gramsci (Said 3–4) and Julien Benda (5–7), conceives the role of the public intellectual as an "outsider," an "amateur," and "disturber of the *status quo*" (x). Said considers that the main function of the intellectual is to "speak the truth to power" and to be "a witness to persecution and suffering, and supplying a dissenting voice in conflicts with authority" ("public role"), and his position is in stark contrast with Richard Posner's, who also sees academics as "outsiders" and "amateurs"; however, for Posner, these epithets cover a naturally inferior status to that of the professional owners of public discourse, such as lawyers, politicians, and so on. The fact that the voices of the Saidian intellectual are often drowned out in the media fray or are absent altogether cries out for public reflection, and this book provides an arena for these essential deliberations.

The authors in the volume do not take a confrontational view; instead, they define the problems and propose creative solutions that have both short- and long-term benefits. One example is "Reflections on Three Decades of the Comparative History of Intellectuals: Beyond the Specialist/Generalist Framework?" by Kjetil Ansgar Jakobsen (University of Oslo) whereby the author advises to go beyond the binary model of generalist versus specialist by proposing a three-prong approach, including the element of "reflective autonomy." Jakobsen examines the term intellectual as a discursive field of controversy to sketch a theory of intellectual practice that is neither structural nor functional but, rather, performative. He replaces the binary distinction between the specialist and the generalist approach with the triangle: specialization, reflective autonomy, and ethics of translation. The functional approach to the problem of the intellectual gives way to a performative approach that limits itself to asking what it is intellectuals do and how they do it, thus establishing a clearer direction for further endeavor.

Falling into two parts, the 13 articles examine the complex relationship between the production of knowledge, the role of the agents producing the discourses whereby this knowledge is transmitted, and the influence of the power structures on these epistemological discourses in a global context. The authors address relevant questions about academics as intellectuals, whether their role should include the production of knowledge or should be limited only to its dissemination (cf. Stanley Fish, "Save the World in your Own Time"). The major context for this debate is the exploration of the interference of power, with its ability to oppress, silence, and censor.

Part I, "Homo Academicus: Making the Case" examines how the epistemological discourse referenced above may be tied to academic disciplines and reconceptualized in a theoretical framework informed by the latest concepts from cultural and media studies that deal with representation, subjectivity, and the manipulability of public discourse, and specifically academic discourse. This approach will contribute to a deeper, historical understanding of the discourses dealing with administrative processes that make up academic structures assisting or hindering the development of multifaceted discourses within academic institutions. Articles included here offer a review of the role of academic intellectuals in the context of modernity (Andrews, Wright, Jakobsen), and discuss the changing role of both the target and the context (Comer, Jensen, and Robertson), namely, the influence of structural changes in academe from educational to corporate models (Servaes), that coincides with a shift from disciplinary pedagogy to the interdisciplinary approach (De Rango). The larger issue—how these changes may affect the process of the production and application of knowledge—is taken up by Robertson and Wright, for whom cultural studies provides the framework in the discussion of various performances by academics who have penetrated public discourse. With models based on Gramsci's notion of the "organic intellectual," Foucault's "specific intellectual," and others, Wright offers a vibrant overview of what can and can't be accomplished from the academic arena. Exemplifying Wright's arguments, Adebe De Rango claims that the documentation of black intellectual production amounts to the management of uncertainty, requiring the displacement of the marginal to the center and an honest critical engagement with the outskirts to solve the current impossibility for an intellectual to be black, American, and intellectual at once. The author argues that white and black identities are predicated on each other, and offers the "jazz man" as a performative figure who has mastered his role, acknowledging that his program must be left radically unfinished as an inventive play between unity and dissonance, a multiplicity of routes and citations in which America is merely one point of departure, and an idiom whose roots are rhizomes, growing scattershot into the ages, confounding all attempts to essentialize it.

All of these articles contribute to the creation of a framework that decenters disciplinary hegemonies by putting forth a collaborative academic model global in scope and transnational in nature. Academe, considered as a community, is at the core of the inquiry of many articles, especially that of J. Scott Andrews who delineates the problems faced by academics with a social conscience when generating knowledge as much for the community as for the university. His approach rejects the dilemma by suggesting that it should not be a choice to direct one's discourse either to the academic community or to the community at large. Since the definition of what counts as "public knowledge" is at least partially inspired by the market-based logic of the university, academics are in a precarious position. Providing an examination of what "public knowledge" is or could be may open the discussion of scholarship to a wider scope of intellectuals within the academic realm, as well as *legitimate* a more inclusive approach to what counts as public knowledge outside academe. This essay argues that (1) traditional analyses of knowledge and methods limit the significance of any one perspective; (2) translation of knowledge from inside to outside academe requires relevance as much as rationality; and (3) a heightened focus on relevance (and rhetoric) democratizes knowledge, and, in turn, promotes public "interest," the same interest that makes the public intellectual "relevant."

On the other hand, Jan Servaes begins by applying Bourdieu's notion of *habitus* to academic elites and their broadening performing terrain; his critique then focuses on how global cultural and economic forces have damaged the work of the United Nations Educational, Scientific and Cultural Organization (UNESCO), community organizations, and nongovernmental organizations (NGOs) in the developing world. Some specifics of this trend include the fact that most academically trained writers work at Western institutions, that funding for development communication has decreased over time, and that activist experts within these organizations are often "promoted" into less powerful administrative jobs. The author counters with strategies for discursive action beyond academia in the quasi-governmental organizations that play a crucial role in developing nations.

The link between intellectual discourse and organized violence (war) in the conditions of globalization and postmodernity is scrutinized by Matteo Stocchetti. Admitting to a pervasive sense of intellectual inadequacy in the academy, the author calls on "distinctively honest intellectuals" to rally in support of their political role and reflect on war and terrorism. In producing critical knowledge, a new form of legitimization will be created, one still credibly associated with authority and from there to the power of discourse.

Stepping into the digital domain of Web 2.0, the essay by Tim Jensen and Kathryn Comer calls for a "public turn" in scholarship, a new praxis of public intellectualism. To this end, the authors recount their experience founding *Harlot: A Revealing Look at the Arts of Persuasion,* an online peer-reviewed journal and open web forum as a venue for reimagining public intellectualism in the twenty-first century. From the outset, *Harlot* was conceived not as an *act of* communication but rather a *space for* scholarly debate about social change and "participation in public-oriented scholarship." Informed by the work of Posner, Fish, West, Wolfe, Said, Chomsky, and Cushman, among others, the authors maintain that digital media and the Internet, with its shared and immense discursive arena, allow academics to interact with a larger public in a give and take of relevant dialogue.

Part II, "Case Studies" outlines several models of intellectual engagement within specific spheres of academe. Contributors defy dichotomist, binary, and other essentialist approaches to the production and dissemination of knowledge as they move their focus from the teacher/student dynamic to a more nuanced approach that includes cooperative models that reflect tolerance and acceptance of various, even conflicting views. Academe is thus conceived as a site where knowledge is not just produced and transmitted, but also dissected and reconceived within a rigorous theoretical framework. The articles demonstrate that inclusion in and exclusion from the realm of power is discursive and deliberate, and that academe proves to be no exception to this dynamic, especially since the corporate models of management have been adopted.

The "case studies" fall into three categories (with some overlap): those that critique the work of a specific scholar, for example, Richard Posner's work on public intellectuals is scrutinized by Samuel C. Rickless; or Norman Finkelstein's writings on the role of power in academe (and more specifically the hotly debated issue of whether a scholar is judged on the quality of his/her work or the ideological position it represents), by David Beard; or Lahcen Ezzaher's metadiscursive reflection on his own work and his own agency as a transitional subject. Other contributions deal with the role of the academic intellectual as a professional associated with a specific discipline, such as philosophy in the Rickless piece in which the author focuses on Richard Posner's criticism of academic philosophers in his *Public*

Intellectuals: A Study in Decline, maintaining that this widely read volume reinforces a public misconception that philosophers are incapable of articulating or unqualified to contribute to public social and political discourse. Philosophers who engage in public commentary on matters of broad social, political, or legal concern in venues with wide readership or viewership (such as newspapers, magazines, popular blogs, and televised programs devoted to analysis of the news of the day) deserve to be read/heard, Rickless maintains, while pointing out the wide discursive range and relevance of philosophical journals that deal with topics such as abortion, euthanasia, assisted suicide, torture, lying, promise breaking, juvenile detention, secession, the targeting of innocent civilians in war, terrorism, self-defense, the death penalty, the moral status of animals, genetic screening and enhancement, privacy, and property. Furthermore, he claims, philosophers receive extensive training in logic and the detection of fallacies. This training puts them in the position to recognize errors of reasoning in *any* area of general concern.

Covering another discipline, that of political science, David Beard's article explores the distinctions between the legal and professional constraints on public intellectual discourse and the ethical obligations that arise from that work. The article scrutinizes Finkelstein's work in two contexts: the academic and the public. Although some may suggest these two entities should be separate, unique, and understood on their own terms, the essay demonstrates that Finkelstein's later work crosses those boundaries, for it engages in a kind of double voicedness, speaking both to the academic community and to the public. Using the concept of *parrhesia* and Foucault's notions of power in discourse, the author states the need for developing a "third voice," speaking "truth to the powerless." How do we differentiate the act of speaking truth to power from the act of encouraging others to speak truth to power, knowing that they lack our institutional protections, is at the core of Beard's inquiry.

The third category of contributions in this section concerns the tension between cultural and national identity (American, Iranian, Moroccan) questioning, once again, the connection of a culture to a specific geographic space while asserting the possibility of hybrid forms of identity both collective and individual. Lahcen Ezzaher describes how his "triple voice" (Arabic, French, and English) provides a map of cultural journeys that informs his teaching of American students who desire to improve their writing skills and make a difference with and by their writing. Making use of postcolonial theory, concepts of representation, the notion of hybridity, and the borderland (as a theoretical device), he reinterprets the Eurocentric history often applied in the teaching of rhetoric and writing, along more effective geocultural paths.

In a collaborative effort, D. Ray Heisey and Ehsan Shaghasemi present an intercultural dialogue on speaking truth to power from a transnational perspective in quite different circumstances and timeframes. Contextualized by their own personal histories, the authors provide a rare glimpse into the experience of defiant academics. The dialogue is constructed by an initial essay by each author, followed by a question and answer section, and a final collaborative conclusion.

Building on the idea of "writing back," or writing as resistance, Amin Emika maintains that a queered examination of identity can call into question limiting discourses of public service. The attitude toward outreach is often demeaning and performed around conceptions of charity, while reifying white, middle-class values as well as patriarchal and heterosexual conventions. This allows the performance of service to be equated with the hierarchical notion of "helping," without ever questioning the ways in which social position and the privileges it confers are part of what creates the community needs in the first place. Students led to address the multifaceted and complex nature of their own social positions may be more likely to locate agency within the communities they attempt to serve.

To incorporate a great variety of perspectives in the volume, the editors have not censored certain points of view but have included the widest possible array of opinions and approaches chosen by the contributors to examine their specific topics. For example, Samuel C. Rickless favors an objectivist view in his analysis of Richard Posner's work on public intellectuals: "objectivity being one of the virtues most prized by philosophers, one would expect them to aim at true, unfiltered understanding of moral wrongs," whereas others prefer the Foucauldian understanding of the prevailing subjectivity in truth claims.

The articles that comprise the book address the topic from multiple perspectives that include historical and ideological variations, in addition to considerations of geographic and pedagogic diversity, while focusing on the articulation of ideas whose relevance originates from the truth claims attributed to them in the social and especially in the political realm. The fundamental question at the core of this book is whether academics are to engage in public discourse or should they be considered "teaching professionals" who transmit knowledge but do not produce it, in which case they cannot be thought of as public intellectuals.

Notes

1. By Europe, they mean the industrialized world, or Western powers, as others call it.
2. See Michael Parenti for a discussion of the relationship between the corporate ownership of news media and the ideologically tilted coverage of events embodied in methods, such as "suppression by omission," "labeling," "preemptive assumption," "false balancing" and others (55–66). A more recent reference regarding the ideological tilt of U.S. mediatic representation is found in the documentary "Orwell Rolls around in His Grave" by Robert Kane Pappas, where Nazi propaganda chief Joseph Goebbels is quoted saying that an ideal media system presents the *ostensible diversity that conceals an actual uniformity* (emphasis added).

Works Cited

Bourdieu, Pierre and Günter Grass. "The Progressive Restoration" *The New Left Review* 14 (2002): 63–77.
Giddens, Anthony. *The Consequences of Modernity*. Cambridge: Polity Press, 1990.
Held, David, Anthony G. McGrew, David Goldblatt, and Jonathan Perraton, eds. *Global Transformations*. Stanford, CA: Stanford UP, 1999.
Hollinger, David A. and Charles Capper, eds. *The American Intellectual Tradition I–II*. Oxford: Oxford UP, 2005.
Johnson, Paul. *Intellectuals: From Marx and Tolstoy to Sartre and Chomsky*. New York: Harper and Collins, 2005, 2007.
Kane Pappas, Robert. *Orwell Rolls Over in His Grave*. Documentary film. 2003.
Krishnaswamy, Revathi, and John Charles Hawley, eds. *The Postcolonial and the Global*. Minneapolis, MN: U of Minnesota P, 2007.
Lee, Benjamin. "Between Nations and Disciplines." *Disciplinarity and Dissent in Cultural Studies*. Nelson, Cary and Dilip Parameshwar Gaonkar, eds. London: Routledge, 1996. 217–34.
Lyotard, Jean Francois. *The Postmodern Condition. A Report on Knowledge*. Trans. Geoff Bennington and Brian Massumi. Minneapolis: U of Minnesota P, 1984.
Melzer, Arthur M., Jerry Weinberger, and M. Richard Zinman, eds. *The Public Intellectual: between Philosophy and Politics*. Lanham, MD: Lexington Books, 2003.
Nagy-Zekmi, Silvia and Karyn Hollis, eds. *Truth to Power. Public Intellectuals In and Out of Academe*. Newcastle upon Tyne, U.K.: Cambridge Scholars Publishing, 2010.
Parenti, Michael. "Monopoly Media Manipulation." *Mediterranean Quarterly* 13, 2 (2002): 56–66.

Posner, Richard. *Public Intellectuals: A Study of Decline*. Boston, MA: Harvard UP, 2001.
Robertson, Roland. *Globalization. Social Theory and Global Culture*. London: Sage, 1992.
Said, Edward. *Representations of the Intellectual. The Reith Lectures*. New York: Vintage Books, 1994.
——"The Public Role of Writers and Intellectuals." *The Nation*. September 17–24, 2001. www.thenation.com/doc/20010917/essay Accessed, April 2011.
Sen, Amartya. "How to Judge Globalism." *The American Prospect* 13, 1 (2002): 1–14.
Small, Helen, ed. *The Public Intellectual*. Malden, MA: Blackwell Publishers, 2002.

Part I

Homo Academicus: Making the Case

Chapter 1

In the Marketplace of Illusion: The Public Intellectual in a Landscape of Mediated Humanness

Joseph Robertson

The question of what role the intellectual should play in society has evolved into an automatic controversy that summons the simplest answers and the most entrenched prejudices. The passion for showing off democratic tendencies while not devoting adequate energies to their exercise has led to an ingrained hostility toward successful thinkers who work to channel their energies into the production of analyses that might make evident the subtle truths the rest of us are living, production that—by extension—means they issue to us an ethical summons, a call, a reminder of the commonness and the humanness of our special human frailties, of our obligations and of what would constitute a better social expression of our selfhood.

Anti-intellectual commentarists, making their living as intellectuals, are fond of suggesting that any information held by any specialized group must necessarily be of little interest to most people. Promoting an ethic of irrelevance, such rhetoric distorts the fabric of ethical summons and response and interferes with the intellectual freedom of those who are taught to denigrate the work of serious inquiry. The sophists of our time use both "intellectual" and "elite" to discredit serious intellectual pursuit, then redeploy their own critique to build an elite space they can inhabit for personal or factional gain. Keeping after the experts and pundits often takes the place of active thought. The work of citing and commenting on citation engines and on commentators who comment on citation engines becomes the model for serious examination of truth, and in this way, our information age is, in fact, not very different from other ages: in many ways, fact is (still) determined by faith.

The vocational thinker, the intellectual who seeks not to pose as expert nor act as instruction manual for opinion consumers, is treated as if he or she must be playing a self-serving game, laboring to undermine the common vocabulary and replace it with one that empowers the intellectual at the expense of the audience. What is most feared is not the failure to know or to see clearly, but the terrible slippage of the customary vocabulary, so that in a landscape of haphazard demarcations, amid vestiges of primal, now *translated,* cravings, the ground will be revealed to be groundless, the arcade of so many comforting clarities destabilized, the viability of the edifice of meaning itself threatened.

Owen Flanagan calls this struggle to hold onto what appears to carry meaning "the really hard problem," in a book of the same title. Meaning is intangible, insubstantial, and the material world often fails to provide useful definitions of meaning, purpose, or whatever it is that brings well-being. In examining the question of *eudaimonia,* conscious flourishing or happiness, Flanagan posits that

> eudaimonia comes, if it does, only if we grow the better seeds in our nature, and weed out or moderate the growth of the "not so hot" stuff. The number of people who have—often by necessity or inattention—cultivated the bad seeds, or been given no resources to care for their own garden, are many. The facts are that their way of living does not achieve what they want, although from the point of view of a sufficiently screwed-up psycho-social-aesthetic it can seem pretty or good.
>
> (Flanagan 54)

By Flanagan's estimation, people often follow a path that leads to an absence of *eudaimonia,* because they are deceived by their own patterns of perception into believing that those particular factors that cultivate an absence of *eudaimonia* in fact do the opposite—cultivate its presence—and should lead to happiness, while others are mired in a lack of *eudaimonia,* because the context of their existence allows for so little conscious flourishing, and their energies are spent in ways that cannot or do not provide for *eudaimonia.* Flanagan's observations invert the conventional wisdom regarding the influence of, and aversion to, cultural elites in a democratic society—for instance, "Our innate conative constitution orients us categorically to seek fitness" (Flanagan 55). There are two important variants in the intellectual landscape for pursuing such fitness: the first is to seek to know as much as well and as extensively as possible, in order to be most fit to deal with what exists; the second is to reframe what exists in terms of more manageable observations and assumptions about what exists.

Flanagan observes that for monks who deliberately choose a life of austerity and seclusion, there is a process of education in their former life that allows them to not only choose the life they do, but to excel at living in that way, and achieve a state of personal harmony, wisdom, serenity, or *eudaimonia*. Understanding is implicit in this process, throughout, and a requirement for living "well and meaningfully." "If there is elitism," Flanagan writes, "it is in social practices that support doing nothing, or not enough, for those who live below the eudaimonistic threshold" (55). There is as much an ethical as an intellectual overtone to Flanagan's approach to the topic: one cannot simply claim that because meaning and *eudaimonia* are connected, and meaning is insubstantial (intangible), that those who are afflicted with severely austere life circumstances require no material assistance to improve their footing, be more fully part of the human realm of meaning, and achieve *eudaimonia;* one cannot simply say it is a matter of spirit, and leave it at that.

That claim is not only based on incomplete information; it is knowingly dependent on the exclusion of important information. It is comforting to view meaning as not only intangible but insubstantial, because then there is no clear way to "provide" for meaning; one is not responsible for its lacking. And so the always implicit ethical call of the other can be ignored, and the substance of complaint about the insufficiencies of the human world gather substance, in that intangible way, and lay the groundwork for a struggle about the nature of meaning..., meaning stolen through the back door, a covert method of locating meaning, or meaning won on the sly.

This manufactured fitness is all too often the preferred course. Where it is not possible to gain control of universal knowledge, it is possible to limit one's definition of the universe, in order to claim control, autonomy, and a verifiable terrain for the project of the self. In the critical work of articulating a verifiable self, a responsible being that is also free of material entanglements, this *fitness-for-what-one-has-chosen* is preferable to the primordial, biological demand, that one be good enough, comprehensive enough, true enough, to survive. In other words, right aligns with the formula for what is right, not with any unknowable complex of complexes from which we, at times, are able to draw something that tastes like truth.

The Decentralized Self

In sections 14, 15, and 16 of *Human, All Too Human,* Friedrich Nietzsche proposes that unities are most often illusions, that there is no inside and no outside in the world and that the "thing in itself" is a dangerous glossing over of vitally important ontological evidence. Taken together, these three passages seek to invalidate our claim that we can draw defined and meaningful boundaries. The proposition is startling, because the implication is that there can be no inward being as against an outward world: there can be no self, such as we imagine it. First, it must be understood, he writes, that the frequent, rapid, and repeated association of specific ideas, closely resembling some deeper truth, leads to the conviction that they are not complexes but unities, and he urges the reader to beware that "as is so often the case, the unity of the word does not guarantee the unity of the thing" (Nietzsche 22).

Second, if unities are really complexes in disguise, their meaningful details glossed over, then the question of boundaries comes to the fore: where exactly is the boundary to delineate, definitively, inside from outside? What separates the body from the world, the mind from the body, the mind from the ideas of which it builds its narrative? Again, Nietzsche warns that "deep feelings" and "deep ideas" are illusions, felt to be deep because we impose a vision of deep inward essence and superficial outward appearance.

Third, to negate the deep sacred inward realm of self is a coextensive jolt to the intellect, because there can be, correspondingly, no superficial material outward realm of other. How, then, do we accumulate understanding? Where does it reside? If there is no essence, then there is no appearance either, no distinction between best self and observable self, no "thing-in-itself" that hovers in the metaphysical ether and no meat of matter that stalks the material, sensory universe. It is not clear that Nietzsche sought to build a cosmology around these observations, but he clearly wanted to state the unequivocal need to explore the idea that in such a world, we must live differently than we are accustomed to living. Though radical, this foray into interrogating the metaphysical framework of relationship between sacred inward self and material outward reality is instructive for redefining the question of what it is we must come to trust, and to what end we search for meaning in the life of the self.

Nietzsche is signaling that there are unanswerable questions—such as *Where is the boundary between the outside and the inside? Can it be drawn, observed, proven, tested, confirmed?*—and that such questions both destabilize our experience of being conscious in this world and are natural, structurally relevant aspects of what our consciousness is, or must be. Can we know meaning, if we cannot know where the boundary is between the inner self and the outer landscape?

If we first admit this insecurity is born from the idea that any reflection coming back from the world "out there" must somehow diminish our claim to a valid, potent, and irrefutable selfhood, then we can start to examine how and why we both seek and flee from, long for and reject, the deep mental involvement of others in our project of creating meaning within which we live. And from there, we can start to assess how the mind needs the very kind of guidance it also needs to refuse. A useful redefinition of the problem requires that we approach this question in wholly different ways: our consciousness may be possible; may be workable; may be relevant, useful, and have some hope of flourishing *only because* the idea of exactly what we are is destabilized by this problem of boundaries. How, after all, does all this information come in? Into where do we take it? From where is it taken? At whose urging?

The terrain of the self is delocalized, and the meaning that would give substance to the insubstantive self is detemporalized. Fact is mediated, and meaning is undetermined—undermined. Traditions fade, and the logic of personal liberty requires novel visions to be both wholly formed and readily applied, precisely in the thrust of the moment in which one experiences something fleeting, and for the first time, only to move on into a universe in which that first time is already past. Emmanuel Lévinas, in *Totality and Infinity*, suggests that "[a]ppearing to representation as a thing among things, the body is in fact the *mode* in which a being, neither spatial nor foreign to geometrical or physical extension, exists separately. It is the regime of separation" (168). The body is a *metaphor* that allows for the description of the process by which one represents one's will to oneself, thus demonstrating, simultaneously, selfhood, volition, potential held in potential, and the possibility of acting and shaping a destiny. The metaphor allows for representation and representation suggests a physical and a temporal self. Representation is the substance of the insubstantial self,[1] but of what, then, is the self made? How can we come to know its shape, its nature, its propensities, its force? Is it nothing more than whatever *happens* to be happening in the space of representation, at any given moment?

Brian Massumi, in his book *Parables for the Virtual: Movement, Affect, Sensation*, explores meaning as mediation. The universe of human experience is a complex registry of sensation, mediated by the body, by artificial media, and by what is perhaps the most elusive of media—of the vehicles to transport meaning: those insubstantial entities so vaguely labeled *facts*. Massumi's book takes as foundational the problem faced in our times where fact cannot be assumed to have weight any more than a deep conviction that one is a uniquely defined, locally bound, definite, and demonstrable self can be assumed to have weight, because all experience is mediated, and because we deliberately *deploy* attempts at meaning via media, engaging the entire space of human experience in ways that might only have been reserved before for the realm of the sensual.

There are many very serious and far-reaching implications for the landscape of human interaction, as a whole, in this analysis. The body and the space of meaning might be, in many ways, equally "virtual." He explains:

> Intensity is *incipience*, incipient action and expression. Intensity is not only incipience. It is also the beginning of a selection... The crowd of pretenders to actualization tend toward completion in a new selective context. Its newness means that their incipience cannot *just* be a conservation and reactivation of a past. They are *tendencies*—in other words, pastnesses opening directly onto a future, but with no present to speak of...
>
> This requires a reworking of how we think about the body. Something that happens too quickly to have happened, actually, is *virtual*. The body is as immediately virtual as it is actual. The virtual, the pressing crowd of incipiencies and tendencies, is a realm of *potential*. In potential is where futurity combines, unmediated, with pastness, where outsides are infolded and sadness is happy (happy because the press to action and expression is life).
>
> (Massumi 30)

It is in the potential of the virtual body, the future allowance for choosing, the possibility of deliberate action, the chosen response to "the press to action and expression" that the notion of the individual acquires meaning. But the individual—the director, the orchestrator, the compiler, and the agent of meaning—is as often mired in crisis as dwelling in security or sanctity. The question might be, then, whether the dwelling of the self is irrefutable and concrete or extensible and evolutionary. Is the self, as we have imagined it, a "pretender to actualization," an "intensity," but not a defined and closed system?

Where traditional spiritual endeavor viewed the crisis of the soul as sacred, and provided for an eternal realm of meaning in the fulfillment of specific noble pursuits, the contemporary human being struggling to verify and enunciate something like an integrated self runs up against Massumi's paradox: "The body is as immediately abstract as it is concrete; its activity and expressivity extend, as on their underside, into an incorporeal, yet perfectly real, dimension of pressing potential" (31). Or rather, what will you show yourself to be? And, will you have existed at all, until you achieve it?

The full and integrated self must be successfully concrete and also successfully intangible, an abstract potential actualization, filtration, flirtation, or implementation matrix, a complex of complexes, a visionary accomplice capable of honest self-seeing and authentic self-propagation. "Conscious reflection is the doubling over of this dynamic abstraction on itself. The order of connection of such dynamic abstractions among themselves, on a level specific to them, is called mind" (Massumi 32). But how can one live the details, the would-be facts of the everyday, and also face the haunting existential crisis of coming to grips with the self as an insubstantial substance, the mind as a groundless ground?

Simplicity to Prove the Self

One important proposed and widely practiced solution is to simplify the design of the crisis—of how it is imagined—so as to escape the need to resolve it. This practice does not aim to achieve a truly simpler landscape of evidence, but rather to pose as true by making simple, by excluding the inconvenient. If true selfhood is somehow the absence of concrete selfhood, and facts in the realm of the concrete must be translatable into the realm of the insubstantial, to be viable as facts, then liberty can be redefined as *absence*—absence of protocols, absence of demands, absence of responses to an ever-absent summons—and the self we seek need not achieve full and free expression of its paradoxical truth in a way that is both concrete and virtual.

The virtual is concrete—what I read on Facebook comprises part of the facts of my existence—and the concrete is increasingly virtual: what is mediated appears in the gallery of my consciousness as concrete, as carrying weight, as graven and defined. It is tempting, as Owen Flanagan noted, to ignore the ways we have cultivated the seeds of a future experience that will be absent of *eudaimonia,* and define as flourishing the very state of absence to which we have—for lack of a better, more complete, more humane vision of this paradox of selfhood—committed ourselves, not seeing that to do so is to undermine our own freedom, to not provide opportunities for choosing to flourish.

Even as science, engineering, economics, and social psychology trace an increasingly epic complexity, requiring an ever-increasing level of dependence on specialized elites, our "globalized"—which might mean artificially unified—landscape of human interaction submits to the temptations of the parochial and sets up as ideal the frame in which all people have a right to defend any perceptual distortion on the grounds of having the right to invent the view, to hold that invented or derived view, to dwell inside a castle of their own devising. Outlook and disposition are elevated above substance, and we resign ourselves to living in the paradox in which we both demand and reject the best efforts of the public intellectual. What lends its momentum to the privileging of the more narrowly defined specialist and the narrow space in which he or she operates also lends its momentum to the culture that pushes aside such advisors, in the realm of meaning? The intellect is commodified, and the cultivation of the intellect is dissuaded in favor of a dispersed mediation aimed at affirming currents of faith and faction.

At times, it almost seems unclear if we are deliberately developing a model of human interrelationship in which the collective field of thought functions as a vast, global organism, or whether we seek the stark and irrevocable atomization of all human identity. The intellectual is, at intervals, the obstacle to collective will or the caretaker of so many lost and fractured souls. Intellectuals themselves are given to a vocational devotion, a self-fashioning as shamanistic vehicles for broader, if imperceptible truths. In some ways, this problematic temptation overrides the most virtuous of intellectual pursuits, the giving of one's life energies to the quest for shared knowledge, and cloaks honest contributions in the imagery of salesmanship and sophistry. Inquiry devolves into commentary as a leading thinker gives priority to the "I think" or the "I have shown" over the significance of tenable, commensurate witness.

We are seduced by the media into believing that we exist beyond a need for mediation, and that everything flows directly to us. Each of us poses as ruler of a microcosm where the wisdom of other voyagers is somehow an indulgence more than a resource. Yet we are immersed in mediation: we are part of language, searching always for meaning that can somehow withstand the impossible journey from one mind to another, looking for ways to impact the fabric of diverse media that color the spaces between us, defined by how we do whatever it is we do in our relationships. We need contact, and we labor to build up to it.

We are more passionate and concerned about trust than almost anything else, yet we are conflicted about what it must mean to admit we are immersed in a tide of mediation by which we breathe a world already made for us and which we claim to be exhaling smoothly into its best, most brilliant form. Trust is about mediation: not just whom we know or how or why, but how successful we are at confirming that *our* experiences, our perceptions have meaning, because trust, if we can find and hold onto it, implies that we can carry over some meaning, some knowledge, some geometrical rendering in the abstract, at the very least, from one moment to the next.

Trusting in Textuality

Julia Kristeva examines how textuality (which implies a desire to fix meaning) carries with it intertextuality (which implies the trauma of unfixed meaning). Specifically, "the poetic word, polyvalent and multideterminated, adheres to a logic exceeding that of codified discourse and fully comes into being only in the margins of recognized culture" (Kristeva 65). Why at the margins? Because recognized culture, or culture hewn and shaped to serve as framework for a life-and-death game of definitions, seeks not polyvalent qualification or multisourced confluence, but defined structure and reliable mapping. Kristeva's work, however, suggests that in textualizing what is "out there," what exists or can be spoken about, the map of the text is, by necessity, a layered and interdimensional map, a map of multiple temporal deviations and source codes, an intertextual *flowing-into*-textuality, which we describe, simply, as text. Any text, whatever its shape, its medium, its aim, or its origin, consists of the latent text, but also of its influences, or rather those confluent *pastnesses* that are, in the text, opening directly onto a future that is other than they were. The present (the text) is the illusion, and the translation (from past to future) is the substance, the confluence of meanings as new meaning, and new meaning again, and again.

Text, then, is a multiplier. There is the text and the past it both obscures and reveals, each layer spanning new traces, positing new approximations of truth—new evidence, new confluence, and a more vast and diverse range of influence. But then, that behavior works against the project of concentrating, centralizing, and minimizing the concrete quality of experience, of mind, which we hope to call self. Kristeva observes the problematic folding over of the insubstantial mechanism at the root of language, so dominant in our shaping of meaning, onto its insubstantial past—the threadwork of past intangibles—until it opens new realms of potential meaning, with rules as yet unwritten:

> The word as minimal textual unit thus turns out to occupy the status of *mediator*, linking structural models to cultural (historical) environment, as well as that of *regulator*, controlling mutations from diachrony to synchrony, i.e. to literary structure. The word is spatialized; through the very notion of status, it functions in three dimensions (subject-addressee-context) as a set of *dialogical*, semic elements or as a set of *ambivalent* elements.
>
> (Kristeva 66)

The polyvalent infrastructure of semiotic history—of significant content coming to be what it becomes, of insubstantial substance, of a given word—pushes the envelope, so to speak, of experience, demands new boundaries, overflows the defined structure of who we are and what we say. Language injects another layer of mediation into the quest for a self, which is more virtual than we like to admit, and whose concrete substance might be, in itself, less concrete than we are capable of dealing with.

Before we can deal with the question of whether or not we, at the individual level of consciousness, prefer to deal with or not to deal with the actions and expressions of certain public intellectuals, or what they do for us, or in what way, we face the deeper question of the self: What is it? Where is it? Can it be shown to exist?

Selfhood in Question, Question Unanswerable

The self is by convention the essence of what an individual claims to be: a mind, a soul, a free-willing entity spanning the divide between the substantial and the insubstantial and assigning sacredness to both and to everything else it touches. But after Nietzsche's intervention, in a universe without inside or outside, deprived of both essence and appearance, the self migrates toward intensity, toward a confluence of observations. The mind as self-awareness made aware of its own value urges the self further along this journey into the nonlinear problem of textuality.

Selfhood is in question, and the question is unanswerable, so selfhood exists primarily as a dialectical category. In a landscape of fevered, virtual, *too-fast-paced-to-be-essence* encounters, of complexes of (and among) complexes, every speech act is an effort at decisive epiphany, a revealing, a shedding of the de facto disguise of not knowing. The concrete-virtual body paradox is echoed in the paradoxical dynamic of speaking as dealing in the substance of what is hidden from view.

What cannot be hidden cannot be spoken, in that the act of speaking is a kind of revealing through the opening up of a closed (silent) code, an expression, a decompression, a recalling and drawing into being. In *Monolingualism of the Other; or, the Prosthesis of Origin*, Jacques Derrida explores this problem of hidden, invented, or discovered selfhood, specifically in relation to the public space, and in direct connection with the social convention of one language having priority over another. One language is privileged where another is not, and so one self is necessarily forced to operate in fundamentally different ways with regard to the prevailing language, as compared to a different self with a different sociopolitical status, as relating to the mother tongue.

Derrida looks to the quiet freedom of writing as indicative of what happens in the space of any disused language or framework for utterance: *écriture*, as he describes it, is

> a certain mode of loving and desperate appropriation of language and through it of a forbidding as well as a forbidden speech ... This gives rise to strange ceremonies, secret and shameful celebrations. Therefore to encrypted operations, to some words under seal circulating in everyone's language.
> (Derrida 33)

The self can remain an undisclosed secret, or an untouchable mystery, and still take shape in the shaping of a language that becomes a dwelling.

For Lévinas, the freedom embodied by the flow of representation allows for "sovereignty in the void," but also for more. Sovereignty is not absolute, because "[r]epresentation is conditioned" (*Totality* 169). The "separation" that demonstrates the difference between beings in space or between moments in time, geographical locations, or perspectives is made through the decision process that forges representations, whose functional space is the dwelling where the self becomes evident, at least to the self-seeking consciousness. The dwelling and the self that inhabits it are not distinguishable; the self is formed dialectically, but can only perceive the "implements" by which dwelling, representation, self, are formulated, through the "recollection which draws me out of submergence" (*Totality* 170).

The proof of the self remains out of reach of all the implements used for fashioning selfhood, because doing, making, witnessing, and speaking are textually interwoven in the demonstration of selfhood and cannot be recalled separately from the self—their active implementation—without calling the self into question. If language is instruction, then the self is instruction, and to be instructed, while suggestive of enrichment of the mind, is a way of negating the same self that takes instruction. If reflected back to you from a (phenomenological) dwelling too remote, "One day, you will see that what you call your mother tongue will no longer even respond to you" (Derrida 34). The self must be involved in the active generation of its own existence in order to be what it seeks to be, what we dream for it, for ourselves.

In *Residencia en la tierra*,[2] Pablo Neruda wrote of a strange uncertain "sound... turning to dust in the grist mill of too distant shapes," the voice lost in imperceptible mysteries, the crisscrossing of actions and expressions—implementations—on the horizon, at the edge of the perceived universe (Neruda 85). Otherness makes the self—the familiar, the knowable—more apparent, even as it posits the decentralization, the opening of the onto-ethical call demanding a response from that same self. In the case of Neruda's "Dead Gallop," events push on, the sacrosanct unsettling demands of selfhood push on, the struggle against what surrounds, the conditions of dwelling in this world, all push on, unsolved, undiminished, uninhibited, despite the pervasive mystery with which they infuse our experience. Self and other are both dialectical, but the information that would clarify their relationship, their boundaries, is ultimately grist for the mill of separation, which suggests that the proof of difference must exist and also breaks it down, confounding our attempts at self-perception and so at holding onto meaning.

Zen tradition holds that the ninth-century master Lin Chi told his disciples, "If you meet the Buddha on the road, kill him" (Harris 73). The admonition is deliberately provocative, and its authenticity has been questioned, but the message is closely linked to the dialectical vision of the making/discovery of the self: Don't believe you can gain access to truth by following an idol; make sure you come to your evolving experience of what is happening, of what is there, of what of who dwells among us, authentically, by a road that runs through the core of who you are and does not falsify your desires and your weaknesses. Or rather, to really achieve wisdom, you must be willing to take responsibility for the process, the lived truth, and the way it all affects the person you turn out to be.

So, where is the place for the sovereign intellectual?

THINKER-AS-EXEMPLAR

The same culture that seeks to narrow the focus of an intellectual's labors, and so to push the space of those labors to the thin edge of prevailing thought, offers also a consolation: that professional intellectual pursuit should be measured as an art form or an athletic performance, with practitioners competing in a visible way for the recognition of having achieved most fully the balance and force possible in such a sport. This view posits the thinker as exemplar, as specimen. The example serves, and so the work of the example serves. One need only witness in order to understand. But then there are grave and ancient questions about what it is to witness and what it is to understand.

René Descartes observed, indispensably, that the senses deceive. If to witness what takes place "out there," we must resort to the senses, then we must be consistently deceived, and our access to understanding is impeded, left wanting, even barred. We see through a glass darkly, and we see what the senses allow us to see. And all of that comes back to us through a universe of complexity we have yet to understand, so the very nature of witness is made suspect.

David Hume shifted focus away from the problems of witnessing, in the direction of the problems of reasoning. If we can observe, through the precise and rigorous synthesis of tested ideas, certain truths about those impressions that come to us through the veils of witness, then we can refine our ideas, build an edifice of understanding, and expand the reach of our reason far enough afield to have a sense of what is true about ourselves and our world. Hume divided "all the perceptions of the mind into two classes or species," specifically ideas and impressions. Ideas he described as "less forcible and lively," though they can be referenced and reused in ways that are ultimately more significant and influential. Impressions he described as "all our more lively perceptions, when we hear, or see, or feel, or love, or hate, or desire, or will" (Hume 12–13).

In each case, we face this crisis of the nature of evidence: we must learn what exists through the filter of what gives us access to that information, through the mediation of body, mind, sense, culture, history, will, frustration of will, experience, or its apparition, the press, political structures, science and research. In *Otherwise than Being, or, beyond Essence,* Lévinas redefines access as vulnerability: "Sensibility is exposedness to the other," so that "at the height of its gnoseological adventure everything in sensibility means intuition, theoretical receptivity from a distance" (75). The evidence, then, is not evidence, but suggestion. This experience can be traced back to Descartes' admonition that we must doubt as far as is reasonable of all things, and the opening up of modern scientific inquiry. Confirmation is harder to come by than even Descartes would have us believe, and yet our incomplete knowledge has made incredible strides. Today, the public intellectual serves to suggest and signal unexpected elements of the landscape of discourse and to marshal the forces of this global human endeavor, but to the public view, that same individual is often seen merely as a useful voice willing to struggle to make clear what those listening have not the time to fully learn or to understand. The thinker displays the thought, serves as an icon of thoughtful inquiry, shapes and delivers examples of what could be considered the best expression of what is, at this moment, knowable.

Descartes, Hume, Lévinas, or Kristeva could be exemplars of specific mindsets. They can be copied, imitated, referenced, and reported. An entire canon can be built to support the hierarchy of exemplars, and then be fitted with the outriggings necessary to render all of their labors applicable to the "man on the street." But this slows the dynamism of the whole human species down to a kind of museum mindset: history is a show and politics an experiment—a show because we are positing examples, an experiment because we are testing vocabularies. And ultimately, those copies will not be the same as the originals; the act of doing as was seen is fundamentally different from the act of doing as one is. But we live with more force than that; we feel the burden, or the joy, of presence much more intensely than to consider serious thought to be part of a museum study and little more. That leads us to the other side of the thinker-as-exemplar mindset: the pioneering thinker is a *justification* for all individuals, an example to which any being that can actively contemplate the "I am" phenomenon can aspire, one of the implements with which one can build and become a dwelling, and then *take place*—be demonstrable—in this world. *You go beyond, and describe the unseen, so I can know that I am here and that being here makes sense.* We tend to long for successful pioneers in thought with whom we can safely align ourselves to give an impression of having secured demonstrable and stable knowledge of the makeup of all the dangers and surprises "out there" which we might face.

Being a Thinking Being, Today

There is, in the work of the thinking being, an implied measure of what it is to exist: since Descartes, the Western world, specifically, has taken the measure of its institutions, including its individual human being, as such, by the standard that humanity consists in *being a thinking being*. But the democratizing principles of advanced Western thought and political infrastructure lead to a competing, implicit aversion to the intellectual "elite." The self might exist not only in the representations of selfhood we manage to conjure up, to formulate, and to express, but better thinking might give more volume to the self, a more viable, more resilient dialectical dwelling to fill out the forms demanded of selfhood by the unknowable vastness of potential experience. But how can this be measured? Is the comparison between one self and another not in some way "the prosthesis of origin," as Derrida suggests in his examination of favored and forbidden languages?

Merit, then, is decentralized, and rooted in potential, "conceived on the basis of the-one-for-the-other proper to sensibility, and not on the basis of a system of terms which are . . . in fact only the situation of the speaker" (*Otherwise* 77). This unsettling diffusion fits with a crucial, virtuous, and very necessary refocusing of human organizational purpose on the liberation of the individual conscience and capability to achieve, but the popularizing standardization of the question in many ways refutes the goal: by freeing questions of merit from institutional centers, something more like democracy can replace something too much like aristocracy, but by positioning merit outside of individual achievement, a kind of antidemocracy emerges, in which those who achieve are barred from practicing the best version of self that they might offer to society, partly because this last, this offering, is considered impossible.

A rethinking of the question may be warranted: Is intellect a secure position, a power base, a coat of arms of noble achievements that can be used to concentrate the world's resources around oneself? No, of course not. Why, then, do we accept that we—as a landscape of human endeavor: spreading, evolving, or discovering itself, renaming and interlacing its potentials with such promising insubstance, in this twenty-first century—should celebrate the marginalization of great intellects, or the sabotage of creative thinking by way of a radical narrowing of disciplines? Why does this idea that anything less would be to sacrifice our individual liberty to a sanctified elite work so well, though it delivers so little?

It is, perhaps, instructive to look at the traces of disused selfhood that linger and lurk at the edges of those spaces we have assigned to operate as intellectualizing dwelling places, to judge what about our interactions, in and around those dwellings, motivates a quest for the expendable Buddha. The temptations of hierarchy, of antidemocracy, are many, and they are primordial. When foundational ideas are destabilized, the recourse to stringent protections against deviation requires a kind of nostalgia for hierarchy. The elite-averse popular consciousness that often prevails in postmodern advanced democracies is, in many ways, the best strategy of hierarchical elites to operate unnoticed high above the fray. In our time, the ideas of origin, of purpose, of sanctity, have been destabilized, and in the contest between knowing more precisely what we do not know and ignoring the intricacies that require professional thinkers to sort them out, the simplified everyday, the answer that allows the individual to both affirm an experienced individuality and override the insubstance of meaning with the seeming substance of detail, wins out.

Heterotopia: Dialectical Selfhood

Nicolas of Cusa, in Djelal Kadir's analysis, saw the need for a moderating influence on the arrogating inclinations of an overriding hierarchy—in fact a perilously split and diverging hierarchy, a system ruled by too-potent pretenders to actualization. In his diplomatic dealings as intermediary between the Roman Catholic Church and the Byzantine Orthodox Church based in Constantinople, Cusa sought cooperative rediscovery, not to contest or delimit orthodoxy. It was necessary, as emissary of the Church of Rome, for Nicolas of Cusa to treat both parties to the negotiations as if they were integral to one broader orthodoxy, which for Cusa was the *maximum absolutum,* an absolute form of indivisible, insuperable selfhood, all-knowing, and wholly unknowable, a shared divine source and purpose (Kadir 71–73).

Kadir describes Cusa's approach to the complex of complexes that was the landscape of the schism between East and West, Rome and Constantinople, as shifting the question of orthodoxy versus heterodoxy into spatial considerations. Both patriarchs stood at the summit of a place where the same unknowable orthodoxy was to be served, and so the problem was not one of heterodoxy, but of *heterotopia.* Steeped in the cultural peculiarities of place and time, these human institutions sought to render service to an unknowable order of infinite knowledge, and so their heterotopia, their multi-polar universe of doctrine, of teachings, of "learned ignorance," could be unified in one immeasurably vast space that transcended earthly cultural specifics. The crisis of culture is a crisis of self-conceptualization, and Cusa perceived the landscape of this heterotopia as what Kadir calls a "phantasm-agora," a marketplace of illusions, of cultures, doctrines, selfhoods, each of them illusion, because they are, of necessity, incomplete, incapable of reaching as far as the *maximum absolutum*, the all-knowing, the infinite.[3] To bring a unified sense of self, of purpose, of culture, of sacred heterodoxy, to this earthly heterotopia, this multiple space in which the language of right and purpose takes place, Cusa offered a *maximum contractum*, an agreement to share in the work of illuminating the landscape, the manner-of-taking-place, of the *unmediated maximum*, the untouchable beyond, the holy infinite (Kadir 73-74).

Kadir describes Cusa's politico-theological innovation as opening the landscape of ideas for the nascent Renaissance, for a full transition out of the problematic, fragmented, and two-dimensional realm of medieval thought. For Cusa—whose aim was to harmonize the otherworldly pretensions of two worldly engines of actualization, to prevent an identity conflict that could countermand all of the doctrinal virtues of either cultural locus— the *maximum absolutum* must be "at once ubiquitous and utopic, the most perfect of circles, in Cusa's own terms, whose center is everywhere and whose circumference is nowhere" (Kadir 74). "Short of this absolute," Kadir continues, "all knowledge is partial and relational, which is to say it is ignorance by degrees. In other words, the space of knowledge is what we would call heterotopic space" (Kadir 74).

The *orthotopia*, the place where the perfect order of knowledge resides, like the *maximum absolutum*, cannot be found in any place we can visit. A "territorial orthotopia," to use Kadir's phrasing, would be a place where doctrine and self-imagining come together in a specific kind of culture that confers to its practitioners powers infused by the supposed virtues of that unreachable beyond (Kadir 74). Such Narcissistic zeal can absorb any leader of any institution that does not adequately perceive that in this world, all knowledge is one or another derivation of ignorance by degrees, because all experience is mediated and all identity is dialectical. Not only is the body virtual, and its connection to the self somewhat more visionary than concrete, the space of human society is by needs a *phantasm-agora*, a commonplace of incomplete subtleties, a marketplace of fragments that hint at truth, but do not speak it (Kadir 68).

The identity of the self is not static, it cannot be. But the drive to know the self takes as its purpose the knowing of a fixed and transcendent truth. The self, after all, must transcend if it is to be responsible, and without responsibility, even a liberty based on absence—of protocols, of legal limits, of a summons—is not clearly discernible as liberty.

There is a tension in the question of dialectical identity that demands eternal alertness and discipline, but that destabilizes the implicit desire for consistency, for identical recognition as evidence of identity:

[T]he "identity," more properly a "simile," serves as descriptor for the relationship of intellect to truth... in the geometry of this simile, equivalence and identity diverge, with identity devolving unto a reduction and equivalence perpetually evading apprehension.

(Kadir 76)

Again, the identity play, to which we are so exhaustively committed, in this time and place, this virtual heterotopia of our age of multilayered ontic mediation, this dialectical exploration of unknowables, deals in the force and relevance of insubstantials, more full of meaning and transcendent than the more trivial material details, the substance, weight, and physics, of whatever everyday experience we call our culture. The identity play is easily transformed into a process of reduction: the evolutionary self is insubstantial, which is too subtle, so a fundamental self is preferred; the dialectical genius of the successful individual intellect is hard-won, intangible and ephemeral, so a right to "live without," to be unburdened, to "express" oneself not by opening up and revealing, but rather by offloading, is not only attractive: it is commodified, fungible; the body as virtual, the organism as collaborative heterotopia cohering beyond our ability to will coherence, is too much a reminder of the frailty of what we are, of mortality, of the unknowability of the unmediated maximum, so the body as magnet for desire, longing for what *feels* like a more substantive, material identity play, must be celebrated.

There is a fundamentalism in this bent to refuse the virtues and the subtle power of the insubstantial, the unknowability of knowing, the unrecoverable origin of consciousness. We seek to know; we seek to be known; we seek to serve as memory that will persist, even if the standards we set up fall away and are replaced by unthinkable, as yet unseen, more vibrant heterotopic phantasm-agorae:

In an epoch such as ours, identity politics and self-empowerment through assertion of one's own putative identity—individual, tribal, ideological, or ethno-national—there seems to be little space for light to sift through to illumine the nature of the paradox for the self-authenticators. This leaves us identical with the ignorance of self-conviction and impervious to the possibilities of nonidentical self-reflection. This hermetic redoubt defines most aptly the impermeable space we call ideology and righteous self-conviction.

(Kadir 77)

As for meaning, we have successfully dismantled much of the meaning handed down from ancient times, but have been less successful at instructing each other in ways to identify and share in new currents of meaning—intentionality, interpretive viewing, store and stock of purpose, reason, clarity: knowing that the full scope of knowledge is, and should be, beyond the reach of any one being. The road to such new currents of meaning cannot be set, charted, defined: there is no way to stage the best example of the clear path to understanding. We have shades of understanding, and degrees of clarity ("ignorance by degrees"), volumes of reasoning (an evolving heterotopia), and stories and variants of power and exchange (*maximum contractum*: our "knowing" can be a dialectical engagement across a landscape of complexes and strategies, a giving of purpose and light, a giving of reason and dignity, despite the uncrossable distances to be crossed).

Power: Relinquished

Power is often understood to be equivalent to force, or to the freedom to exert force without constraint, but mathematical imperatives limit the degree to which any one individual can secure or implement power of this kind—the one always runs into the many, and power as force fails in the face of greater force. With the breakdown of traditional hierarchies, it is more useful to describe power as a negotiated constellation of potential relations and constraints. It is possible to accumulate and to exercise more influence by relinquishing power, by giving up the right to act without constraint, though this is often not well understood by anyone other than the generous practitioner. Nevertheless, the method does exist and examples of its vibrant viability abound. They are, however, often humble, local, untranslatable examples, and popularizing standardizations simply breeze past them, rejecting the possibility of localized humanness or humane peculiarities.

The question is no longer, in this light, Why should a merit-privileging democratic culture marginalize a concentration of cultured thought, as if it were a tyrannical elite, when it is not? The question becomes, rather, What motivates this aversion to the idea that the influence of complex and advanced ideas, shared and debated by a vanguard of public thinkers, as if it could not be a form of powerful empowerment of the other, of accumulation of information for the purpose of relinquishing power consistently to empower the other, the learner, the future, the society at large?

The desire for an expendable Buddha is not so much the desire to be free of the thinker or of the enlightened example—and so of the influence implied by that enlightenment and that example—but rather a convenient manifestation of the desire to enact one's own freedom by reducing someone else's. This noblesse-tinged view of what democracy is for and how to enact it is both anti-intellectual and antidemocratic. It is a holdover from the absolutist culture against which modern democracy was an elaborate ethical response. It uses the vocabulary of legitimizing, negotiated democratic politics to perpetuate—however unconsciously—the *concentration-without-relinquishing* model of power, by alleging that only by countering those who use their knowledge to help disperse power among the rest of a people can one—that is, the powerful—be free of undesired constraints.

The next distortion then comes to the question of the public intellectual, when it becomes clear that it can be convenient to have powerful intellects helping to spread one's ideas in unique and unpredictable ways. The thinker as fellow-traveler is sanctioned in ways uniquely reserved not for the pioneer, not for the free practice of human action, abstract or otherwise, but for predictive models, conventions that demand compliance, for the self-perpetuating mythology of the known and certain. The independent thinker, who would freely relinquish the personal influence that might accumulate around his or her ideas in exchange for a more viable, sustainable, humane universe of ontic involvement, is co-opted by forces that seek to suppress awareness that *topos* (place) among so many concentrations of *ontos* (being) must be an evolving heterotopia.

To preclude the free thinker from contributing to the wider culture by executing a personalized campaign of creative thought, thinking uniquely, genuinely, in not only human fashion but in excellent fashion, is to isolate the individual, to atomize the fabric of human learning and provide for the dubious comfort to be found in the idea that no one is required to act as guide. This serves not to reinforce the freedom of choice, but to negate the possibility that it might play an active role in determining the state of affairs among human beings. When what is knowable and discernible about the realm of truth is so disconcerting to the uninitiated, and fixed identity is the popular standard for whole selfhood, the view that order can be hewn out of chaos by force of will gathers momentum, and "identity emerges as a compensatory gesture or as a residual reparation for the unattainable" (Kadir 76).

We do not have access to static determining structures. We have to deal with an evolving landscape: ecosystems, topographical quanta, ethical uncertainties. There is genuine need for active, engaged, well-informed, diverse, deliberative human thought, to inform the responsible free will in a heterotopic landscape of mediated experience, but the root structures of meaning are not so obvious as we like to think, and sometimes, when we let ourselves be free, we can not only see that, witness it actively being so, but see also that what we are looking for is precisely that they not be so obvious. Power is too easily misunderstood as force, and the real freedom of intellect, the openness that allows for actual (if mediated, temporal and evolutionary) grasping of certain aspects of what is true and knowable, is too often brushed aside in favor of far weaker, apparently substantial, but ultimately less viable assertions of self-predictive fact.

The idea of the thinker as exemplar is incomplete, held back amid the flood of phantasms and momentary, uncertain positionings of thought. The expendable Buddha is a metaphor among metaphors, a virtual embodiment of a paradigm of sound thinking: idolatry leads into material desire, and away from understanding. The relationship of thinker as fellow traveler to institution as defined vanguard is more often a relationship tied to falsifying identity plays, and the commodification of thought (sophistry) than a pure exploration of the landscape of ideas. Our contemporary culture is a self-aware heterotopia that has just as artfully expressed the needs and limitations of the human mind as it has labored to suppress the evidence that identity is diffuse, mediated, partial, networked, a fabric. What we most celebrate is also what we most often keep at arm's length.

It is the present that is the illusion, and the translation, the mediated transfer of what is, from pastness to futurity, that builds the weight of presence into our experience. "Communicational technologies *give body to relationality as such* and as set in motion—as the passing-on of the event" (Massumi 86). A concentration of selfhood's implements, of culture's practices, of heterotopia's facets posing as actualization, is what Massumi calls "enclosure":

> Every "enclosure" is encompassed by a pure immanence of transition. The medium of "communication" is not the technology. It is the interval itself: the moveability of the event, the displacement of change, relationality outside its terms, "communication" without content, communicability.
>
> (Massumi 86)

That enclosure is intensity, the space of decision, the room for acting freely, the dwelling that both *is* and *houses* the self, never entirely closed, never entirely fluid, the insubstantial substance of what we seek to affirm. Affirmation of self need not be negation of other, if only because the other's selfhood, and the implication of a self-aware heterotopia, an informed democracy of seeing, is the foundation for any dialectical examination (evidence) of my own selfhood. For Lévinas "[i]t is only in approaching the Other that I attend to myself" (*Totality* 178) and for Kadir "[i]t turns out that there are no lines in the sand here, after all." (83) Or, rather, the life of the self does not depend on the refutation of the other, but on the fabric that demonstrates a shared openness between self and other.

To come to grips with the question of the role played by public intellectuals in the landscape of temptations, language games, fecundities, and frictions, which we refer to as twenty-first century democracy, it is more instructive to look at what we demand in the space, the interval, the dwelling, that we populate with the politics of identity. Do we demand proof of the right to steadfast identifying "enclosure"? If so, we are limiting the language of evidence and curbing personal intellectual freedoms in important ways, privileging a paradigm of sophistry for the public intellectual. Do we demand persistent explorations of the "dwelling," the "enclosure" that poses as identity, as opening onto multiple planes of futurity, diversely informed and consequential? If so, then we are empowering not a narrow elite to serve as intellectual guides, but the lives of individuals to serve as genuine agents acting freely in a networked landscape, expanding the boundaries of what is knowable. We face not a question of whether there is such a thing as the public intellectual in our times, but rather of how that public figure interacts with the networked intellect of the uncelebrated individual, the identity not known or recognized, not constant or resounding enough to accumulate power, but just as integral to the quality of the overall heterotopia that is the quest for a genuine, just, and liberated life of the human self.

Notes

1. I use the word insubstantial, here, as an extension of this problematic (and pervasive) opposition/concurrence involving the substance-insubstance of selfhood (relating to the implacable desire to capture intangibles), the not-being-there that is both the possibility of being there and the being there itself.
2. *Residencia en la tierra* is a three-volume collection of poems that explore what I prefer to call the experience of "Dwelling on Earth": the translations into English are my own, and the citation for the original text is from Neruda's original Spanish, from the opening poem of the collection, "Galope muerto."

3. *Agorah*, transliterated into English, from the ancient Hebrew, was a "small coin," so that the etymology—according to the Oxford American Dictionary—gives us in one word the idea of marketplace, exchange, and currency. The dwelling space of Kadir's *phantasm-agora* is not only a space in which the self can make or encounter meaning; it is also a substance to be exchanged in the realm of insubstance—suggestion of existence (truth) in exchange for value/meaning (experienced truth). It is a thing that acts, inhabits, is inhabited, perceives, and yet does not perceive itself, which is singular and collective, which is and is not, *phantasm-agora*.

Works Cited

Derrida, Jacques. *Monolingualism of the Other; or, the Prosthesis of Origin*. Trans. Patrick Mensah. Stanford: Stanford UP, 1996.

Flanagan, Owen. *The Really Hard Problem: Meaning in a Material World*. Cambridge: MIT Press, 2009.

Harris, Sam. "Killing the Buddha." *Shambhala Sun*, March 2006, pp. 73–75.

Hume, David. *An Enquiry Concerning Human Understanding*. Oxford: Oxford UP, 2008.

Kadir, Djelal. *Memos from the Besieged City: Lifelines for Cultural Sustainability*. Stanford: Stanford UP, 2011.

Kristeva, Julia. *Desire in Language*. New York, NY: Columbia UP, 1941.

Lévinas, Emmanuel. *Otherwise than Being, or, Beyond Essence*. Trans. Alphonso Lingis. Pittsburgh: Duquesne UP, 1998.

Lévinas, Emmanuel. *Totality and Infinity*. Trans. Alphonso Lingis. Pittsburgh: Duquesne UP, 1969.

Massumi, Brian. *Parables for the Virtual: Movement, Affect, Sensation*. Durham: Duke UP, 2002.

Neruda, Pablo. *Residencia en la tierra*. Ed. Hernán Loyola. Madrid: Cátedra, 1991.

Nietzsche, Friedrich. *Human, All too Human*. Trans. Marion Fabor, with Stephen Lehmann. Lincoln, NE: U of Nebraska P, 1984.

Chapter 2

From Rational to Relevant: What Counts as "Public" Knowledge?

J. Scott Andrews

> Life is confused and superabundant,
> and what the younger generation appears to crave is
> more of the temperament of life in its philosophy,
> even though it were at some cost of logical rigor and formal purity
>
> William James

Inaccessibility has long been cited as a factor explaining the limited and declining role of the intellectual in society. Changing political economies, the argument goes, dictate who can enter the public domain, hamstringing both the efforts of academics to intervene in critical moments when society "needs" their work most and the efforts of a given public to understand those efforts, condemned as they are to be spectators. From a "uses and gratifications" perspective (Blumler and Katz 1974), however, the narrow import of the public intellectual might be attributed to the limited "public" quality of his or her discoveries. According to one characterization, the sort of knowledge produced today "does not offer answers to many, probably the overwhelming majority, of the questions that most concern people," "its deliverances are not equally reliable," and "the information gained ... is inaccessible to almost all living people" (Kitcher 1208–9). In 1927, John Dewey warned us that the most critical "problems" of "the public" would be the twin legacies of technology, an explosion of information and a corresponding decline in public dialogue. As the need to listen grows, so shrinks the time for talking.

In response to these twin forces, a new wave of academics that see their work as bearing on "public" matters craft what has come to be known as "public scholarship" (Boyer 1996). In this mode, knowledge of "such multidisciplinary issues as citizenship and patriotism, ethnicity and language, space and place, and the cultural dimensions of health and religion" (Cantor and Lavine B20) is seen to be generated in, by, and for the community as much as the university, discipline, or scholar that may sponsor it. This academic vanguard advances at its own risk, however, under the patronage of institutions whose increasingly market-based logic is fundamentally incompatible with the social goals and outcomes of public scholarship. The narrowing of the range of valued scholarship limits, among other things, the potential public scholar's ability to help in the creation of "public knowledge." Equally complicit in the obstruction, this essay argues, is a lack of clarity on what a *public* knowledge is or could be. Indeed, the fate of public scholarship is tied to definitions of what counts as "public knowledge."

A number of thinkers in the wake of modernity have made thematic the existence, nature, quality, and foundation of public knowledge. The effect of their categorizing, this essay will show, is a limited and therefore contested space for public knowledge, insofar as each rendering of knowledge further specializes the very act of knowledge making. Where there is incompatibility between "knowledges" and "rationalities" *inside* academe, there can only be an incommunicado condition *outside* academe as far as the fruits of knowledge making are concerned. Thinking about what makes knowledge "public" could open the enterprise of public scholarship to a wider scope of "intellectuals" within academe, as well as legitimate a more inclusive sense of what counts as public knowledge outside academe.

Paralysis by Analysis

Aristotle appears to be the first to distinguish *kinds* of knowledge. In *Nichomachean Ethics* (Book VI), he argues that the rational part of the soul contemplates two sorts of objects: "those kinds of beings, the principles of which cannot subsist otherwise than they do" as well as "things of a contingent nature." Corresponding to this division, there must be two "different species of knowledge," where "the knowledge of that which is necessary should be necessary, but contingent of that which is contingent" (209–10) and never the 'twain shall meet. The best knowledge making within these two paradigms culminate in the virtues of *sophia*, or theoretical wisdom, and *phronesis*, or practical wisdom. Both virtues, it should be noted, are manifested as *individual habits*, and Aristotle was always wont to encourage a *mean*—"neither excess nor deficiency"—in this case a unique balance of *sophia* and *phronesis* for each human:

Hence the multitude say that Anaxagoras and Thales, and such-like persons, were indeed wise, but not prudent men, in consequence of perceiving that they were ignorant of what was advantageous to them [with respect to a corporeal life;] and they say, that they knew indeed things superfluous and admirable, difficult and divine, but which are useless, because they did not investigate human good.

(222)

Despite this individual dispositional orientation, Aristotle's rendering of two kinds of *beings* seems to have been interpreted as two kinds of *being*, a distinction hardly less stark than Plato's dividing line separating the intelligible and visible worlds. Given the particularity and mutability of "the public" and public matters, public knowledge after Aristotle would be confined to the realm of contingency.

Max Weber's epistemology expands Aristotle's dichotomy of knowledge in search of a more comprehensive sorting. In order to incorporate *social cognition*, Weber's account conceptualizes four "rationalities" attending the production of knowledge: theoretical, practical, formal, and substantive. While the first two reflect Aristotle's distinction between (individual) theoretical and practical knowledge, Weber's formal and substantive rationality operate exclusively in the social realm. On the one hand, *formal* rationality operates in deference to rules or laws, and thus depends upon the "actual consensus" of all its users (Goodnight 429; Farrell 2). Weber attributes this "bureaucratic" sort of thinking to industrialization and the economic, legal, and scientific institutions to which it gave rise (Kalberg 1159). *Substantive* rationality, on the other hand, negotiates the "clusters of values" that constitute, for example, friendships, and thus it operates within a *working* consensus realized in communication, the ongoing and deliberate process of "making common" individual experience (Kalberg 1155). As the only type of knowledge that references *values*, substantive knowledge appears after Weber to be the only sort that can be generally publicly held; his other ways of thinking (theoretical, practical, formal) all respond to specialized *interests*. The larger problem with this quarter-share is that historically, when theoretical, practical, and formal interests contradict a given public's substantive values, the crises of humankind occur, such as (in Weber's time) the Great War.

Alfred Schutz fortifies Weber's distinction between formal and substantive rationality by identifying the different species of knowledge that result from these respective social ways of thinking. For Schutz, *socially derived* knowledge is made and evaluated using agreed-upon methods and aims, while *socially approved* knowledge is manifested in "mores, folkways, habits," and public opinion, and is fortified by "members of our in-group" (132–4). However, because "mere" social approval lacks the systematic precision of informed inquiry, Schutz finds problematic that popular, socially approved knowledge sometimes supersedes deliberate, socially derived knowledge. By qualifying the "publics" of public knowledge, he reinforces a familiar hierarchy—in his terms—between the "expert," the "man in the street," and the "well-informed citizen." Conceiving the public in segments, of course, minimizes the particular public an intellectual might engage. But Schutz's conclusion, "[i]t is the duty and the privilege, therefore, of the well-informed citizen...to make his private opinion prevail over the public opinion of the man on the street" (134) runs patently counter to the spirit of public knowledge. But it reflects a reality worth revisiting.

Dire Warnings

The brief survey above offers no pretense of exhaustiveness or exhaustibility.[1] But we have seen enough to realize that a major problem with these analyses of knowledge is that each slice carves away more and more of the space that may be occupied by public knowledge and public knowledge making. T. S. Eliot captures this loss when he asks, "Where is the wisdom we have lost in knowledge? Where is the knowledge we have lost in information?" (96). The larger problem, however, is that partial knowledge is as much factional as fractional. Indeed, values and valuations post-Kant *may* carry comparable weight as facts, but cast as discrete parts of life may still be hierarchized in a Platonic (or Schutzian) fashion. In academe, for example, divisions of labor between empirical, interpretative, and critical work contradict and contravene the comprehensiveness these methods independently claim to offer, and the power given over to those with the means to issue in facts increasingly overwhelms that afforded to those whose work treats of values.

For Richard Bernstein, this trend carries with it a "potentially ominous consequence," in that absent a critical element, fact-driven technical knowledge cannot sustain itself among the "good and just lives" that make a community, the lives that in many cases underwrite the production of this knowledge (53–4). In its worst moments, it "towers" over that community, neglecting or rejecting outright what a public may value, an antagonism captured well by Kurt Vonnegut in *Player Piano,* where he has Finnerty remark, "If it weren't for the people, the god-damn people always getting tangled up in the machinery. If it weren't for them the world would be an engineer's paradise" (332).

The "habit of regarding as true—as knowledge—those propositions which issue from accepted scientific procedures of investigation and confirmation" comes at the expense of "principles of moral conduct and maxims of political and social life" (Bitzer 92). In a genuine attempt to normalize thinking in a form exploitable *across* contexts, such work can proceed, ironically, only by *controlling* the conditions of particular contexts—by eliminating the "total social framework of interests" (Bitzer 99). It may be argued that the reason social and political science and other attempts at systems fail to result in intelligent policymaking and social problem solving is because these offer no account of the particular contingencies communities and individuals outside the academe must evaluate daily. "What's wrong with technology," opines a character from Robert Pirsig's *Zen and the Art of Motorcycle Maintenance,* "is that it's not connected in any real way with matters of the spirit and of the heart. And so it does blind, ugly things quite by accident and gets hated for that" (168).

John Dewey in 1920 surmised that "the greatest dualism which now weighs humanity down [is] the split between the material, the mechanical, the scientific, and the moral and the ideal" (*Reconstruction* 256). To the extent that the quest for certainty *demands* the exclusion of values, it *cannot* inform its own (contingent) social and moral contexts, most apparently in decisive moments, crises, and turning points in history. For Habermas, war represents the ultimate case "when information is exploited for the development of productive or destructive forces" (82), and an uninformed public can only play the indecisive role of a spectator. Only after the fact "can its revolutionary practical results penetrate the literary consciousness of the life-world: poems arise from consideration of Hiroshima and not from the elaboration of hypotheses about the transformation of mass into energy" (82).

In these moments of crisis, the "knowledge of atomic physics remains without consequence for the interpretation of our life-world, and to this extent the cleavage between the two cultures is inevitable" (Habermas 82). In referencing C. P. Snow's 1959 lecture, Habermas suggests that the linchpin of his anxiety is a failure on the part of scientists and humanists to work together to solve complex human problems. Beyond the walls of the academe, "the muddled words of the tribe and the too precise words of the textbooks" are incapable of "harmonizing" (52), and Habermas takes this too as symptomatic that specialists and "the public" may be living entirely different experiences. He seems to suggest that the fruits of technical rationality can achieve practical significance only by means of their communication as such—practical, significant, valuable. If this is in fact the goal, then only work that is "*at once* empirical, interpretative, and critical" (Bernstein 235) can form the basis for intellectual responsibility and public responsiveness. A more fulsome knowledge that synthesizes the operations of matter and spirit could "operat[e] as an immense release, a liberation" (Dewey, "Absolutism" 10) of a public's power to deliberate its own future to perform its own critical problem solving.

Toward this reconciliation, Habermas upholds a more general *communicative* rationality. Grounded in consensual social norms, communicative rationality takes shape in ordinary language, and thus depends upon an "intersubjectivity" of meanings, rather than the more limited precision and accuracy demanded of logical systems. Because communicative rationality seeks a "mutual understanding of intentions" and a "general recognition of obligations" (92) among *all* implicated parties, it suggests a means by which *any* community may intervene in knowledge making. In this mode, matters of controversy are settled in decision as much as experimentation, and thus the sort of knowledge made is not only explanatory but evaluative. Ideally, "the lay public provides the shortest path of internal understanding between mutually estranged specialists" (77), for public knowledge is ultimately validated—made so—by the public. There is plenty of room in public for both science and praxis if both adopt the same spirit of communicative fallibility.

Relevance by Rhetoric

To be concerned with public relevance and public deliberation is to give thought to the rhetorical nature of one's scholarship. Rhetoric, as a general practice, attempts to redress imbalances of relevance by insisting that public knowledge "be shared by knowers in their unique capacity as an audience" (Farrell 4). Rhetoric's work is ever toward a public, and rhetoric's goal is always maximum relevance to a total public on whatever scale. Rhetoric thus recommends itself to public knowledge making insofar as it seeks its end from among "local knowledge and fallibilistic theories" rather than from a "top-down epistemological tyranny" (Eberly 32). Rhetoric begins with problems that "grow out of the stresses and strains in the community life" of a public (Dewey, *Reconstruction* iii) and seeks its end in "the resolution of new problems ... the formation of new inclusive communities" (McKeon 198).

From a rhetorical perspective, then, any sort of knowledge becomes "public" by its adjudication and sustainment in its broader context, by its suitability to "enter the day-to-day routines of physical existence, ensure the excellent performance of crafts and duties, and in some degree answer to the intellectual, moral, aesthetic, and spiritual impulses" (Bitzer 81). Public knowledge from this vantage may include *any* kind of knowledge "needful to public life and actually present somewhat to all who dwell in community" because it has been judged to be "sufficiently reliable" (Bitzer 68) for meeting community needs or satisfying community interests. We may take as models of public knowledge that which has *already* been publicly authorized, including, for example,

> principles of public life to which we submit as conditions of living together; shared interests and aspirations; values which embody our common goals and virtues; our constitutions, laws, and rules; definitions and conceptual systems; truths expressed in literatures of poetry, criticism, philosophy, aesthetics, politics, and science; the accumulated wisdom proffered by our cultural pasts; and to this we add the personal facts of our public life (87).

The fullest sense of public knowledge, then, warrants expansion of the meaning of the adjective "public" from merely "known to or accessible to" to include a broader sense of "relevant to" (Brouwer and Squires 212). For Dewey, such an approach demands a "casting off of that intellectual timidity which hampers the wings of imagination, a plea for speculative audacity, for more faith in ideas, sloughing off a cowardly reliance upon those partial ideas to which we are wont to give the name facts" (*Philosophy* 12). This enlarged spirit widens the scope of what counts as public knowledge, provided that ideas are articulated in such a manner as to be available to public scrutiny.

More than this, though, *all* the spheres of knowledge making (Goodnight) are contained within the rhetorical sphere, insofar as the particular knowledge advanced in each has been "treated, shaped, and given meaning by one or a combination of the faculties of invention, interpretation, sequencing, and explanation" (Carleton 323). More generally, rhetoric has been characterized as "an art of structuring all principles and products of knowing, doing, and making" (McKeon 198), *simultaneously* "a way of being, a way of knowing, and a way of doing" (Benson 318). Carried to its limit, if rhetoric is the "source or carrier of truths and values thought to be indispensable" to *any* particular public, then rhetorical rationality is "*the* way, the *generic* way, *all* ways of coming to know" (Bitzer 69) for all publics.

Cast this widely, rhetorical rationality becomes accessible to the public and the public intellectual alike. Knowledge making on these terms makes its end the narrowing of a variety of knowledge gaps. Per one characterization, "Engaged scholarship in rhetoric integrates theory, practice, and production. It is inter-disciplinary and cross-disciplinary, igniting and facilitating a dialectic between the generalist and the specialist" (Hartelius and Cherwitz 436). In "retreating" to a level inclusive of all these modes of knowledge making, a rhetorical orientation aims at a unity of knowledge.[2] Louis Mink is helpful here in distinguishing rhetoric as a particular method and as a general intellectual orientation: "Is unity of science possible? No, because the several modes of comprehension generate and justify several methods. Is unity of knowledge possible? Yes, as knowledge of a world for a mind whose mode of comprehension gives structure to that world" (41).

Real Challenges

Presumably, the institution best positioned to foster a diversity of knowledge making toward a unity of knowledge is the "university," and the etymological implication of the term is not lost on rhetorical scholars who see their work as productive of public knowledge.[3] From this central site, public scholarship can utilize "the university's intellectual and creative resources in the service of those obligations...of democratic participation" (Cohen 8). In its capacity as "the premier knowledge institution in an era of exploding knowledge and knowledge technologies," the university can be fundamental to the formation of critical public knowledge, but only to the extent that what is encouraged by "[e]ducation as a public resource" is "scholarship as a public good" (Boyte 80; Cohen 9–10).

Even so, a number of internal logics run counter to this conception of "the public" as a principal to knowledge making.[4] The logic of accountability and tenure, for example, drives wedges between a scholar's research, teaching, and service, such that the potential "knowledges" derived from each are "isolated from each other at best; at worst they are allowed to become structural antagonists" (Eberly 28). The logic of disciplinarity "restricts our ability to see the various kinds of work we do as parts of a coherent whole called scholarship" (Eberly 27) and "fracture[s] the commonwealth of learning and undermine[s] our sense of commitment to general understanding and integration of knowledge" (Gregorian B12).[5] Even the logic of form—the journal article, the study, the monograph—narrows the scope of what may be admitted as knowledge. As a result, the work of the university is often *defined* by difference, not only generating "detached expertise" but also fostering a "culture of critique and estrangement from middle class Americans" (Boyte 94).

One response to this characterization has been increased calls for collaborative projects. In 2007, a consortium of scholars gathered in Washington, D.C., to discuss "The Public Good: Knowledge as the Foundation for a Democratic Society." This event marked the first-ever convocation of the American Academy of Arts and Sciences, the American Philosophical Society, and the National Academies of the Sciences, Engineering, and Medicine, and the Congressional citation commemorating the occasion emphasized that Franklin, Adams, and Lincoln shared with these the same "conviction that knowledge in service to the public good is an indispensable pillar of our Nation." Significantly, complementing this institutional presence were government representatives, journalists, historians, poets, singers, attorneys, business leaders, foundation directors, and economists, a striking reminder that "to help advance 'useful knowledge' in the colonies" meant "promoting enlightened leaders *and* an engaged citizenry."[6]

What is needed to prevent the increasing irrelevance of intellectual work is a democratization of public knowledge itself, a more inclusive sense of what public knowledge could be, per the spirit of the 2007 convocation. The recognition of this broadened scope on institutional and scholarly levels makes necessary the attitude that theorizing, criticizing, testing, and articulating are all general *practices,* and are by that very nature public acts. Ideally, public scholarship would "bridg[e] different interests and perspectives" between a university and a community and "creat[e] public relationships" (Boyte 87). From a rhetorical perspective, publics *actually are* vested with the same *authority* to participate in the production of public knowledge, insofar as they become a vital part of the process, locus of its evaluation and application. The investment of the public as stakeholders in such knowledge aims to engender and sustain public interest in acts of creating, affirming, adapting, and discarding this knowledge as public conditions warrant. From the public's perspective, then, knowledge is "public" when it "*demands* that a decision be made," even when that decision is "to do nothing" (Farrell 10). Relevant public knowledge provides the opportunity for valuation and to that extent is rhetorical.

Acknowledging and treating the rhetoricity of knowledge and knowledge making admits the reasonable and the relevant as much as the rational (Toulmin 13). It reminds the academic that we are all craftspeople, in greater and lesser degrees aware of the obligations of our work to a democratic community. Stephen Toulmin has this in mind in pointing out the etymological relationship between the terms *experiment* and *experience* (187). In any experience lies the potential for the generation of new knowledge, within or outside the walls of the academy. As a rhetorical litmus, we might say that insofar as the individual lives of intellectuals are experienced publicly, that far must a legitimate public knowledge extend.

Notes

1. Arguably—for example—another profound rift was created by Kant's characterizations of "is" and "ought," a move originally intended to "justify the autonomy, objectivity, and universality of moral judgment" as much as scientific ontology (Bernstein 46–7). This is a very familiar theme.
2. I use the term "retreating" to provide an alternative to the top-down connotations of "transcending," as much as to signify a return in time to rhetoric's precategorical roots.
3. Ackerman and Coogan (2010), Cherwitz and Hartelius (2007), and Hikins and Cherwitz (2010) go far toward considering the individual and institutional advantages of adopting a rhetorical worldview university-wide.
4. A forum in the Winter 2010 issue of the *Quarterly Journal of Speech* (96.4) highlights, from a rhetorical perspective, the real concerns and contradictions of pursuing public "engagement."
5. For Louis Mink, "The limits of the world are the limits of the discipline we adopt to inquire into it" (41).
6. My italics. The Conference program (with audio) is accessible online at <http://www.amacad.org/audio/publicgood.aspx>. Randel (2009) reprints his keynote address.

Works Cited

Ackerman, John M., and David J. Coogan, Eds. *The Public Work of Rhetoric: Citizen-Scholars and Civic Engagement.* Columbia: U of South Carolina P, 2010.
Aristotle. *The Rhetoric, Poetic, and Nicomachean Ethics of Aristotle.* Trans. Thomas Taylor. Vol. 2. London: James Black and Son, 1818.
Benson, Thomas W. "Rhetoric as a Way of Being." *American Rhetoric: Context and Criticism.* Ed. Thomas W. Benson. Carbondale: SIU Press, 1989. 293–322.
Bernstein, Richard J. *The Restructuring of Social and Political Theory.* Oxford: Blackwell, 1976.
Bitzer, Lloyd. "Rhetoric and Public Knowledge." *Rhetoric, Philosophy, and Literature: An Exploration.* Ed. Don Burks. West Lafayette: Purdue UP, 1978. 67–93.
Blumler, J.G., and E. Katz. *The Uses of Mass Communications: Current Perspectives on Gratifications Research.* Beverly Hills, CA: Sage, 1974.
Boyer, Ernest L. "The Scholarship of Engagement." *Journal of Public Service and Outreach* 1.1 (1996): 11–20.
Boyte, Harry C. "Public Work: Civic Populism versus Technocracy in Higher Education." *Agent of Democracy: Higher Education and the HEX Journey.* Ed. David Brown and Deborah Witte. Dayton, OH: The Kettering Foundation Press, 2008. 79–102.
Brouwer, Daniel C., and Catherine R. Squires. "Public Intellectuals, Public Life, and the University." *Argumentation & Advocacy* 39.3 (2003): 201–13.
Cantor, Nancy, and Steven D. Lavine. "Taking Public Scholarship Seriously." *Chronicle of Higher Education* 52.40 (2006): B20. Web. 3 Mar. 2011.
Carleton, Walter M. "What Is Rhetorical Knowledge? A Response to Farrell—and More." *Quarterly Journal of Speech* 64.3 (1978): 313–28.
Cherwitz, Richard A., and E. Johanna Hartelius. "Making a 'Great "Engaged" University' Requires Rhetoric." *Fixing the Fragmented University: Decentralization with Direction.* Ed. Joseph C. Burke. Boston: Anker, 2007. 265–88.
Cohen, Jeremy. "A Laboratory for Public Scholarship and Democracy." *A Laboratory for Public Scholarship and Democracy.* Ed. Rosa A. Eberly and Jeremy Cohen. Hoboken, NJ: Jossey-Bass, 2006. 7–15.
Dewey, John. "From Absolutism to Experimentalism." *John Dewey: On Experience, Nature, and Freedom.* Ed. Richard J. Bernstein. New York: Liberal Arts Press, 1960. 70–87.
——. *Reconstruction in Philosophy.* Mineola, NY: Courier Dover Publications, 2004.
——. *Philosophy and Civilization.* New York: Minton, Balch, 1931.
Eberly, Rosa A. "Rhetorics of Public Scholarship: Democracy, Doxa, and the Human Barnyard." *A Laboratory for Public Scholarship and Democracy.*

Ed. Rosa A. Eberly and Jeremy Cohen. Hoboken, NJ: Jossey-Bass, 2006. 27–39.

Eliot, T.S. "Choruses from 'The Rock.' " *Complete Poems and Plays.* New York: Houghton Mifflin Harcourt, 1952. 96–114.

Farrell, Thomas B. "Knowledge, Consensus, and Rhetorical Theory." *Quarterly Journal of Speech* 62.1 (1976): 1–14.

Goodnight, G. Thomas. "The Personal, Technical, and Public Spheres of Argument: A Speculative Inquiry into the Art of Public Deliberation." *Journal of the American Forensic Association* 18.4 (1982): 214–27.

Gregorian, Vartan. "Colleges Must Reconstruct the Unity of Knowledge." *Chronicle of Higher Education* 50.39 (2004): B12. Web. 3 Mar. 2011.

Habermas, Jürgen. *Toward a Rational Society: Student Protest, Science, and Politics.* Trans. Jeremy J. Shapiro. Boston: Beacon Press, 1971.

Hartelius, E. Johanna, and Richard A. Cherwitz. "The Dorothy Doctrine of Engaged Scholarship: The Rhetorical Discipline 'Had It All Along.' " *Quarterly Journal of Speech* 96.4 (2010): 436–42.

Hikins, James W., and Richard A. Cherwitz. "The Engaged University Where Rhetorical Theory Matters." *Journal of Applied Communication Research* 38.2 (2010): 115–26.

James, William. "A World of Pure Experience." *Journal of Philosophy, Psychology, and Scientific Methods* 1.20–1 (1904): 533–43, 61–70.

Kalberg, Stephen. "Max Weber's Types of Rationality: Cornerstones for the Analysis of Rationalization Processes in History." *American Journal of Sociology* 85.5 (1980): 1145–79.

Kitcher, Philip. "Public Knowledge and the Difficulties of Democracy." *Social Research* 73.4 (2006): 1205–24.

McKeon, Richard P. *Selected Writings of Richard McKeon: Culture, Education, and the Arts.* Vol. 2. Ed. Zahava, Karl McKeon, and William G. Swenson. Chicago: U Chicago P, 2005.

Mink, Louis O. *Historical Understanding.* Ed. Brian Fay, Eugene O. Golob, and Richard T. Vann. Ithaca: Cornell UP, 1987.

Pirsig, Robert M. *Zen and the Art of Motorcycle Maintenance: An Inquiry into Values.* New York: HarperCollins, 2005.

Randel, Don Michael. "The Public Good: Knowledge as the Foundation for a Democratic Society." *Daedalus* 138.1 (2009): 8–12.

Schutz, Alfred. "The Well Informed Citizen: An Essay in the Social Distribution of Knowledge." *Collected Papers.* Vol. 2. The Hague: M. Nijhoff, 1954. 120–34.

Toulmin, Stephen E. *Return to Reason.* Cambridge: Harvard UP, 2001.

Vonnegut, Kurt. *Player Piano: America in the Coming Age of Electronics.* New York: Charles Scribner's Sons, 1952.

CHAPTER 3

FROM THE ORGANIC THROUGH THE
SPECIFIC TO THE ACCIDENTAL:
CULTURAL STUDIES AND THE
(POTENTIAL) PROLIFERATION OF
CONTEMPORARY CATEGORIES OF
THE ACADEMIC AS PUBLIC
INTELLECTUAL

Handel K. Wright

Academics are traditionally thought of as rather different from activists and while some of them are sometimes thought of as intellectuals, the idea of the academic as public intellectual is not universally embraced. This brief essay addresses the idea of the academic as potential or de facto public intellectual. The primary intention in the essay is to open up the topic and point to a few permutations and possibilities rather than to define and delineate. No attempt will be made, therefore, to define the notion of the public intellectual, nor to provide a definitive answer to the question, "What constitutes the public intellectual?" As Edward Said observed in *Representation of the Intellectual,* "[i]n the outpouring of studies about intellectuals there has been far too much defining of the intellectual" (13). Rather, the idea is to raise questions that further complicate the issue of the academic as public intellectual, suggest types of academic public intellectual, and, hopefully, provoke some reflection. Six points will be made on the topic and the essay will end with a decidedly inconclusive conclusion. The focus will be on academics and their relationship to the term "public intellectual," and cultural studies will be employed as a loose framework for the arguments.

Choosing to explore the question of academics as intellectuals implies an assumption that well-established or budding academics have something to do with it; that academics might be or ought to be public intellectuals. However, such suppositions should not be taken for granted. Some academics hold that being a public intellectual is not part of their job description and are adamant about pursuing knowledge for knowledge's sake and therefore resistant to attempts to have them play the role of the public intellectual. In terms of the topic at hand, in their extreme form, such academics are what we might call antiutilitarian academics.

The first version of this essay was presented at the Second Global Conference on Intellectuals: Knowledge, Power Ideas (Budapest, Hungary, May 2009). The work of the organizers of the conference was quite definitively situated within the discourse of knowledge for knowledge's sake. This is not to say that the conference focused on knowledge for knowledge's sake: rather the organizers mentioned it as an almost taken-for-granted framework of the entire project. The following excerpt from the organizers' description of the project is illustrative:

> In 2005 ID.Net formally and legally came into existence as a not-for-profit network, constitutionally "limited by guarantee." The phrase is deliberate, for the following reasons; Inter-Disciplinary.Net is founded on the time-honoured motto: knowledge for knowledge's sake, education for education's sake. These are worth pursuing because they are inherently valuable, not they may be "useful" in some way.
> (Inter-Disciplinary.Net, 2005)

Inter-Disciplinary.Net is only one example of numerous projects that take up the knowledge for knowledge's sake as an academic motto and framework. Such a commonsense and taken-for-granted approach to academic work is deeply ideological and constitutes the foundations of what might be considered the antiutilitarian intellectual stance. Even if they are not antiutilitarian, those academics who insist that their work should not extend beyond the immediate bounds of their traditional job description can be said to be taking an important stance, not only ideologically but also politically. This is true, especially in these times when academics are overwhelmed with traditional academic tasks (pressure to "publish or perish," to teach upwardly creeping courseloads, to write, administer and report on more and bigger grants, to serve on increasing numbers of university, faculty, departmental and program committees, to advise and mentor increasing numbers of students, to serve on more journal boards and society committees and to keep up with bewilderingly burgeoning developments in our fields, and so on). Given all that academics do as routine part of their work, is it not unreasonable to expect that they resist adding the role of public intellectual to what are already virtually impossible workloads? Should not the expectation that academics also be public intellectuals be seen for what it is, namely, yet another way of increasing the workload and exploiting labor of academics, almost always without additional compensation? Although it is tempting to consider the antiutilitarian academic as one who avoids public intellectual work or even intellectual work in general, it can also be argued that as a stance, antiutilitarianism is in fact important academic activist work.

Another way of looking at things is to declare, as Antonio Gramsci famously did in his *Prison Notebooks,* that "all men are intellectuals... but not all men have in society the function of intellectuals" (9). Perhaps we can say something similar about academics: all academics are intellectuals but only some are granted or actively take on the role of intellectual, especially public intellectual. Alternatively, Jean Genet, who paradoxically disdained the term intellectual and yet was the consummate activist intellectual, holds that we are always already political the moment we engage in public debate, whether or not we consciously take on the role of public intellectual. Edward Said quotes him: "The moment you publish essays in a society you have entered public life, so if you want not to be political, do not write essays or speak out" (Genet in Said, *Representations* 110). So is everyone in society an intellectual or is one an intellectual only when one takes on the role, is assigned the role, or at least is acknowledged as an intellectual? Does the very work of academics make them political and therefore always already intellectuals or are only those academics who declare themselves public intellectuals to be regarded as such? This question is a version of how wide or narrow the category academic public intellectual is and is in fact a variation on the same question that could be asked of public intellectuals in general. At the very opening of *Representations of the Intellectual,* Said asks, "Are intellectuals a very large or an extremely small and highly selective group of people?" (3).

Cultural studies as a field include some exploration of the variety of ways in which we can conceptualize the academic as intellectual. As the preeminent cultural studies scholar Stuart Hall once pointed out, cultural studies involves "bringing the dirty outside world" into the university and the academy and even his account of its early theoretical work ("Emergence..." 12) depicts cultural studies not as a traditional discipline but as a "project" that of necessity involves the imbrications of critical theory, practice, progressive politics, pedagogy and social justice activism. In particular, what I referred to as "cultural studies praxis" exemplifies this by taking up theory, practice and research as inextricably linked. The aim of cultural studies in its Birmingham origin, Hall once declared, was to produce what Antonio Gramsci identified as the ideal progressive public intellectual, namely, the "organic intellectual" ("Cultural Studies" 282–84).

The traditional intellectual, according to Gramsci, is engaged in discussion of issues with other intellectuals and with the powers that be and serves the status quo. The organic intellectual, by contrast, works for the marginalized in society: he or she takes on the double burden of all the work of the traditional intellectual plus the work of being an advocate for and someone who explains things to the marginalized, with the alternative aim of working for a more just and equitable society. The organic intellectual thus is not only politically engaged (as in Jean Paul Sartre's notion of the engaged intellectual), but by specifically and exclusively aligning with and working for the marginalized is, to appropriate Paulo Freire's notion of *conscientização*, the "conscenticized" intellectual.

The organic intellectual is an ideal that is quite difficult to achieve because the threshold of success is so high. Indeed, Hall readily concedes they did not succeed in becoming true organic intellectuals at Birmingham. In fact Tony Bennett disputes Hall's assertion that Birmingham attempted to produce organic intellectuals since he feels the academy is too unsuited to the task, another reason for arguing that the threshold is so high. Michel Foucault is one figure who argues simultaneously for more complexity and modesty in progressive intellectual work. Rather than positioning themselves as possessing and professing "the truth," and working assuredly for social justice, Foucault argues that progressive intellectuals ought to undertake work that explores what constitutes truth and how it is produced and put to work economically and politically (cf. *Foucault Reader*). And in response to the difficulty of being an expert in the exponentially increased and diversified topics and areas of public discourse and in acknowledgment of the fact that our expertise is often confined to specific fields, Foucault proposes in the section "Truth and Power" of *Power/Knowledge* that we can only aim to become "specific intellectuals" rather than "universal, organic intellectuals." If academics are to be public intellectuals (and if all identities are about becoming rather than being), should the process of academic as public intellectual identity be one of becoming organic intellectuals or more modestly of becoming specific intellectuals?

Of course, the inclusion of the word "public" in the term public intellectual fixes our attention on participation in the public sphere and therefore begs the question of whether there can be such a thing as a private intellectual? Edward Said, in *Representations of the Intellectual,* points out that there is "no such thing as a private intellectual, certainly not a private organic intellectual, since the moment you set down words and then publish them you have entered the public world" (110). Gilles Deleuze, on the other hand, makes the following observation: "Private thinkers are in a way opposed to public professors.... Private thinkers have a double character: a kind of solitude that remains their own in every situation; but also a particular agitation, a particular disorder of the world in which they rise up and speak. Hence they speak in their own name, without 'representing' anything, and they solicit those raw presences, those naked powers in the world which are hardly more 'representable' " (78).

Thus Deleuze draws a sharp distinction between "private thinkers" and "public professors" and in discussing the work of the former makes the case for how their work ends up being particularly instructive and influential, obfuscating and even running contrary to what one would expect of the dichotomy suggested between private and public. Rather than the nominal public nature of the work of teaching (which may or may not prove to be public intellectual work), the private work of productive thinking ends up being the truly radical public intellectual work. Deleuze's characterization can be read as an endorsement of Said's position that acknowledging that one's work cannot exist in a hermetically sealed cosmos but rather is necessarily "worldly" means that the work of the private intellectual does in fact constitute public intellectual work (*Representation* passim). In fact, with the caveat that the progressive private thinker in his or her conception does not overtly take on the burden/privilege of representing the marginalized, Deleuze goes further and asserts that the best pedagogical and public intellectual work is often produced by "private thinkers."

What does all of this mean for the academic as public intellectual? It would appear that it means that in the course of performing the normal functions of their work as graduate students or faculty (e.g., publishing a journal article, presenting a conference paper), academics step into the public sphere and therefore, in some nascent form, their work can be considered the work of the public intellectual. Of course, for those who take on the role more consciously it means actively going out into the public sphere, a concerted and sustained engagement beyond the so-called ivory tower: We should note that in this sense of the term public intellectual requires more than producing texts about things like social justice, revisionist history, and protection of the environment. As the Chicago Cultural Study Group warns, "It is too easy to suppose that mere academics can rise to become activist intellectuals simply by force of moral will, or fail to do so by failure of will—rather than through the mediation of publics, media, institutions, roles, discourses, and other conditions" (115). Thus, to avoid what the Chicago Cultural Study Group calls "the temptation...to resort to heroic fantasies about intellectual work" (115), we should realize that true public intellectual work means venturing beyond the normal course of academic work, no matter how radically antidiscriminatory and prosocial, ecological, and historically just that work might be. It means venturing out beyond the "ivory tower," it means "civic engagement," "town-gown relationships," the taking on of university-community partnerships, involvement in local, national, and international activist groups, writing letters to newspapers and giving interviews to various mass media outlets on topical issues, and so on.

Somewhere between the academic who goes about their traditional role only and the academic as an engaged public intellectual lies the work of academics who are not necessarily going outside but working within their institutions and profession for a more just and representative university and academy. Is such work intellectual work and are such academics public intellectuals? Russell Jacoby would say they are not, or if they are, then they are a very flawed version of intellectuals. In his book, *The Last Intellectuals,* Jacoby warns of academics who are altogether too absorbed with change within the narrow confines of academia and who are motivated principally by a thirst for greater academic privilege for themselves. On the other hand, Carol Becker in her essay on "The Artist as Public Intellectual" would insist that they are, making—as she does—a similar strong argument for artists who on the one hand stand outside of mainstream society and on the other work for change within institutions to be regarded as public intellectuals.

From the above discussion we might conclude that it is not altogether paradoxical to speak of the academic as public intellectual. Six points have been put forward in this essay, which suggests that rather than thinking of this issue in definitive, unitary terms, we could discern six categories of the academic as a public intellectual.

1. "Intellectuals in denial"—those academics who actively eschew the role but could be said to play it nonetheless.
2. "Accidental intellectuals"—those who enter the public sphere by merely doing their traditional roles.
3. "Traditional intellectuals"—those who support the status quo and merely transmit knowledge.
4. "Organic intellectuals"—the Gramscian term for those who represent the oppressed and marginalized and work for a just and equitable society.
5. "specific intellectuals"—the Foucauldian term for those who are questioning truth claims, eschew universalisms, and limit themselves to discussion of issues in their specific areas of expertise.
6. "Institutional intellectuals"—academics who work on making the same goal of a just and equitable society come to fruition within their own profession and individual institutions.

To raise again one of the questions brought up in the introduction to this essay, Is academic intellectual a very large, multiple, and politically pliant category or is it a very small, politically conscious, social justice—driven category? Are the six categories outlined above valid or does such an overcrowded and overly inclusive field make nonsense of the very idea of the public intellectual, in much the same way that the declaration that all children are gifted in their own way makes no sense, and does no justice to the idea of giftedness, or the declaration that all babies are beautiful make nonsense of the notion of beauty? We can conclude either that a very expansive set of categories, perhaps even larger and more varied than has been identified in this essay, is possible or that the meaning of the academic as intellectual is to be limited to a very small category of organic and/or specific academics who are risk takers, who work consistently for social justice, and who are never willing to be co-opted by the status quo. This very small category are defined by Said in this way:

At bottom the intellectual, in my sense of the word, is neither a pacifier nor a consensus-builder but someone whose whole being is staked on a critical sense, a sense of being unwilling to accept easy formulas, or ready-made clichés, or the smooth, ever-so-accommodating confirmations of what the powerful or conventional have to say, or what they do. Not just passively unwillingly but actively willing to say so in public.

(*Representations* 23)

In the end, whether academics are or can be public intellectuals and if so what that conception is or ought to be depends largely on one's own politics and whether one sees academic, intellectual, and activist work as quite distinct or potentially productively intertwined.

WORKS CITED

Becker, Carol. "The Artist as Public Intellectual." Ed. Bradford, Gigi, Michael Gray, and Wallach, Glenn. *The Politics of Culture: Policy Perspectives for Individuals, Institutions and Communities.* New York: The New Press, 2000: 236–46.

Bennett, Tony et al., *Culture, Ideology and Social Process.* London: Open UP, 1981.

Berubé, Michael. "Public Academy." *The New Yorker,* Jan. 9, 1995: 78.

Chicago Cultural Studies Group. "Critical Multiuculturalism." *Critical Inquiry* 18 (Spring 1992): 530–55.

Deleuze, Gilles. "He was My Teacher." *Desert Islands and Other Texts 1953–1974.* Los Angeles: Semiotext(e), 77–81.

Foucault, Michel. *Power/Knowledge: Selected Interviews and Other Writings, 1972–1979.* Ed. C. Gordon. New York: Pantheon Books, 1980.

——*The Foucault Reader.* Ed. Paul Rabinow. New York: Vintage Books, 1984.

Freire, Paulo. *Pedagogy of the Oppressed.* 1970. Trans. Myra Bergman Ramos. New York: Continuum, 2000.

Goldberg, David Theo. *Multiculturalism: A Critical Reader.* Oxford: Blackwell, 1994.

Gramsci, Antonio. *Prison Notebook* 2. New York: Columbia UP, 1975.

Habermas, Jürgen. *The Structural Transformation of the Public Sphere.* Cambridge: MIT Press, 1989.

Hall, Stuart. "Cultural Studies and its Theoretical Legacies." Ed. Cary Nelson, Paula Treichler and Lawrence Grossberg *Cultural Studies.* London: Routledge, 1992. 277–94.

——"The Emergence of Cultural Studies and the Crisis of the Humanities." *The Humanities as Social Technology.* 53 (Summer, 1990): 11–23.

Inter-Disciplinary.Net. www.inter-disciplinary.net/about-us/history/. Jesse Peterson and Radoslav Kolarov. Accessed Apr. 10, 2011.

Jacoby, Russell. *The Last Intellectuals: American Culture in the Age of Academe.* New York: Basic Books, 1987.

Said, Edward. *Representations of the Intellectual: The 1993 Reith Lectures.* New York: Vintage Books, 1994.
——*The World, the Text and the Critic.* Cambridge, MA: Harvard UP, 1983.
Wright, Handel Kashope. "Cultural Studies as Praxis: (Making) an Autobiographical Case." *Cultural Studies* 17.6 (2003): 805–22.

Chapter 4

Beyond the Specialist/Generalist Framework: Reflections on Three Decades of the Comparative History of Intellectuals Discourse

Kjetil Ansgar Jakobsen

The adjective *intellectual* has long been used and is still being used in a general sense (as in "intellectual life"). It was in France during the Dreyfus affair in the 1890s that the noun *intellectual* caught on and started to circulate widely. *Intellectuals* then appeared in the media, and discussion broke out over who was and who was not a true intellectual. From there the idea quickly spread to most other nations, always as a source of controversy and contest. Indeed, the death, decline, or treason of the intellectual has been proclaimed incessantly for more than a century. Yet the intellectual is still a prominent public figure. Why is it that the question of the intellectual became so urgent suddenly in the late nineteenth century? And why has remained so today? Why do modern societies seem to have a need for such a term, even if the concept is by no means clear?

As a research field the study of intellectuals is almost as old as the term itself. The structural and functional approaches of Karl

Mannheim, Antonio Gramsci, Seymour Martin Lipset, and Edward Shils were conceived as socio-scientific alternatives to more common-sensical biographical approaches. Since the 1980s, focus has turned away from sociological modeling toward a more open-ended comparative discursive approach, founded in intellectual history. "The intellectual" is treated as a discursive field of controversy. The comparative study of intellectuals, as exemplified by the works of Charle, Lepenies, Ringer, Trebitsch, Granjon, Casanova, and Collini, is very much a history of a concept, of how "intellectual" (and related notions) has been employed in various contexts sine the nineteenth century. The virtue of the comparative turn is threefold. First, it widens the horizon, challenging national *doxa*. Second, it renders a sharper methodology. As Durkheim noted, comparison is to the social sciences what experiment is to the sciences of nature (45). Finally, it produces much new knowledge. The program has been extremely successful. We now have profound knowledge of how the discourse of the intellectual developed in many countries and cultural areas of the world. Indeed, empirical knowledge is so great that it may be time to step back and do a new round of theoretical debate. This chapter overviews the study of intellectuals as a research field and sketches a theory of intellectual practice that is neither structural nor functional but rather performative. This work of conceptualization based on the results of comparative intellectual history will serve to show that the intellectual is not an outdated discourse based on untenable universals and absolutes and on an outdated concept of the public sphere. Intellectuals do important things in contemporary society qua intellectuals rather than qua researchers, artists, teachers, or journalists. It is therefore important to continue discussing and refining the concept.

Common Usages

The comparative history of intellectuals has flourished for nearly two decades since the pioneering works of Wolff Lepenies, Fritz Ringer, and Christophe Charle, despite the unusual epistemic challenges posed by the study of intellectuals. It would an exaggeration to say that there is no agreement at all on what an intellectual is, but opinions certainly differ. Sister fields, such as art history or political science, also have problems in delineating their objects of study. Those studying the field of contemporary art must entertain the illusion that there is really no specialized art field in the sense of Pierre Bourdieu's sociology, but that the production and enjoyment of art flows, so to speak, from human nature. A similar phenomenon is true of democratic politics, which must necessarily entertain the illusion that everyone can participate in political life on equal footing even though politics in modern democracies is obviously a highly specialized and hierarchal activity. Key controversies among arts scholars involve exclusive and inclusive notions of art, just as key struggles among political scientists concern issues of technocracy and participation, professionalization, and populism. But even if field boundaries are in both cases subjective, fluid, and paradoxical, it would still be easy to pick out a kernel of people who are unquestionably artists or politicians. Academic controversies over who is and who is not an artist and who is or is not a politician may never be decided, but the designations do have a kind of intersubjective reality due to the fact that they correspond to specialized fields of activity in modern society. The term *intellectual* tends to be given to people who are active in very different fields and who mediate between specialist discourses as well as between those discourses and various publics.

I propose that we start the discussion by looking at the common usages of the word intellectual in ordinary language. Collini distinguishes the following uses of the word intellectual: (1) "the sociological sense," defining the intellectual as a socio-professional; (2) "the subjective sense," focusing on an individual's attitude about and degree of interest in ideas; (3) "the cultural sense," involving both a level of achievement in a specific cultural field and the expression of general views to a wider public; and finally, (4) "the political sense," emphasizing political interventions from the cultural domain. A fifth common usage of the term (mentioned only en passant by Collini) is that which focuses on the "free intellectual" understood as self-employed and institutionally independent. These meanings are not mutually exclusive and are often used together. One may easily imagine an educated person active in the cultural domain (usage 1), having shown persistent engagement with ideas (usage 2), being institutionally independent (usage 5), having achieved a level of recognition in a specialized field of culture (usage 3), and intervening in politics (usage 4).

According to Collini, the hegemonic use in the English language is usage 3. All the uses observed by Collini have, however, been developed into concepts by scholars. Usage 4 is the starting point for one of the most influential French schools of thought for the study of intellectuals, that is, that of Pascale Ory and Jean-François Sirinelli and his associates. For the Sirinelli school, the history of intellectuals is a subspecies of political history, dealing with the political interventions from the cultural and scientific domain since the time of Dreyfus. Collini notes that this restrictive use is much more common in French than in English and also that it is more properly a subset of usage 3, politics being a field of general interest.

Usage 2 and 5 are prominent in biographical approaches whereby it is common to define the intellectual in terms of personal qualities such as independence of spirit, curiosity of mind, interest in ideas, personal autonomy, and integrity. Institutional independence is also a commonly invoked hallmark of the "free intellectual." Discussing the intellectual involves the naming of great examples: Ibsen, Tolstoy and Zola, Bertrand Russell, George Orwell and Aldous Huxley, Sartre, de Beauvoir and Foucault, Rushdie and Derrida. Most scholars within the comparative study of intellectuals tend, however, to dismiss the subjective or romantic conception of the intellectual as naive as it involves no reflection on the social and historical conditions for intellectual practice, but define the intellectual as someone who stands outside of society with lofty loyalty to the world of ideas. The word *intellectual* has been denounced by some as a hoax, an inherently ideological discourse that reinforces a misplaced romantic notion of knowledge (just like art) as the product of the individual genius. Several schools of thought, the Bourdieusian school among others, have sought to develop a notion of the collective intellectual, organizing, among other things, collective interventions.[1]

To Seymour Martin Lipset, intellectuals are "all those who create, distribute and apply *culture*—the symbolic world of man, including art, science and religion" (quoted in Collini 46). Other sociologists have identified the term with the university-educated segment of society. Several schools of research applied this structural approach to the study of intellectuals, whereby intellectuals are thought of as a class, a social strata or socio-professional group. Defining the intellectuals as those who work with culture or hold a university education renders a relatively objective and operative concept of the sort favored by empirical social science. Unfortunately, it fails to do justice to the discourse in question.

As mentioned before, controversies over the nature of intellectuals have raged ever since the term emerged in the 1890s. A staple of those controversies has been the lament over the absence or "death of" intellectuals. Yet the number of people who make their living working with "culture" and/or who have a university education runs to the millions in larger countries and appears to be constantly expanding. If the field of intellectuals is constituted to a large extent by struggles over what an intellectual is and who the true intellectuals are, the "objective" concept somehow betrays the nature of the object. Furthermore, in structural usage, "intellectual" becomes a rather general notion often exchangeable with a series of other concepts of mainstream sociology, such as professionals, the educated middle class, cultural capital, *Bildungsbürgertum,* and so on.

Closely related to the structural approach of the study of intellectuals is what one could call the functional approach according to which someone is an intellectual not because of who he or she *is*, but because of what he or she *does*. Gramsci famously pronounced that "all men are intellectuals...but not all men have in society the function of intellectuals." His concept of the organic intellectual answers the question "what is the function of intellectuals in the revolutionary movement?" In his influential books about sociology and intellectual history, Edward Shils proposes a wide functional notion of intellectuals as those who produce the symbolic order of society: "Through their provision of models and standards, by the presentation of symbols to be appreciated, intellectuals elicit, guide, and form the expressive dispositions within a society" (5). In French research, intellectuals are routinely described as a necessary *counterpower* to the established authorities of society. One argues or assumes that there is a need for social and political critique in modern society, fulfilled by people who are thus called intellectuals.

Function, however, functions within some kind of social order. This is true even for Marxists, like Gramsci, who give intellectuals the function of a being an organ (the head?) in the proletarian body. The issue of functionality and the concept of the intellectual is a hard one. One must avoid a full-blown functional explanation, wherein the part is explained by its utility for the reproduction of the totality. Such functionalism undercuts the criticality of the intellectual. Besides, what kind of totality are we referring to—the nation-state, the proletariat, humankind, the global social system, the ecosystem of the earth, or the universe? Moreover, who is in a position to conceptualize that totality?[2]

A Two-Source Term

Turning now from uses to genealogy, one may note that contemporary discourses on the intellectual largely spring from two historical sources: the mid-nineteenth-century Russian discourse on the *intelligentsia* and the late nineteenth-century French discourse on the *intellectuels*. Both terms carried, in their original contexts, strong connotations of marginality and protest. In contemporary Slavic languages *intelligentsia* is simply the word which corresponds to the Western term *intellectuals*. In English and many other languages, *intelligentsia* and *intellectual* cohabit with a nuance of semantic difference. *Intelligentsia* is—generally speaking—a less affirmative term than intellectual. It tends to denote a relatively closed social group that lays claim to authority based on *who they are* rather than *what they do*. Thus when conservatives denounce intellectuals for being unwilling or unable to argue their cause publicly in an understandable language, they tend to use the term *intelligentsia*. The historical trajectory of the two terms helps to explain why they mean slightly different things. Before spreading worldwide, the Russianized form intelligentsia was imported to Russian from German, along with national Romanticism and idealist philosophy, in the first half of the nineteenth century.[3] The peculiar marginality of the *intelligentsia* was the paradoxical and undesirable result of the program formulated in the eighteenth century by czars Peter and Catherine to ensure Russia's status as a great power. The program, continued by their successors, consisted in importing as much Western technology, science and "enlightenment" as possible while ignoring Western political and social institutions. A few people were trained in the Western sciences and arts, thus facilitating the importation of science and technology to an empire facing competition from the West. This small group—the *intelligentsia*—lived strangely isolated in the feudal and authoritarian megaempire. Shut out from real social and political power by the nobility, they developed exalted notions of their mission and that of the "people," of which they, by the way, often knew very little. Nevertheless, with the sciences of the West came Western political ideals; however, the *intelligentsia* did not obtain the political rights achieved by their professional colleagues in the West. When the *intelligentsia* engaged in political activity, they tended to be driven into illegality. Confrontation with the authorities inspired extreme positions. For various reasons the attempts made by certain tsars to establish ties of loyalty with the *intelligentsia* through political reform failed and led to a new wave of repression, driving parts of the *intelligentsia* into exile. This *intelligentsia*, with its sprouting flora of spectacular terrorists, self-declared *nihilists* and anarchists, poets and dreamers, sharp-minded theoreticians and incurable drunkards, Jews and politically active women, was frequently used as a scapegoat in conservative and right-wing propaganda all over Europe.[4]

It was in France during the Dreyfus affair in the 1890s, a moment of marginality and protest, that the noun *intellectual* started to circulate widely. The army, the courts, the government, and the mainstream media were caught lying in the Dreyfus affair. Out of conviction, convenience or cowardice, they had been playing along with the fake spy charges instigated by anti-Semites against Captain Dreyfus. In *Les Règles de l'Art* Bourdieu forcefully argues that the preponderance of literary avant-gardists like Émile Zola, Anatole France, Marcel Proust, and André Gide during the affair—somewhat paradoxically—stems from the high levels of autonomy from society at large, manifest in experimental literature by the generation following the "nomothetic" or "legislative" work of Baudelaire and Flaubert (Charle, *Naissance*). When it became apparent to many that power was corrupt, faith was placed in sectors of society renowned for relative autonomy in relation to power, notably literature and the science.

Paradoxes of Power

The question of the intellectual then may be framed in the following manner: How does one make the achievements of the specialized fields of art, scholarship, and science relevant to each other and to politics, and to a wider social context, notably that of mass-mediated culture? What, if any, cultural and political authority do artists, writers, scientists, and scholars have *beyond* their specific status as experts of a particular, limited field of craft or knowledge? In a jargon that seems outmoded today, one would speak of the intellectual as involving the *spiritual authority* of artists, writers, scholars, and scientists. One should note, however, that the authority of the intellectual involves a profound paradox, that of the authority of the marginal, the power of those who hold no power! Intellectual discourse entails a certain marginality and criticality. The intellectual should therefore be distinguished both from the expert advisor and from the professor-politician. Intellectual discourse is different from the power-knowledge of the expert, even if the same person may practice both types of discourses, in different contexts. The professor-politician is a key figure of nation building in many countries—for instance, in the young democracies of Eastern Europe where politics was less professionalized than in the West—at least up until recently. Academics and artists, like anyone else, may perform public duty and engage in civic life, for instance, by joining a political party and running for office. It is, however, not in the exercise of practical authority and formal power, as, say, a member of parliament, that the characteristics of intellectual discourse play themselves out. Under the July monarchy (1830–48) France was ruled by a circle of university professors known as *Les doctrinaires*. They included the historians François Guizot and Adolphe Thiers, the philosopher Victor Cousin, and Abel-Francois Villemain, a professor of literature. If asked to draw up a list of the leading French intellectuals of those times I would, however, shy away from these figures of authority and rather look in the direction of a critical and yet engaged writer like Victor Hugo or even relatively apolitical, but extremely critical and reflective figures like Charles Baudelaire or Gustave Flaubert.

According to the Bourdieu school, there is an inherent tension between economic, socio-political, and cultural capital. The Bourdieusian theory of the three dimensions of power explains in a general way why marginality is intrinsic to most discourses on and by the intellectual. Elite groups that specialize in cultural capital are marginalized to a certain degree due to the dominance of the economic dimension in capitalist societies. Cultural capital is obliged to engage in all sorts of struggles to maintain autonomy relative to money and the state and is therefore deemed to be the basis of a counter power.[5]

THE COMPARATIVE DISCURSIVE APPROACH

Whereas proponents of the structural and functional approaches started with a rigid concept of the intellectual, the contemporary comparative research on intellectuals tends to be conceptually open. Historians opt for *Begriffgeschichte* as does Collini in his *Absent Minds* (2006) where he intends to write the history of the word in England. Rather than defining what an intellectual is, Collini recounts the history of the word *intellectual* in England and the controversies that have surrounded it. He then compares the word in other key cultural contexts, notably France, Germany and the United States. In sociology, the hegemonic approach is probably the Bourdieusian. Field theory is a more rigid conceptual framework than that usually employed by historians, but it points to the uniqueness of the object studied. Despite a more rigid conceptual framework, the comparative approach favored by the Bourdieusians precisely maps the way the discourse of the intellectual developed in various national contexts.[6] One seeks to identify and render explicit the *doxa*, the cultural schemata, which motivated the controversies. Thus, the "field of intellectuals" is a more fluid and subjective entity than the "field of art," "field of literature," or "field of science." It is seen as self-reflectively constituted through continuous debate about what an intellectual is and who the true intellectuals are. The intellectual field is very much a field of people proposing concepts to marginalize opponents through a struggle that involves paradoxical terms, such as margin and *marginal,* that tend to be positive labels among intellectuals. In some cases *intellectual* may be a negative label that one seeks to attach to one's opponent in order to exclude him or her from the field; this was long the case in Germany (cf. Bering). Both the *Begriffgeschichte* and the field theory approach bring out how the intellectual was conceived in various cultural and political contexts, and the struggles that took place over this notion.

The discursive-comparative approach makes a major sacrifice of scope compared to previous theories by Edward Shils and Karl Mannheim. Shils proposed a wide comparison, pointing out that all societies have their symbol producers across time and space, though usually of a religious nature (9). Shils favors the model of a *polyhistor,* the intellectual as a person of religion as much as of science and art. Intellectuals are "persons with an unusual sensitivity to the sacred, an uncommon reflectiveness about the nature of their universe and the rules which govern their society" (3). In the discursive approach, the field of research and comparison is limited to contexts where the word *intellectual* is actually at stake. The study of intellectuals thus becomes the study of modern or contemporary intellectuals and thus largely of secular intellectuals. In the comparative discursive approach, the distinction between premodern and modern intellectuals becomes meaningless as the discursive position of the intellectual is only available in modern societies. I prefer this approach for reasons of conceptual and methodological clarification, but as a historian of ideas I would be the last to deny that there is a loss involved in this clarification.

The virtue of the comparative turn is threefold. First, it widens the horizon, challenging national *doxa.* Second, it renders a sharper methodology, and it produces new knowledge. So what are the chief results of 20 years of comparative study of intellectuals? That question cannot be answered in a short article, but to mention only one trait: the similarity of the various national discourses on the intellectual. This finding is important, since intellectuals tend to think their national trajectory is unique. Most notably two paradoxical traits can be found in all discourses, whether in major cultural centers like Germany or England, small peripheries like Norway or Quebec, or postcolonial societies like Brazil or Senegal, namely, the eternal death of the intellectual and the provincialism of them all.

Death of the Intellectual

The rich literature on the comparative history of the intellectual shows us that the death or absence of the intellectual has been deplored or celebrated incessantly ever since the notion was established in the late nineteenth century. One of the more recent examples mentioned by Collini is Michael Ignatieff's affirmation that "the death of the intellectual has left a void in public life." The "independent intellectual" is gone, leaving us with "worthy professors, cultural bureaucrats, carnival barkers and entertainers" (9). Similar examples can be found in Maurice Barrès' *Scènes et Doctrines du Nationalisme* (1902). This text by the French novelist and right-wing leader is perhaps the first to elaborate at length on the concept of the intellectual. *Intellectual* had begun as an insult, a charge against the "Dreyfusards" echoing Edmund Burke's charge of intellectualism against the Revolutionaries of 1789. But the Dreyfusards, in a classic gesture of resistance, had reappropriated the intended insult, making it a honorific title. Barrès' long chapter entitled "Intellectuels ou Logiciens de l'Absolu" is, in terms of its motivation, a conservative attempt to return the word to its original pejorative sense. The tone that Barrès aims for at the outset is one of high-minded "scientific" reflection, and he discusses various definitions, notably one drawn from Henrik Ibsen's 1886 play *Rosmersholm* where Ulric Brendel says to Rosmer: "Peder Mortensgaard never wants more than he can obtain. Peder Mortensgaard is capable of living life without ideals. The intellectual, on the other hand, is an artist or scientist who does not hold power and yet forms a social ideal" (44). In Ibsen's play the representation of the tortured aristocrat, Rosmer, wandering in his manor amidst crowded bookshelves and somber portraits of distinguished ancestors, is an anachronism, a lofty man of spirit whose vague attempt at political intervention "above party politics" is effortlessly sidelined by the conservative headmaster Kroll, a master of intrigue in the circles of power, acting for once in conjunction with his opponent, the leftist leader Peder Mortensgaard, editor of a successful popular newspaper. Barrès charges "the logicians of the absolute" with mistaking scientific and artistic authority for political and social authority and thus for not recognizing the nature of modern society. Interestingly, the concept of the intellectual is *launched* in a text where this social figure is portrayed as an anachronism that should be thrown into the dustbin of history.

The three reasons given for the purported decline or death of the intellectual have remained remarkably stable across time and cultural barriers. First, the media and the general public are blamed for celebrity culture, commercialism, superficiality, and a decline in literacy. I'll call this the Mortensgaard effect. Second, a finger is pointed at the snobbism and reclusion of scholars and scientists and the growing incomprehensibility of their discourse. I'll call this the Magic Mountain effect. Finally, there is the recurring worry over the purported decline of universal standards and values with which intellectuals are supposed to engage. This could be called the Unbearable Lightness of Being effect. The first two are just different examples of differentiation and specialization at work. In an age when journalists use every trick in the book to reach larger audiences, while scholars specialize in refining expert language, there is, it seems, no room for the generalist addressing the "enlightened public" anymore, or so the argument goes.[7]

Why does every generation suggest that the age of the intellectual is past and that there are no great intellectuals anymore? This could be explained in various ways. First, calling someone a "great intellectual" is a form of canonization, and one does not willingly, and least of all in intellectual circles, bestows larger-than-life qualities on one's contemporaries, especially when disagreeing with them. According to this logic, Salman Rushdie, Slavoj Žižek, and Judith Butler may seem like midgets of the mind compared to George Orwell, Jean Paul Sartre, and Simone de Beauvoir (but so did Orwell, Sartre, and de Beauvoir in their time compared to an earlier generation.) Yet, the complaint that the age of the intellectual has passed and that the intellectuals have betrayed their true mission is so common and has changed so little since the word *intellectual* was first used in the modern media that there is reason to ask if this accusation is actually intrinsic to the discourse on and by the intellectual. The death of the intellectual has followed or even foreshadowed the notion of the intellectual in much the same way as "the death of art" (first developed as a theory by Hegel) did the modern art institution from its origins in Romanticism up till the contemporary period.[8]

My claim would be that "the death of the intellectual" is intrinsic to the modern concept of the intellectual because this is a discourse brought on by modern tendencies toward contingency, decenteredness, and specialization. When one says "there are no real intellectuals anymore," one implies a series of difficult and important inclinations concerning the overspecialization of academic life, the nature of the mass media, and the professionalization of politics. Chronology shows that the fear of specialization predates by far the notion of the intellectual, and the intellectual is only one of many answers that have been proposed. German romanticism and neo-humanism were perhaps the first two great cultural currents to be motivated largely by fear of specialization. The ambitious (alternative) notions of philosophy in Kant and Hegel were set to counter the malaise. So was Hölderlin's notion of the poet as well as Humboldt's of the translator. Comte's notion of sociology, Coleridge's of the "clerisy," and Arnold's of culture were posterior responses to the problem. It is also common to point to the critic as part of the answer to the problem of specialization. To some critique is really the culminating point of a specialized effort of art and scholarship, the work of an author not being complete until the critic has made the author's insights available for the general public and initiated discussion of them. The influential U.S. notion of the "think tank" denotes another important strategy that has been proposed to mobilize the cognitive achievements of various specialized fields for a nonspecialist purpose.

The intellectual appears on the scene of history to confront a three-headed ogre: The Mortensgaard effect, the Magic Mountain effect, and the Unbearable Lightness of Being effect. Without the ogre there would be no intellectual and, on the face of it, the ogre always comes out on top in their deadly struggle. The ogre is part of progress, and a modern society can hardly be conceived without it. Thus the death of the intellectual is intrinsic to the discourse of the intellectual just as the death of art is intrinsic to contemporary art.

The Universal Provincialism

The "death of the intellectual" is not the only paradoxical trait of the discourse brought out by the many comparative studies of the intellectual appearing over the last decade. Not only has the age of intellectuals been long gone, but one's own country is and was always peculiarly anti-intellectual. Much U.S. literature on the intellectual deplores the peculiar anti-intellectualism of North Americans. Brazilians deplore the peculiar anti-intellectualism of Brazil, the Brits that of Britain, Norwegians that of Norway. To Belgians Belgium is *the* nation *par excellence* of anti-intellectualism.[9] Often this anti-intellectualism is presented with a positive twist. The British may see it in the light of presumed qualities of Englishness like moderation, empiricism, and good common sense. Norwegian intellectuals will typically waver: in one phrase they deplore the presumed anti-intellectualism of Norwegians, while in the next acknowledge that it may be the price to pay for the antielitism and strong democratic cohesion of Scandinavian societies. In all cases, the counterexample given is usually France, the supposed paradise of intellectuals (the French themselves may not subscribe to that description though).

The paradox that intellectuals of all cultures (except possibly France) consider their own culture to be peculiarly anti-intellectual is neatly explained by the Bourdieu school, notably Charle, Gisèle Sapiro, and Pascale Casanova. To this school, the intellectual gesture typically involves a recycling of specific cultural capital, accumulated in the transnational fields of art, science, and scholarship, into general cultural and political capital, in national contexts. The intellectual, also called the counterpower of the avant-garde, is said to have arisen due to the autonomization of art and literature in relation to the nation-state in the nineteenth century and as a result of a similar autonomization of philosophy and social science in the twentieth century. A gap arises between the field of power—that is, politics, money, and the mass media, closely tied in with the nation-state—and the more internationalized fields of art and knowledge production. In this gap a space is opened for a specifically intellectual field where artistic, scholarly, and scientific avant-gardes actualize themselves relative to the symbolic capital of the special fields they represent, as Zola, France, Proust, and Gide did when intervening for Captain Dreyfus. Intellectuals are thus not "free moving" like Karl Mannheim thought, but anchored in transnational art and knowledge-producing networks. We now see why one's own culture is usually felt to be peculiarly anti-intellectual. Intellectual intervention *is* internationalism (or better, transnationalism) faced with the constraints of the national contexts. In peer-to-peer talk internationally, discourse may reflect a specifically scientific or artistic logic. When returning to the national scene, the impure obligations of politics and commerce make themselves felt in the cultural domain again. The intellectual is thus structurally disposed to lament the anti-intellectualism of his or her national context. As shown by Casanova, this has been the case in France somewhat less than elsewhere due to the special status of Paris as "world capital of culture" and the French claims to universalism in culture and politics (Enlightenment values, cradle of the rights of man, avant-garde art, etc.).[10]

Specialization and the Generalist

The Bourdieusians note that the discourse on the intellectual arises with specialization and is concerned with making the fantastic achievements of the most differentiated and specialized fields of modernity available to other fields. The intellectual is thus not seen as a kind of leftover from a prespecialist stage, a renaissance man of the media age, constantly threatened by modernization processes. Even researchers who are critical of Bourdieu's social theory follow the Bourdieusians in seeing the intellectual as defined by the two poles of specialization and generalization. This is the case with Collini's 2006 book, *Absent Minds,* for instance, which brings two decades of continental research on the intellectual to bear on British experiences. Collini does not propose a theory of the intellectual, but he does propose a concept of the intellectual, made up of four criteria.

1. The attainment of a level of achievement in an activity that is esteemed for the noninstrumental, creative, analytical, or scholarly capacities it involves.
2. The availability of media and channels of expression that reach publics other than that at which the initial "qualifying" activity itself is aimed.
3. The expression of views, themes, or topics that successfully articulate or engage with some of the general concerns of those publics.
4. The establishment of a reputation for advancing important and interesting ideas and for the willingness to express them effectively through the appropriate media.

This concept is really very close to that of the Bourdieusians, even though he avoids the trademark concept of capital. Both see the intellectual as a mediator between the achievements of a specialized cultural domain and a more general public. Collini refuses to base his concept of the intellectual on a Habermasian notion of the uniqueness of the public sphere, insisting that there is a multitude of different publics, not one "public sphere." Even so, his concept presupposes such a theory or at least a tacit or normative consensus as to what does and what does not constitute a "general concern." That is a problematical assumption, I believe. Take the example of the Norwegian modernist novelist and football commentator Dag Solstad who publishes a book of reportage and reflection on the latest FIFA World cup every four years with another writer. The football (i.e., soccer) books are read by a different and wider public than his novels. Solstad generally refuses to express artistic or political views in national newspapers or television, claiming that such media have deteriorated to such a degree that they are now "unfit for the discussion of serious issues." He, however, liberally shares his views on football issues.

In Norway, as in most European countries, nothing—except possibly the sex life of celebrities—seems to be of more general interest to various publics than soccer football. The modernist novel, in the tradition of Proust and Thomas Mann, is certainly a field that is esteemed for the noninstrumental, creative, analytical, or scholarly capacities it involves. A prized author like Solstad, translated into many languages, has achieved a level of accomplishment that meets Collini's first condition. As a football commentator, he also expresses himself through media and channels of expression directed to publics different from the one at which the initial "qualifying" activity was aimed. He has developed a reputation for saying important and interesting things effectively about football through the appropriate media. Therefore, is Solstad to be considered as the perfect intellectual, not only an esteemed experimental artist but also someone who expresses himself to a different and wider public on a quite different set of issues? Something is wrong with this line of reasoning. If Solstad is an intellectual, and I think he is, it is because he writes novels that deal critically and reflectively with the various languages and media that make up modern societies and with ethical and political issues involved in contemporary life. My point is that the notion of "general concern" presupposes a normative theory on the relative value and importance of different publics. Today such normative presuppositions can no longer remain tacit; if you rely on them, they must be specified since the traditional quality media are clearly on the defensive in relation to new media. Major newspapers are sparsely read among people under 50 (Alterman). The concept of the public sphere raises enormous conceptual difficulties due to globalization, the rate of media change, and the rapid fragmentation and multiplication of publics. Is it necessary to involve the theory of the intellectual in those difficulties? This is what the specialist/generalist framework does. I will suggest, therefore, giving up that framework. The opposite of a specialist is not and cannot be a generalist.

Cultural Translation

Is there an alternative to mindless specialization other than "general culture"? What should intellectuals do if they cannot step out of discourse and take the panoptic view of things? For a long time, the intellectual was characterized in terms of universalist concepts like "truth," "justice," "history," "autonomy," and "the public sphere." These concepts and their presuppositions are hotly contested in contemporary theory. The intellectual is deemed neither as a specialist that generalizes nor as a modern-day Don Quixote valiantly patrolling the spectra of the public sphere to defend the graves of Truth, Reason, Justice, and History. What alternatives do we have for making sense of discourses on the intellectual since the concept first emerged a good century ago?

Roland Barthes in his essay on the Dreyfus affair addressed the historical significance that resides in the moment in history when it becomes apparent that unitary bourgeois culture has been blown apart. The bourgeoisie has lost its cultural voice. The affair signals the advent of a society where the elites of finance, politics, the military, and the mainstream media "no longer have access to experimental intellectual, literary and artistic languages." Social elites no longer share common cultural ground. "Une séparation dramatique des langages" (1191) has occurred, a dramatic internal untranslatability having risen in the midst of culture. How does one respond to this "séparation dramatique des langages"? Aside from attempts to bring back the generalist, part of the answer must certainly be about translation.

One thing that may sound surprising to those not well versed in the history of translation philosophy is that modern theory of translation began with the discovery of *untranslatability* in the works by Friedrich Hölderlin, the Schlegel brothers, and Wilhelm von Humboldt.[11] The great philosopher of translation—Humboldt—wrote in the early nineteenth century that

> man lives with his objects chiefly—in fact, since his feeling and acting depends on his perceptions, one may say exclusively—as language presents them to him. By the same process whereby he spins language out of his own being, he ensnares himself in it, and each language draws a magic circle round the people it belongs, a circle from which there is no escape, save by stepping out of it into another.
>
> (Humboldt qtd. in Cassirer 9)

These observations on the untranslatability of language may be extended to the discourses of modern society. Awareness of untranslatability endows the translator with a major ethical and political mission, to be the caretaker of the untranslatability of the other. Translation aims to expand the recipient language by making otherness felt. Acknowledgment of the otherness of the other involves an opening up of one's own language. Translation in this line of thought from Hölderlin and Humboldt to Benjamin, Derrida, and Lévinas is the key mission of intellectuals. The first step toward a theory of what intellectuals actually do would be to replace some of the usual universals by a philosophy of translation that should be one of practice, pragmatics, and performativity. Intellectuals are performers that specialize in recontextualizing knowledge and creating new meanings.

SYMMETRIC CRITICALITY

Intellectual discourse operates within historically specific cultural and social relations. It should be noted, however, that even if idealist notions of the intellectual seem naive, it is hard to think of an affirmative notion of the intellectual that does not assume some qualifications in terms of personal culture, creativity, reflectivity, and mental seriousness even though these might be hard to assess with an objective criteria. Even if it is naive to think that "independent" intellectuals are by nature more autonomous than employed scholars or artists, autonomy may still form the basis for the concept of the intellectual. It is hard to think of a notion of the intellectual that disregards independence and autonomy entirely. This is evident in the fact that the intellectual who is not free (unfree) is a contradiction in terms. The thinker who is not free appears to betray any conceivable ideal for what an intellectual should be. Intellectuals are by definition among the freest thinkers in the land, somehow unconstrained even by the professional norms of a specialized discipline. Contemporary cultural theory is, however, largely hostile to the notion of autonomy. It is, therefore, my purpose to develop an up-to-date nation of intellectual autonomy. Any relapse into idealism would be regressive. As Bourdieu points out it is "on the backdrop of illusionary freedom from social determinations ... that such determinations are free to compel" (26). The artist, scientist, or philosopher is the most unfree when he or she feels free from all determinations. We need a framework wherein intellectuals who are by definition free are understood socio-historically. I will call this framework "symmetric criticality."

The term is inspired by Clement Greenberg's famous essay on "Modernist painting," in which he distinguished between two forms of critique. Enlightenment critique is holistic and totalizing. Modernist critique, on the other hand, is specific and self-referential.

> The essence of Modernism lies, as I see it, in the use of characteristic methods of a discipline to criticize the discipline itself, not in order to subvert it but in order to entrench it more firmly in its area of competence. Kant used logic to establish the limits of logic, and while he withdrew much from its old jurisdiction, logic was left all the more secure in what there remained to it.
>
> (Greenberg 1960)

As Greenberg sees it, the characteristic methods of a discipline are used to criticize the discipline, not in order to subvert it but in order to entrench it more firmly in its areas of competence. Modernism in this sense began with Kant's philosophy, and has since become a staple of modern society. Greenberg traced symmetric critique as a major factor in the development of modern painting. In my opinion, however, symmetric criticality is not just a characteristic of Modernist painting or critical philosophy, but of intellectual practice in general. Take journalism as an example. Who is the true intellectual? Is it the journalist of grand cultural orientation, posing as social philosopher? Or is it the journalist using the powerful tools of his or her trade to scrutinize and uncover the power of the media, thus achieving reflective autonomy in relation to media discourse? The symmetry principle explains why the avant-garde deconstruction of the art institution, that is, the artist disclosing the magic formula of art such as Duchamp promoting a mass-produced urinal as art, seems peculiarly intellectual, as does the Bourdieu school's objectification of the "homo academicus," or the critique of science and education in Michel Foucault, Jacques Derrida, or Bruno Latour. There are perhaps two main reasons why symmetric criticality has become so important to contemporary seekers of the truth. First, the totalizing (panoptic) claims implicit in the ideals of the Enlightenment are losing credibility. Symmetric criticality offers a way to counteract the ills of specialization, which does not depend on Enlightenment reason being able to see the "big picture." Second, the efforts made by modernizers to limit issues of power and confrontation to a specific functional space called politics is being questioned. We have become accustomed instead to think that power is everywhere. Before Foucault it seemed reasonable to think of the practice of intellectuals as delimited by two ironical phrases, the "court intellectual" and the "ivory tower intellectual." The "court intellectual" or advisor to the sovereign is too close to power to be a true intellectual. The "ivory tower intellectual" is on the other hand a contradiction in terms since being an intellectual implies a willingness to go beyond one's specialized professional domain. With this new self-understanding, intellectuals are obliged to be "specific intellectuals," questioning in a radical manner the mental closure, power practices, and even violence implicit in their own professional practices, in universities, media institutions, hospitals, and institutions of taste and artistic production. If power is everywhere, then all intellectuals are, so to speak, court intellectuals, buffoons of the king, looking to unleash a discourse, perhaps one of suspended responsibility (such as fiction), wherein it will finally be possible to speak the truth.

Still, most symmetric self-referentiality is not really critical, just playful and inconsequential like contemporary advertising that pokes fun at the manipulative techniques of advertising. Symmetry does not guarantee seriousness, unless there is an intention to be critical. Also, critique in itself may be a necessary but is not a sufficient condition for a practice to be labeled intellectual, in the sense I'm proposing. Critique is part of the normal function of science specifically and reason in general. The intellectual must go beyond the normal critical procedures of the field and what Bourdieu calls field *doxa*, that is, the tacit normative content and implications of practices. An atomic physicist is not an intellectual just because he's good at questioning the papers of his colleagues but only when he signs a petition against nuclear testing. Several interpretations have been proposed as the quote strikes a chord in general sensibilities. To Sartre the remark illustrates his own comic self-description of the intellectual as "quelqu'un qui se mêle de ce qui ne le regarde pas" (someone who interferes with what does not concern him) (9). Collini is in relative agreement with Sartre, taking the antinuclear protest of the atomic physicist to be a case of the renowned specialist addressing a different public on an issue of general concern (Collini 61). But why does the antinuclear protest of a nuclear physicist concern us more than would his engagement in any other socio-political issue? Isn't it because the symmetry principle is at work? The protester knows what he's talking about and his talking out (one can imagine) involves moral and intellectual courage and sacrifice, precisely because of the self-referentiality involved. Foucault took Robert Oppenheimer's opposition to the atomic bomb as the starting point for his famous argument about the need for specific, as opposed to general, intellectuals. The specific intellectual no longer engages with the universals of Truth, Justice, and History. He is neither Julien Benda, nor Jean Paul Sartre, but engages his specific professional competence in critique of the various power-knowledge spheres of society.[12] What I call symmetric criticality is the logical mechanism at work in Foucault's description of the task of the specific intellectual. What Foucault adds to this Kantian mode of thinking is an original concept of politics. Modernity sought to limit controversy over power by delegating decisions to professionals who draw their authority from science. The Foucaultian intellectual helps bring this process into reverse by repoliticizing the domains of experts and specialists. In Greenberg symmetric criticality is used in order to entrench the discipline more firmly in its areas of competence; in Foucault it is used to question discipline and open closed domains for body politics.

As shown by Lev Manovich, digitization has made "the media universe more self-referential" because when all media objects are designed, stored, and distributed using a single machine—the computer—it becomes much easier to borrow elements from existing objects (131). In a sense we have all become Duchampians. The problem is that the symmetric critiques of modernity often remain ignorant of each other. Philosophers often take the Kantian critique of reason to be the one truly reflective critique. Sociologists like Bourdieu tend to absolutize their form of symmetric critique. In the growing field of cultural studies, reflexivity often denotes the use of approaches, of a literary sort, that question the rhetoric of science (cf. Hopper 58–70). But science is more than a set of textual norms, and the linguistic turn does not exhaust the concept of symmetric critique in science. Artists tend to see science as a unitary block, overlooking the radicalism of the critique of science, which is such an important aspect of contemporary research and higher education. One lacks awareness of how reflective institutional critique is going in many places in society, often based on the specific competence of the field in the question and in its own language.

I have proposed to replace the binary distinction between specialization and generalization with the triangle of specialization, reflective autonomy, and ethics of translation. The functional approach to the problem of the intellectual gives way to a performative approach that limits itself to asking what it is intellectuals do and how they do it instead of who they are.

Notes

1. Is there hope for a biography? Writing the lives of great intellectuals is a veritable cultural industry in which, however, an admirable tradition has developed for intellectual biographies that seek to clarify the intellectual environment and cultural forces that are at work in the great works of art, science, and scholarship, demonstrating that the great spiritual realizations of humankind are collective rather than individual efforts. Examples could be Sartre's and Bourdieu's work on Flaubert or Stephen Greenberg's work on Shakespeare. My favorite in this genre is Joseph Frank's five-volume biography of Dostoyevsky, offering a fantastically detailed and extraordinarily moving panorama of Russian intellectual life in the nineteenth century, seen through the prism of the nineteenth-century author who so brilliantly deconstructed the discourse of the intelligentsia in his works.

2. There is an obvious logical problem involved here. In order to observe something objectively, one needs to observe it from somewhere else, from a point beyond. But how do you step out of the totality?
3. *Intelligenz* was also imported from German into Scandinavian languages at the same time and in the same philosophical context. Here, however, the term took on very different connotations more similar to its original German meaning. The young Norwegian students who in the 1830s and 1840s called themselves *intelligenz* and who formulated a program of nation building and modernization based on the ideas of Herder, Kant, Humboldt, and Hegel went on to become the leading figures of Norwegian politics and society of the next generation. With their "German mandarin" blend of romantic and pro-industrial beliefs, the professor-politicians dominated the country until full parliamentary government and general suffrage was finally introduced under great controversy in the 1880s and 1890s. In Russia no such opportunities existed for the educated bourgeoisie. The positions of power were reserved for the aristocracy.
4. Frank's aforementioned five-volume intellectual biography on Dostoyevsky offers an excellent perspective on the Russian *intelligentsia*. For a more social scientific perspective, see Christophe Charle, *Les intellectuels* 246–55.
5. Bourdieu, *Les Règles de l'Art: Genèse et Structure du Champ Littéraire*. It should be stressed, however, that even counterpower is a power, and that cultural capital is "dirty" in the sense that it is—as capital is by definition—a source of power over people.
6. Charle (*Naissance*) offers an impressive synthesis in this tradition , in addition to the two special issues of *Liber* edited by Pierre Bourdieu in the mid 1990s on the status and situation of the intellectual in various European countries.
7. From the point of view of an advanced social theory like that of Niklas Luhmann, the decline of universals may also be seen as a symptom of a deepening differentiation. Society is being cognitively decentered by the *autopoiesis* of functional systems. Science still produces truths (that is what that particular discourse machine has been programmed to do) but in order to be put to use, those truths need to be renegotiated for nonscientific social contexts like those of law, politics, media discourse, and everyday life, contexts that produce "truths" of their own. That process of negotiation is proving to be more painful as semantic differentiation deepens (Luhmann, *Die Wissenschaft*, passim).
8. "The death of art" is intrinsic to contemporary art, since every work of art asks raises the question: Is this art, is art still possible, and can there be "works" of art?
9. Multiple examples of this paradox can be found in Trebitsch and Granjon.

10. The study of intellectuals demands much conceptual work. The problem of delimitating conceptually the object studied is even more challenging than studies in sister fields like art or science. The Bourdieu school has notably contributed to conceptual clarification, even though several notions of the "intellectual field" are actually at play in Bourdieusian texts. In the early stages of his career, Bourdieu favored a very wide notion of the intellectual. In *La Distinction* intellectuals are defined as "the dominated fraction of the dominating class," those who possess a large volume of cultural capital, but little economic capital (196). In *Choses Dites,* Bourdieu still tends to use "intellectual field" as a general term covering the various fields of scientific, scholarly, and artistic production. In late works and in some important works by his associates, attention is focused on the relation of the most autonomous cultural fields with politics and the mass media, and toward the possibility of a counterpower.
11. The best introduction to this history is A. Berman, *L'épreuve de l'étranger.*
12. "Les intellectuels ont pris l'habitude de travailler non pas dans l'universel, l'exemplaire, le juste-et-le-vrai-pour-tous, mais dans des secteurs déterminés, en des points précis où les situaient soit leurs conditions de travail, soit leurs conditions de vie (le logement, l'hôpital, l'asile, le laboratoire, l'université, les rapports familiaux ou sexuels)." (Foucault, *Dits et écrits* 109).

Works Cited

Alterman, Eric. "Out of Print. The Death and Life of the American Newspaper." *The New Yorker.* March 31, 2008. Internet. April 2011. http://www.newyorker.com/reporting/2008/03/31/080331fa_fact_alterman.

Barthes, Roland. *Œuvres Complètes II.* Paris: Seuil, 1994.

Barrès, Maurice. *Scènes et Doctrines du Nationalisme.* Paris: Felix Juven, 1902.

Bering, Dietz *Die intellektuellen. Geschichte eines Schimpswortes.* Stuttgart: Klett-Cotta, 1978.

Berman, Antoine. *L'Épreuve de l'Étranger. Culture et traduction dans l'Allemagne Romantique.* Paris: Gallimard, 1996.

Bourdieu, Pierre. *La Distinction. Critique sociale du Jugement.* Les Éditions de Minuit, Paris: 1979.

——*Choses dits.* Paris: Les Éditions de Minuit 1987.

——*Les règles de l'art. Genèse et structure du champ littéraire.* Paris: Seuil, 1992.

——Ed. "Les intellectuels." *Liber* 25, December 1995 and *Liber* 31, June 1997.

Casanova, Pascale. *La République Mondiale des Lettres.* Paris: Seuil, 1999.

Cassirer, Ernst. *Language and Myth.* Trans. S. K. Langer. New York: Harper and Bros, 1946.

Charle, Christophe. *Naissance des Intellectuels 1880–1900*. Paris: Éditions de Minuit, 1990.
——*Les Intellectuels en Europe au XIXème siècle*. Paris: Seuil, 1996.
Collini, Stefan. *Absent Minds*. Oxford: Oxford UP, 2006.
Durkheim, Émile [1895] *The Rules of Sociological Method*. 8th edition, trans. Sarah A. Solovay and John M. Mueller, Ed. George E. G. Catlin. New York: The Free Press, 1982.
Foucault, Michel. "What Is Enlightenment." *The Foucault Reader*. Ed. Paul Rabinow. New York: Pantheon, 1984.
——"La Fonction politique de l'intellectuel." *Dits et écrits III*. Paris: Gallimard 1994. 109–21.
Frank, Joseph. *Dostoevsky, The Seeds of Revolt 1821–184*. Princeton: Princeton UP, 1979.
Gramsci, Antonio. *Selections from Prison Notebooks*. Trans. and Ed. Quintin Hoare and Geoffrey Nowell Smith. London: Lawrence and Wishardt, 1971.
Greenberg, Clement. "Modernist painting." Web. June 17, 2008. homepage.newschool.edu/~quigleyt/vcs/modpaint.pdf.
Habermas, Jürgen. "Ene Politische Verfassung für die Pluralistische Weltgesellschaft." *Zwischen Naturalismus und Religion*. Frankfurt: Suhrkampf, 2005.
Hopper, Simon. "Reflexivity in Academic Culture." *Theorizing Culture. An Interdisciplinary Critique after Postmodernism*. Ed. Barbara Adam and Stuart Allan. London: UCL Press, 1995. 58–70.
Ibsen, Henrik. *Rosmersholm. Samlede Verker (Hundreårsutgave)*. Oslo: Bind X, 1932.
Lepenies, Wolf. *Die Drei Kulturen. Soziologie Zwischen Literatur und Wissenschaft*. Frankfurt am Main: S. Fischer Verlag. 1985.
Luhmann, Niklas. *Die Wissenschaft der Gesellschaft*. Frankfurt: Suhrkamp, 1990.
——*Social Systems*.Trans. John Bednarz Jr. and Dirk Baeker. Stanford: Stanford UP, 1996.
——*Die Realität der Massenmedien als Soziales System*. Opladen: GRIN Verlag, 1996.
——*Observing modernity (Beobachtung der Moderne* 1989) Stanford: Stanford UP, 1998.
Mannheim, Karl. *Ideology and Utopia*. London: Routledge, 1936.
Manovich, Lev. *The Language of the New Media*. Boston: MIT Press, 2001.
Ory, Pascale, and Jean-François Sirinelli. *Les Intellectuels en France de l'Affaire Dreyfus à nos jours*. 3rd ed. Paris: Armand Colin, 2002.
Philosophy of Education. An Encyclopedia. Ed. J. J. Chambliss. London: Rutledge, 1996.
Ringer, Fritz. *Fields of Knowledge. French Academic Culture in Comparative Perspective 1890–1920*. Cambridge: Cambridge UP, 1992.
Sapiro, Gisèle. *La guerre des Écrivains 1940–53*. Paris: Fayard, 1999.

Sartre, Jean Paul. *Plaidoyer pour les intellectuels*. Paris: Gallimard, 1972.
Shils, Edward. *The Intellectuals and the Powers and Other Essays*. Chicago: U of Chicago P, 1972.
Solstad, Dag. *Shyness and Dignity*. London: Harvill, 1994.
——*Novel 11, Book 18*. London: Harvill, 1992.
Trebitsch, Michel and Marie-Christine Granjon. *Pour une Histoire comparée des Intellectuels*. Paris: Complex, 1998.

Chapter 5

Homo Academicus, Quo Vadis?

Jan Servaes

> Insiders promote special interests, but intellectuals should be the ones to question patriotic nationalism, corporate thinking, and a sense of class, racial or gender privilege
>
> Edward Said (xiii)

In a recent assessment of the history of communication studies from a sociology of science approach, Maria Loblich and Andreas Mathias Scheu argued that both "internal" conditions (such as social interests, norms, reputation system, social structure, and organization of science) and "external" influences (the relationships between science and other areas of society) affect the development of a scientific community. I attempt to highlight some of these internal and external aspects emerging from intellectual, biographical, and institutional histories to arrive at a rather sobering conclusion regarding the role and place of academics or public intellectuals[1] in today's society.

"Esprit de corps"

In his famous analysis of the French academia, Pierre Bourdieu (*La Noblesse*) analyzes tensions and trends in French higher education, with particular attention to the historical circumstances of the student protests in May 1968. *Habitus* is a term featured in much of Bourdieu's work and is a useful shorthand expression for much of the socialization that individuals of particular groups have undergone. Habitus is what forms faculty opinions about what represents legitimate expectations for junior scholars, the length of time appropriate to spend developing a thesis, their prospects for appointment and promotion, and so on. Using both statistical and qualitative assessments, Bourdieu eloquently describes how the backgrounds and agendas of different academic groups first led to conflict and then uneasy transitions as a result of changes in university demographics and economics. His discussion of the different ideological positions taken by faculty as a result of their socio-cultural background provides insight into the ways that academic elites tend to react to changes and pressures on the circumstances of higher education. The influence faculty exercise within an academic institution is often associated with the prestige and "power" of certain disciplines. In France the greatest prestige was accrued to the faculties of medicine and law. These disciplines had a different concept of research and scholarship than that of disciplines within the arts and humanities. Medical doctors and lawyers, especially those who teach at prestigious universities, Bourdieu observed, usually come from a bourgeois or elite class. Consequently, research and teaching in medicine and law is often more pragmatic, formal, and technological in nature, less concerned about the social implications it may have. In other words, Bourdieu identifies a more or less direct relationship between disciplinary prestige and original social class of member faculty. He investigates this further regarding the academic grading and performance systems for students, and what Bourdieu calls the reproduction of the "corps," or the way new faculty members are hired and tenured. The "changing of the guard" in academic transition and power is considered crucial in most disciplines. Hence, a lot of time and energy is spent on "turf wars" and the "greening" of junior scholars. Those who control the circumstances of the transition hold the reins to the future. Those who are willing to follow the advice of their mentors are often guaranteed a secure career path.

Bourdieu characterizes academia as a *fundamentally conservative institution* that reproduces and reinforces social class distinctions as a result of internalized faculty outlooks and expectations. Attempts to challenge this conservatism in academia meet with resistance by the vested power interests of the faculty. Therefore, in line with Bourdieu, Mariette Hellemans asks herself whether the "real" academics and intellectuals are a "dying breed" of weird figures that lost their original habitus and are consequently condemned to "survive" in ivory towers called universities. Bourdieu maintains that fundamental change in academia is more likely to be driven by changes in the demographics of students and the economic needs of society as a whole.

Two English scholars, Frank Furedi and Mary Evans, start from Bourdieu's analysis and position it in the British university landscape.[2] By doing so they also broaden the argument to a critique of the way in which intellectual life has been degraded. Mary Evans describes the process that has turned the British university from a "collective world in which independent and critical thought was valued, to a collective world in which universities are expected to fulfill not these values but those of the marketplace and the economy" (Evans 3), where academics and students are enslaved by the principles of audit, assessment, and regulation.

Regulatory bodies, such as the Quality Assurance Agency (QAA) and the Research Assessment Exercise (RAE), have, according to Evans, pushed knowledge, creativity, and education out of British universities, to be transformed into "the painting-by numbers exercise of the hand-out culture and of much research into an atavistic battle for funds" (Evans ix). In other words, contemporary society seems to value knowledge, culture, and education only in as much as they can play a practical role in people's lives.

Furedi argues that two of the key objects of intellectual inquiry are the disinterested search for the "truth" and determining what constitutes a "good society." Furedi reminds us that ridiculing these endeavors will have serious consequences for everyone, not just political philosophers. Once the truth loses its importance, we cease to care when our leaders lie and, once we accept that they do so, regularly, we lose our respect for them. Once we stop caring about what a good society is, ideals cease to matter, and instead of being a clash of competing ideas in the public sphere, democracy becomes technocratic, dull, and election campaigns become a series of appeals to our xenophobia, fear, and greed.[3]

Assuming that the issues are too complex for the public to understand, Furedi argues, politicians make the problem worse by simplifying their messages. The result is, he concludes, a further *dumbing down* in our institutions and a loss of confidence in our cultural and intellectual leaders:

Sadly the authority of the past has been replaced by a far worse option, which is the unacknowledged authority of a disparate group of professionals, hucksters, celebrities and cultural entrepreneurs. This is a group without a mission, a sense of purpose or a coherent worldview. They have a lot to say about the virtues of inclusion but very little about what it is that is worth being included in. They are good at undermining the legacy of the past but inept in constructing an alternative focus for authority. Their main accomplishment is to call into question conventional forms of authority and dumb down our cultural and intellectual life. What they offer is not progress but intellectual and cultural stasis.

(Furedi 175–6)

Cultural institutions like universities no longer challenge us or encourage us to question what we know. Instead *they flatter us*: "Flattering students is fast becoming an important institutional norm. Students are frequently not expected to study but to learn. Because complex ideas are not in fact learned, but studied, the intellectual horizon of the learner is restricted to the assimilation of information and the acquisition of skills" (Furedi 116). Instead of flattering the public and appealing to the lowest common denominator, Furedi wants to challenge them to aspire to better themselves and the society they live in. Therefore, it is time for intellectuals to engage with the public's desire to be taken more seriously in all areas of public life, media, culture, economics, education, politics instead of "reviewing each other's books" (Eagleton 107).

Business as Usual

I am afraid that the above-described situation in France and England is not fundamentally different from other countries. Universities worldwide have transformed or are about to transform themselves from educational institutions into business-like corporations where quantity rules over quality, form over substance, and management over the *homo academicus*. The United States (Arum and Roksa;[4] Giroux; Gitlin; Jacoby; Keohane; Taylor), Mexico (Ordorika), or Australia (ERA, Gare) are no exceptions (Tehranian).

President Eisenhower originally included "academic" in the draft of his oft-quoted speech on the military-industrial complex. Giroux explains why Eisenhower saw the academy as part of the famous complex and how his warning was vitally prescient for twenty-first-century America. After 9/11, Giroux contends, an assault has being waged on the academy by militarization, corporatization, and right-wing fundamentalists who increasingly view critical thought itself as a threat to the dominant political order. Giroux argues that the university has become a handmaiden of the Pentagon and corporate interests; it has lost its claim to independence and critical learning and has compromised its role as a democratic public sphere. Susan Jacoby goes one step further and calls it "the age of American Unreason: In today's America, intellectuals and nonintellectuals alike, whether on the left or right, tend to tune out any voice that is not an echo. This obduracy is both a manifestation of mental laziness and the essence of anti-intellectualism" (Jacoby xx). And, yet, in spite of all this, Giroux defends the university as one of the few public spaces left capable of raising important questions and educating students to be critical and engaged agents. He concludes by making a strong case for reclaiming the university as a democratic public sphere.

At the time that the British RAE system was on its way out, the Australian government decided to introduce from 2008 onwards a similar system, initially called RQF (Research Quality Framework), later *Excellence in Research in Australia* (ERA). The first report was published in February 2011 and concluded that more than two-thirds of the 41 Australian universities have an overall research performance that is below international benchmarks. The report ranked the universities in eight broad disciplines, like "engineering and environmental sciences," on a scale of one to five, with five indicating that a university was well above world standards in a certain area. In all, a significant number of institutions performed at or above world standards in the physical, biological, environmental, and medical sciences. However, with a few exceptions, they performed poorly in the arts, humanities, and social sciences. *The Australian* newspaper commented that the findings could shape government financing, force some poor-performing colleges to focus more on teaching, and lead some institutions to devote more resources to the humanities and other weak research areas.

This doesn't mean that the above-described processes weren't already visible before in the Australian context. If you are not convinced, read Peter Coaldrake and Lawrence Stedman's historical overview, or Shelley Gare's popular analysis, *The Triumph of the Airheads and the Retreat from Commonsense*. Under the chapter "How to Educate a Goldfish" she assesses the Australian education system:

The trend now in OECD countries is for the university system not to be academic-driven but to be performance-driven and market-oriented. Australian universities now operate more like large businesses. That has had universities chasing the dollar, doing research for industry, and concentrating on full fee-paying students, especially those from overseas. The sideshows, introduced to raise funds, have ended up changing the main show. Now that overseas enrolments have dropped, several universities are in trouble. Academic standards have fallen because of workloads and lower staff numbers, but they have also been affected by the way students, especially the full fee-paying ones, see themselves as "clients" with a client's privileges and expectations. Academics have come under pressure to give degrees to students who should have failed or to give them higher grades generally... The move towards the business model has also led to a host of performance indicators and benchmarks being developed and imposed so that managerialism is now entrenched.

(Gare 144)

In other words, a combination of political, cultural, and especially economic agendas has set the modern university and its "employees" on a disastrous trajectory.

Do Consultants, Social Engineers, and Spin Doctors Rule the World?

Is the situation in other sectors of society different? For instance, is the field of communication for development with its local, national, regional and international bureaucracies managing it? *I am afraid not.* In the course of the last decades one can observe similar trends as the ones described for universities and academics. My experience, since 1989, mainly through the UN Educational, Scientific, and Cultural Organization (UNESCO), in the U N Agency Roundtable Biannual Meetings on Development Communication (Servaes "Harnessing the U.N. system"), as the coordinator of the biannual International Association for Media and Communication Research (IAMCR)-UNESCO seminars, my membership of the high-level panel on the future of the Sustainable Development Department of the Food and Agriculture Organization in 2005, and my chairmanship of the Scientific Committee of the World Congress on Communication for Development (Rome October 2006), organized by the World Bank, the Food and Agriculture Organization, and the Communication Initiative (Servaes "Communication for Development"), has been quite sobering.

As a result of bureaucracy and managerialism, more than in the past, many United Nations agencies *outsource* their intellectual capacity to consultants, sometimes nongovernmental organizations (NGOs) but more often to for-profit foundations. These agencies often prefer consultants because consultants are always available on short-term notice, while academics often cannot be easily freed up, or have become "too costly." A range of self-proclaimed experts and consultants fill the gap and provide the background papers and policy recommendations as commissioned by the system. Anthony Judge calls it "the art of non-decision-making" and lists 9 basic practices in non-decision-making and 14 forms of category manipulation, all meant to maintain the status quo: "Indeed decision avoidance has become an art form in its own right" (Judge 1).

The process is more or less similar to what has happened in the political arena (see Louw). It is therefore not surprising that these consultants are often former journalists, or public relations (PR) people, or retired members of UN agencies. Recently, Hernant Shah completed an analysis of 167 items (123 journal articles, 38 book chapters, and 6 books) on development communication, covering the 1997–2005 period. Christine Ogan and her students analyzed 211 on- and off-line peer-reviewed articles on communication and development between *1998 and 2007*. These are the latest in a series of systematic meta-research projects over 3 ten-year time frames (see also Fair; and Fair and Shah). Though the meta-research technique may still need some fine-tuning, some of the findings confirm my worries:

1. *Most authors work at Western institutions* (mainly North America, then Western Europe), rather than in the non-Western world, although the majority of authors actually come from developing countries.
2. Surveys, secondary data analysis, content analysis, and meta-research were the most popular quantitative methods used in 1997–2007; whereas on the qualitative side interviews, case studies, observation, focus groups, and ethnography were used.
3. On the content side, as in earlier studies, the trend to conduct atheoretical research in this field persists. Three-quarters of all the studies used no theory to define their work.

> Though many of those articles may have mentioned theory used in other work, the majority of the authors did not use it to build (2.8%), test (10.4%) or extend (2.8%) that theory in their own work. Even if they did not use theory for their own studies, 9% did include a critique of previous theory, however.
>
> (Ogan 662)

In those studies that build on theories, *modernization theories remain dominant,* followed by participatory development, dependency, and feminist development. Globalization did not feature prominently in most studies.

4. A comparative analysis of media theories used to assess media impact on national development,[5] leads to the following interesting observations:

> First, *Lerner's model of media and development has reappeared in the 1997–2005 time period* after totally disappearing in the 1987–1996 period. Second, only two other theories from the traditional U.S.-based behavioral science approach, social learning theory and knowledge gap, appear in the 1997–2005 period... The third trend to note is that the two most prominently mentioned theories in 1997–2005, participatory communication and social learning, reflect two popular development communication project orientations that were mentioned as innovations in the 1987–1996 study: *participatory development and edu-tainment.*
>
> (Shah 13)

Shah explains the persistence of "old" ideas, especially Lerner's model (1958, 1977), from a technological deterministic perspective: "Each new technological innovation in the postcolonial world since 1958—television, satellites, microwave, computers, call centers, wireless technology—has been accompanied by determined hope that Lerner's modernization model will increase growth and productivity and produce modern cosmopolitan citizens" (Shah 24).

5. The *consequences of development communication* are very much associated with the more traditional views on modernization; that is, media activate modernity, and media raise knowledge levels. This more traditional perspective makes a strong return, as it was less pronounced during the 1987–1996 timeframe. The three other consequences listed are more critical to modernization: media create participatory society, media benefit certain classes, and media create development problems.

6. The *optimistic belief* that there are overall positive impacts of development communication on individuals, dominant in 1958–1986, has consistently dropped from 25% (in 1958–1986) to 6% (in 1997–2005). Increasingly, however, it is pointed out that *more attention needs to be paid to theory and research.* "Aside from the conclusions urging attention to development theory, the studies also urged more attention to development communication campaign planning by taking into account, as implied by other conclusions, local culture, gender issues, and multimedia delivery of information, and to improving research methods" (Shah 20).

7. *Suggestions for future research* prioritize the development of new development communication models and the examination of

content relevance (both 27%), the need for indigenous models (24%), the study of new technologies (21%), more comparative research (18%), the need for more policy research (8%), and the development of a new normative framework (5%).

Ogan concludes that studies have moved away from mass communication and toward the examination of the role of the Institute for Creative Technologies (ICT) in development that they infrequently address development in the context of globalization and often continue to embrace a modernization paradigm despite its many criticisms:

We believe that the more recent attention to ICTs has to do with the constant search for the magic solution to bringing information to people to transform their lives, allowing them to improve their economic condition, educate their children, increase literacy and the levels of education and spread democracy in their countries. Despite years of research that tells us that information is necessary but insufficient to bring about this change, ICTs have become the most recent iteration of the holy grail for development. And even if communication scholars know better because critical scholarship written over the last 30 years has told them so, newcomers to this field from other information-based disciplines may not have such close acquaintance with that literature. Furthermore, because of the appeal of the modernization paradigm, there is a tendency to forget that it cannot work

(Ogan 667–8)

Obviously, this was clearly different in the past. For instance, let's remind ourselves that the IAMCR was established about 50 years ago on the initiative of UNESCO and "at one time constituted its research arm in the field of journalism and mass communication" (Nordenstreng 4; see also Hamelink and Nordenstreng).

The quality of the service men and women in many of the UN agencies is also deteriorating as a result of a "politicized" selection process and quota system. Often the few remaining "experts" have been promoted into bureaucratic or managerial positions and are no longer available for more content-based jobs. Therefore, Thomas Weiss and Peter Hoffman, on the occasion of the inauguration of the new UN Secretary-General Ban Ki-Moon, pleaded for the removal of spin doctors from the UN system:

Communication with constituents—from diplomatic missions of member states to NGOs and to global public spaces—should be informed and direct. Hollow rhetorical flourishes and dodging duties and responsibilities in the past had sometimes contributed to a dwindling of support for the U.N., and therefore the new Secretary-General should have a media strategy based on transparency.

(Weiss and Hoffman 21)

They recommend the following actions to be taken at the level of the UN Secretariat and its management: reinvigorate the International Civil Service, improve the transparency of senior appointments, invest in analytical capabilities, increase transparency as a media strategy, develop International Civil Service Career Tracks and tap the global human resources market, build and preserve institutional memory, and strengthen accountability standards for staff (Weiss and Hoffman 20–4).

KERMIT IN THE BOILER

The above findings speak to a larger problem in society and higher education: universities being run more like corporations than educational institutions, with students viewed as consumers who come for a degree and move on, and academics expected to adjust to ever-increasing workloads. Is the situation really this desperate? Have most academics lost the capacity to, what Todd Gitlin calls their prime obligation, "to improve the capacity of citizens to govern themselves ... to cultivate reason and to deepen understanding of the world" (113–4). After all, there are only few academics (often the same ones) featured as talking heads in news shows and debating fests. Bourdieu would call them "heretics," intellectuals who have often become marginalized for their viewpoints within their own institutions but have gained a following elsewhere in society. I am afraid that such a status is only reserved for the happy few. In addition, one can also observe the incestuous behavior of some of these "celebrities," who either use their tenured position as a revolving door to accept high-level jobs in Wall Street or Washington or accept an "academic position" after a career in the dungeons of power. No ethical questions are asked; university administrations obviously believe this must be the right way forward.

The rest of us may have to face the following dilemma: Systems thinkers and marketers have given us a useful metaphor for a certain kind of human behavior in the urban legend of the *boiled frog* placed in boiling water. It will jump out, but if it is placed in cold water that is slowly heated, it will unresistingly allow itself to be boiled to death. (Real scientists argue that the story is not true biologically, see Gibbons.) The story has been reprinted many times and used to illustrate many different points, for instance, as a caveat against people sympathetic to the Soviet Union during the cold war, as a warning about the impending collapse of civilization, as a warning against being in abusive relationships, or as a caution against inaction in response to climate change. Al Gore used the analogy in his *An Inconvenient Truth* to describe people's ignorance toward the issue of global warming. What would we do, if we were the frogs? Jump out? Or did this opportunity pass already and are we slowly being boiled to death in our role as academics and researchers?

Notes

1. A public intellectual is "someone who writes knowledgeably about ideas for a popular audience on matters of public concern" (Rhode 113).
2. In early February 2010 UK universities were informed by the Higher Education Funding Council for England (HEFCE) that £449m—equivalent to more than a 5% reduction nationally—would be stripped out of university budgets. As a result many UK university authorities announced the axing of thousands of teaching jobs, closing of campuses and ditching of courses to cope with government funding cuts. Other plans include using postgraduates rather than professors for teaching and the delay of major building projects. The funding squeezes led to union actions and student protests. According to a group of vice-chancellors and other senior staff at 25 universities, "UK universities were being pushed towards becoming U.S.-style, quasi-privatized institutions" (The Guardian February 7, 2010, http://www.guardian.co.uk/education/2010/feb/07/job-losses-universities-cuts, accessed on March 23, 2011).
3. For an interesting discussion of universal values, such as "truth," in a global and ethical perspective, see Appiah; Elliott and Lemert; or Christians and Traber.
4. This book argues that for a large portion of the seemingly successful American undergraduates the years in college barely improve their skills in critical thinking, complex reasoning, and writing: "Many students come to college not only poorly prepared by prior schooling for highly demanding academic tasks that ideally lie in front of them, but—more troubling still—they enter college with attitudes, norms, values, and behaviors that are often at odds with academic commitment" (3). For an in-depth review and summary of this book, see David Glenn.
5. For an overview of the different approaches and paradigms on communication and development, see Servaes "Communication for Development" 1999, 2006, 2007.

WORKS CITED

Appiah, Kwame Anthony. *The Ethics of Identity*. Princeton NJ: Princeton UP, 2005.
Arum, Richard and Roksa, Josipa. *Academically Adrift: Limited Learning on College Campuses*. Chicago: U of Chicago P, 2011.
Australian Research Council. *Era 2010*. Canberra: Australian Government, 2011 http://www.arc.gov.au/era/era_2010.htm (accessed on September 7, 2011).
Bourdieau Pierre. *Homo Academicus*. Trans. Peter Collier Paris: Stanford, CA: Stanford UP, 1988.
——*La noblesse d'État. Grandes écoles et esprit de corps*. Paris: Ed. De Minuit, 1989.
Christians, Clifford and Michael Traber. *Communication Ethics and Universal Values*. Thousand Oaks: Sage, 1997.
Coaldrake, Peter and Lawrence Stedman. *On the Brink. Australia's Universities Confronting Their Future*. St. Lucia: U of Queensland P, 1998.
Eagleton, Terry. *The Function of Criticism*. London: Verso, 2005.
Elliott, Anthony and Charles Lemert. *The New Individualism. The Emotional Costs of Globalization*. London: Routlege. 2006.
Evans, Mary. *Killing Thinking: The Death of the Universities*. London: Continuum, 2005.
Fair, J. E. *A Meta-Research of Mass Media Effects on Audiences in Developing Countries from 1958 through 1986*, Unpublished doctoral dissertation Indiana University, Bloomington IN, 1988.
——"29 Years of Theory and Research on Media and Development: The Dominant Paradigm Impact" *Gazette* 44, 1989: 129–50.
——and H. Shah. "Continuities and Discontinuities in Communication and Development Research since 1958" *Journal of International Communication* 4.2 1989: 3–23.
Furedi, Frank. *Where Have all the Intellectuals Gone? Confronting 21st Century Philistinism*. London: Continuum, 2006.
Gare, Shelley. *The Triumph of the Airheads and the Retreat from Commonsense*. Sydney: Park Street Press, 2006.
Gibbons, Whit. "The Legend of the Boiling Frog Is Just a Legend," *Ecoviews 2007* http://www.uga.edu/srel/ecoview11-18-02.htm (accessed on July 11, 2007).
Giroux, Henry. *The University in Chains: Confronting the Military-Industrial-Academic Complex*. Boulder, CO: Paradigm Pubs. 2007.
Gitlin, Todd. *The Intellectuals and the Flag*. New York: Columbia UP, 2006.
Glenn, David. "New Book Lays Failure to Learn on Colleges' Doorsteps." *The Chronicle of Higher Education* January 18, 2011. http://chronicle.com/article/New-Book-Lays-Failure-to-Learn/125983/?sid= at&utm_source= at&utm_medium= en? (accessed on January 24, 2011).
Gore, Al. *An Inconvenient Truth*. Documentary. Dir. Davis Guggenheim. 2006.

Hamelink, Cees and Kaarle Nordenstreng. *A Short History of IAMCR, IAMCR in Retrospect 1957–2007.* Paris: Maison des Sciences de l'Homme, 2007.
Hellemans, Mariette, *Een schitterende onschuld. Over de intellectueel.* Leuven: Acco, 2007.
Jacoby, Susan. *The Age of American Unreason.* New York: Vintage Books, 2009.
Judge, Anthony. *The Art of Non-Decision-Making and the Manipulation of Categories.* 1997 http://www.laetusinpraesens.org/docs/nondee.php (accessed on August 7, 2007).
Keohane, Nannerl. *Higher Ground. Ethics and Leadership in the Modern University.* Durham: Duke UP, 2006.
Loblich, Maria and Andreas Matthias Scheu. "Writing the History of Communication Studies. A Sociology of Science Approach." *Communication Theory* 21.1 February 2011: 1–22.
Louw, Eric. *The Media and Political Process.* London: Sage, 2005.
Nordenstreng, Kaarle. "IAMCR as NGO" *IAMCR Newsletter,* 17.1, April 2007.
Ogan, Christine L., Bashir Manaf, Lindita Camaj, Yunjuan Luo, Brian Gaddie, Rosemary Pennington, Sonia Rana and Mohammed Salih. "Development Communication. The State of Research in an Era of ICTs and Globalization" *The International Communication Gazette* 71.8 2009: 655–70.
Ordorika, Imanol. *Power, Politics, and Change in Higher Education: The Case of the National Autonomous University of Mexico,* Unpublished doctoral dissertation, Stanford, CA: Stanford University, 1999.
Rhode, Deborah. *In Pursuit of Knowledge. Scholars, Status, and Academic Culture.* Stanford, CA: Stanford UP, 2006.
Said, Edward. *Representations of the Intellectual. The Reith Lectures.* New York: Vintage Books, 1994.
Servaes, Jan. *Communication for Development. One World, Multiple Cultures.* Creskill: Hampton Press, 1999.
———"Communication for Development. Making a Difference" Background paper for the World Congress on Communication for Development. Rome, October 25–27, 2006.
———"Harnessing the U.N. System into a Common Approach on Communication for Development," *The International Communication Gazette,* 69.5 2007: 483–507 http://gaz.sagepub.com (accessed on August 7, 2007).
———ed. *Communication for Development and Social Change.* London: Sage, 2008.
Shah, Hernant. "Meta-Research of Development Communication Studies, 1997–2005: Patterns and Trends Since 1958," Paper ICA Conference, San Francisco, May 2007.
Taylor, Mark C. *Crisis on Campus: A Bold Plan for Reforming Our Colleges and Universities.* New York: Knopf Doubleday, 2010.

Tehranian, Majid, Jim Dator and Walter Truett Anderson, eds. *Learning to Seek: Globalization, Governance, and the Futures of Higher Education.* Peace and Policy 11. Transaction Publishing, 2006.

Weiss, Thomas and Peter G. Hoffman. "A Priority Agenda for the next U.N. Secretary-General, New York: Friedrich Ebert Stiftung, 2006. http://www.fes-globalization.org/publications/FESOCP28_Weiss _Hoffman_Priority_Agenda_for_UNSG.pdf (accessed on August 15, 2010).

Chapter 6

The Enemy Within?: Intellectuals, Violence, and the "Postmodern Condition"

Matteo Stocchetti

Introduction

After September 11, 2001, Baudrillard wrote a comment that outraged many:[1]

> The fact that we have dreamt of this event and that everyone without exception has dreamt of it—because no one can avoid dreaming of the destruction of any power that has become hegemonic to this degree—is unacceptable. Yet it is a fact, and one which can indeed be measured by the motive of violence of all that has been said and written in the effort to dispel it. At a pinch, we can say that they *did it*, but we *wished for* it. If this is not taken into account, the event loses any symbolic dimension.... This goes far beyond hatred for the dominant world power among the disinherited and the exploited, among those who have ended up on the wrong side of the global order. Even those who share in the advantages of that order have this malicious desire in their hearts. Allergy to any definitive order, to any definitive power, is happily universal, and the two towers of the World Trade Center were perfect embodiments, in their very twinness, of that order.
>
> (*The Spirit* 6)

If one reread those lines thinking about "us intellectuals" where Baudrillard wrote the whole essay simply in the first-person plural— that scandalous and still unacceptable interpretation of the single most important act of organized violence of the twenty-first century to date will provide some insights about the problem I am addressing here: the relations between intellectuals and organized violence in the context of globalization and postmodernity.

The comment above is even more surprising considering that the same Baudrillard claimed, ironically, that *The Gulf War Did Not Take Place* (1995). One is tempted to recall that denial and identification with the supposed aggressor are both defensive reactions to trauma, and wonder, if such is the case here, in which way these two episodes are—or should be—traumatic on intellectual grounds.

My starting point is the possibility that the trauma produced by these events arises from the realization of intellectual inadequacy—a painful occurrence that requires some intellectual training to be experienced—that afflicts distinctively honest intellectuals, those who believe in their work and in their role.

This problem, as such, would only be the concern of a few if it were not for the mutually constitutive relationship between social reality and the intellectual reflection on it. The emotional problems of intellectuals would be of little concern, indeed, were it not for the fact that the actual meaning of war and organized violence more broadly, just like virtually all forms of social interaction, depended on and are affected by the way we think about them.

Instead of discussing constructivist epistemology, I would like to examine briefly some of the implications of this mutual dependence. More precisely, I would like to show the practical implications of the "postmodern condition" on the intellectuals' capacity to think and discuss war as a politically meaningful phenomenon. If one accepts the idea that social reality is constructed, my main point would then read as follows: intellectual authority in the social reflection on war has lost its political nature because intellectuals have lost the capacity of producing critical knowledge. Or, to put it differently, since too many intellectuals have ceased to consider war as a political issue, the social relevance of war is now reduced to a technical or moral problem—and war itself is waged neglecting its political consequences. As I shall argue, the demise of critical knowledge by intellectuals is also the beginning of the end for the authority of the intellectual as a distinctive social profile.

Intellectuals

Who are the intellectuals, or rather, what makes an intellectual? Frank Furedi agrees with Lewis Coser and Ron Eyerman on that intellectuals are not those who depend on ideas to earn a living—an offensive description that reflects conservatives' fear of the moral authority and political influence of this group of people—but rather those who live for ideas: their own and those of others. This definition not only describes and prescribes the fundamental traits of the intellectual profile, but it also gives us more than a hint regarding the nature and role of intellectual authority as a distinctive form of power.

In his account, Furedi quotes Pierre Bourdieu and others to argue that aspects such as "mental distancing from the conventions and pressures of everyday affairs...an uneasy relationship with the status quo...detachment from any particular identity and interest," "social engagement" and "the assumption of social responsibility" are fundamental "to feel and behave like an intellectual" (Baudrillard qtd. in Furedi 33–5).

The authority of this position within the broader society is not only connected to the value of truth as could be the case with other social profiles such as that of the scientist or the expert. The truth of science is authoritative because it is based on certainty or reliability resulting from the production of knowledge through available scientific methods. The truth of the expert or the consultant is worth its value only if it provides the commissioners with useful knowledge for the pursuit of their interests. The same interests inspire the "expert's construction of truth and the production of performative knowledge. The authority of intellectual truth, however, does not necessarily rely on scientific truth, or on the performative capacity to serve a particular interest: it is a moral truth with universal claims. An important element that distinguishes the value of intellectual truth is the element of risk. As Edward Said put it,

> Universality means taking a risk in order to go beyond the easy certainties provided us by our background, language, nationality, which so often shields us from the reality of others.
>
> (Qtd. in Furedi xii)

I think this quote is particularly effective, because it not only expresses the element of risk that distinguishes moral truth—what Foucault called *parrhesia*—from scientific truth, but it also suggests the specific value of this truth for the rest of society: the possibility of producing an understanding of important aspects of the world beyond the limits—social, cognitive, political, ideological, and so on—of the social world itself.

The element of risk that this function or communicative behavior implies is referred to even more explicitly in Foucault's discussion of *parrhesia*, which he describes as

a verbal activity in which a speaker expresses his personal relationship to truth, and risks his life because he recognizes truth-telling as a duty to improve or help other people (as well as himself). In *parrhesia*, the speaker uses his freedom and chooses frankness instead of persuasion, truth instead of falsehood or silence, the risk of death instead of life and security, criticism instead of flattery, and moral duty instead of self-interest and moral apathy (5). The risk and the freedom to take that risk are the constitutive elements of the moral authority of the *parrhesiaste*—the one who speaks the truth at his/her own risk.

It is tempting to consider the intellectual as someone who can see beyond the limit of social reality as it is, and looks into what it could be: some sort of oracle in the age of modernity, whose voice introduces an element of complexity and ultimately chaos in the "order of things" and the apparent immunity to change of the "present."

In this sense, and independently from more specific ideological affiliations, the role of the intellectual is always subversive because the possibility of nonincremental changes in society depends on subversion: the subversion of ideas before subversive action. The acceptance of or resistance to this subversive role may depend on many factors. What remains rather constant is the fact that the intellectual authority and the subversive potential of intellectual work depend on the successful positioning of intellectuals in the politics of knowledge.

I will use some of the insights by Baudrillard and Lyotard to discuss how intellectuals have lost a fundamental battle, misconstruing the meaning of violence, confusing universalism and globalization, and ignoring the performative role of human rights in the discussion over the humanitarian wars of the West.

Incredulity and Performativity

The first problem I would like to address here is what Lyotard called the "postmodern condition," the unmaking of intellectual authority and the repression of the risks of subversion associated with the practical exercise of this authority, when intellectuals speak as *parrhesiastes* at their own risk against hegemonic power. It would seem that this unmaking has been brought about by the intellectuals themselves through the radicalization of that disenchantment that Max Weber believed to be an inherent characteristic of the "professional intellectual." This would have produced a sort of self-immunity syndrome, which—under the name of postmodernism—would have succeeded where the Inquisition, fascism, nazism, communism and other totalitarian institutions have failed: shielding the existing order from the practical effects of intellectual criticism.

The terms of this alleged unmaking of intellectual authority are well-known. The crisis of great narratives produces the crisis of the idea of truth and justice, of science and politics. If truth is no more, the authority of knowledge is no more. Lyotard saw the beginning of the end in the ontological indeterminacy of quantum physics. Others, criticizing Lyotard, explained this "incredulity" as a result of the disappointment of Left intellectuals after the political defeat of the 1980s (Anderson 17–36, Hammond 81–105.).

The main criticism that can be levered against this description is that the crippling effects of conceptual indeterminacy have affected the intellectual community rather selectively, disabling only the Left. "Incredulity" seems, indeed, to strike selectively, affecting only some ideologies and values but not others; for example, neoliberalism is a fully functioning and almost unchallenged dogma. More dramatically, the crisis of incredulity did not affect the proponents of the "revolution in military affairs" (or RMA),[2] the believers in the prophecy of the "clash of civilizations" (Huntington), or the "end of History" (Fukuyama)—the new "great" narratives that legitimized the prominence of the West (constructed mostly as an Anglo-Saxon or North Atlantic agency) and the global claim of capitalism over competing ideologies. More specifically, the organization of violence requires that certain myths and their respective narratives—such as the sacrifice for a higher good—still have currency among a fairly large part of the population, at least among the target groups of recruitment officers if not in larger strata of civilian and military bureaucracy. In other words, war can happen only if sufficient people (are made to) believe that the war in question is just, and it can be won.

But why do only Left intellectuals seem affected by disenchantment? Why does incredulity afflict only those who believe in social justice, egalitarianism, welfare, and public transportation? If one acknowledges that the relation between knowledge and power is, indeed, a close one, one may assuredly agree that the crisis of truth has important political repercussions, as Lyotard suggests. But the sense of this connection goes both ways: the hegemonic power may affect beliefs concerning the nature of authoritative knowledge.

Ultimately, one may suspect that the incredulity that seems to threaten the practical possibility of authoritative knowledge and its high priests—the intellectuals—poses a problem only for some of the intellectuals themselves. The forces of globalization and those of the opposition do not seem to be affected by it. The indeterminacy that seems unbearable to some is actually what motivates the engagement of others, and it may even be considered a necessary condition for the survival of "singular" others—as the only nonincremental alternative to the system itself. Shortly put, politics in the age of terror can do without the notion of truth that intellectuals believed to be a necessary element of the political as a distinctive domain. In this regard, I suspect that even Baudrillard makes the grave error of confusing two problems: the epistemological problem of conceptual indeterminacy and the political problem of the use of violence against a hegemonic power. While the first problem affects relatively few intellectuals of the Left, the latter problem presumably affects many more people, if, with Baudrillard, one believes that "allergy to any definitive order, to any definitive power, is—happily—universal" (Baudrillard, *The Spirit* 6). The association between the epistemological and the political problem of postmodernism seemingly led him to write that

> this is terror against terror—there is no longer any ideology behind it. We are far beyond ideology and politics now. No ideology, no cause—not even the Islamic cause—can account for the energy which fuels terror. The aim is no longer even to transform the world, but (as the heresies did in their day) to radicalize the world by sacrifice. Whereas the system aims to realize it by force.
> (Baudrillard, *The Spirit* 9–10)

My argument against Baudrillard is that terrorism is not "beyond politics" but rather, for those interested in the political use of violence, a very political form of social behavior. This point is important because the idea that terrorism is beyond politics has been, in my view, the single most important factor in defusing intellectual criticism about the political role of violence and in the construction of war as a technological possibility or a moral imperative—with technological and moral implications, respectively—rather than as a form of political behavior with political consequences.

The postmodern condition and the "incredulity" resulting from the crisis of great narratives—including that of the Enlightenment—brings about the crisis of the universalism that is the very standpoint for the otherwise contradictory traits of "distance" and "engagement" supporting the moral authority of the intellectual profile. This crisis hits the intellectual and the scientist, but not the expert because "performativity"—which values the "knowledge that works" rather than the knowledge that is methodologically or morally true—is the grounds or the standpoint of the latter.

In his famous essay, Lyotard convincingly explains that the crisis of truth is associated with the crisis of justice and that the crisis of legitimization that afflicts science has a parallel in the crisis of legitimization that afflicts authority. In this perspective, once the disenchantment with modernity has translated into "incredulity" and in the crisis of truth, the result is not emancipation from the repressive use of science but the impossibility of authoritative knowledge. Once this happens, once knowledge is deprived of its moral leverage on human affairs and political order, the subversive role of ideas is neutralized, and the intellectual becomes a vestige of the past.

"Incredulity" for Lyotard is a result of indeterminism and, more precisely, the discovery of indeterminacy in quantum physics—the famous Heisenberg principle. For others, the postmodern disenchantment was a more personal problem of Left intellectuals, like Lyotard (Anderson 24–36), who had to live through the failure of the socialist "utopia" after the 1960s.

The defeat of the Left, if anything, only proves that history cannot be trusted to work on the behalf of the masses—and maybe not even on anybody's behalf. Perhaps no such thing as "historical necessities" may be relied upon in the efforts to reduce the inequalities in the distribution of power in society (Elliott 32). And that truth is not discovered but rather constructed.

For some, the defeat of the Left has triggered the crisis of the Right, opening the ideological vacuum of the West, which—most importantly for our discussion—motivated Western engagements in the "humanitarian wars" of the last decade or so, between the disappearance of the Soviet threat and the beginning of the "war on terror" (Hammond 94). This thesis is interesting, because it denies the ideology of the Right from any other ambition than to oppose the Left. This notion, though, is also misleading since it suggests the idea of an ideological vacuum where, I would claim, the problem is indeed one of ideological saturation. But beneath the conceptual linkage between the crisis of the Left and the crisis of truth, or the political relevance of truth, lies an epistemological trap: the belief that the end of one form of opposition was indeed the end of opposition *tout court*: the "end of history." That trap and that belief are the fundamental traits of globalization: the essential "violence of the global." But the important point here is that truth and power are connected: if one disappears, the other becomes invisible; if one is reconstituted, the other is as well. This is the equation considered essential by Foucault but whose conceptual implications Baudrillard used to refute Foucault himself (Baudrillard, *Forget Foucault*). It is ironic that about three decades later Baudrillard felt the need "to go over a genealogy of globalization" to discuss terrorism as a form of resistance to it (87).

The result is an ambivalent notion of incredulity, based on the association of power and knowledge, which refuses not only globalization but the "performative" rationality that it supports. This notion of incredulity establishes the possibility of truth and politics on a dimension incommensurable with and therefore invulnerable to the effects of the truth and the politics of globalization. In this view, and with a move that deliberately avoids the epistemological trap of "the end of history," incredulity is not construed as the impossibility of politics, or power play, but as the cause of a transformation where politics is waged by other means: not antagonistic global ideologies but irreconcilable forms of singularities:

Behind the increasingly sharp resistance to globalization, social and political resistance, we should see more than mere archaic rejection: a kind of painful revisionism regarding the achievements of modernity and "progress," a rejection not only of the global technostructure, but of the mental structure of equivalence of all cultures.... It would be a mistake to condemn these upsurges as populist, archaic, or even terroristic.... What can thwart the system is not positive alternatives, but singularities. But these are neither positive nor negative. They are not an alternative; they are of another order. They do not conform to any value judgement, or obey any political reality principle. They can, as a consequence, be the best or the worst. They cannot be united in a general historical action. They thwart any dominant, single-track thinking, but they are not a single-track counter-thinking: they invent their own game and their own rules.

(Baudrillard, *The Spirit* 94–5)

In this perspective, violence acquires the fundamentally political role of reaffirming the irreducible "autonomy of the political" as the capacity to "treat, distinguish, and comprehend the friend-enemy antithesis independently of other antithesis" (Schmitt 27), but also the "singularities" that the ideology of globalization aims to efface:

Singularities are not necessarily violence, and there are some subtle ones, such as those of language, art, the body or culture. But there are some violent ones, and terrorism is one of these. It is the one that avenges all the singular cultures that have paid with their disappearance for the establishment of this single global power... It is not a question, then, of a "clash of civilizations," but of an—almost anthropological—confrontation between an undifferentiated universal culture and everything which, in any field whatever, retains something of an irreducible alterity.

(Baudrillard, *The Spirit* 94–7)

As Naomi Klein suggests in *No Logo,* the generation of intellectuals at the end of the twentieth century has been struggling to preserve their intellectual lives from the privatization of culture and the colonization of universities by corporate interests and—even more deeply—by the neoliberal dogma (McKinley). "Publish or perish" became an unchallenged truth when productivity—a fundamental corporate value—became an uncontested academic value. And since the will to power is a form of knowledge that cannot be understood as a "theory" but only as practice—intellectuals may have simply "lost" it as such. If, with Eric Fromm (28–33), knowledge is experienced as a state of being rather than a commodity to be possessed, one may suspect that a generation of intellectuals has lost the fundamental form of knowledge necessary for the comprehension of the political. Thus, from an intellectual point of view, war may be conceived as an empty object. If we cannot see the political in the organized use of violence—because we are blinded by hegemonic consensus—we will not be able to deal with violence as an intellectual problem.

The first and most fundamental challenge of the intellectual reflection on organized violence in our age, therefore, is the avoidance of the epistemological trap of incredulity/end of history: the idea that the decline of one truth is the decline of the possibility of truth and that the end of the ideological confrontation between socialism and capitalism is the end of the political, as such.

From Universalism to Globalization

For those who fell into the "incredulity" trap, globalization could appear as the "mature" stage of universalism: the stage in which the "end of history" legitimizes the enforcement of Western "values," the reliance on coercion rather than on consensus. What has been lost is the idea that someone might not only have different interests but, more radically, she or he may refuse to comply with the adaptation of the world to the needs of a single "victorious" ideology—and the corporate management of the material and immaterial values of human life whenever and wherever it occurs.

This is a story of how intellectuals have lost their souls. If one agrees with Furedi and others who state that modern intellectuals are the incarnation of Enlightenment and its universalist spirit, the decline of universalism should "naturally" spell the decline of modern intellectuals. What has happened here, in my view, is even worse. Universalism has not technically declined—that would revitalize its opposites, localism, regionalism, particularism—but it has actually mutated into something else. According to Baudrillard, "the universal comes to grief in globalization."

In fact, the universal comes to grief in globalization. The globalization of trade puts an end to the universality of values. It is the triumph of single-track thinking over universal thought. What globalizes first is the market, the profusion of exchanges and of all products, the perpetual flow of money. Culturally, it is the promiscuity of all signs and all values or, in other words, pornography.... At the end of this process, there is no longer any difference between the global and the universal. The universal itself is globalized, democracy and human rights circulate just like any other global product like oil or capital.
(Baudrillard, *The Spirit* 89–90)

If universalism and globalization are considered as two separate ideologies, one has to explain this separation by looking at changes in the distribution of power among elites that supported one or the other ideology. My inclination, at least within the terms of this discussion, would rather be to consider both as forms of ideological formulations originally located in a specific point in time and space. The notions of *liberté, égalité, fraternité* were originally born as an ideological tool to foster the interests of some, that is the French bourgeoisie, within a distribution of power that privileged the interests of others, that is, the French aristocracy. The coalition of European aristocracy against revolutionary France was a move that made the exporting of the French Revolution almost a political necessity. But the key factor in this ideological struggle was the elite's awareness that in the eighteenth-century (Western) world the transnational intelligibility of an ideological program was an important political resource. In this sense, whereas it is usually considered as a "cause," universalism may also be seen as an effect and, more precisely, the effect of a change not in the nature of the elite competing for power, but rather in the condition and eventually the scope of this competition: from within the narrow borders of the local community to the larger spaces of humankind. The "disembedding" that, according to Anthony Giddens (22), accompanied the development of modern institutions had its *raison d'être* and was simultaneously a result of this fundamental effort: to equip traditional ideologies with the conceptual devices to extend their claims in time and space and therefore to reach "fellow humans" whenever and wherever they are.

Take these conceptual attachments to traditional theories and apply them to capitalism and there you are: globalization! Where universalism was still about ideological struggle among irreducible interests and world visions—and actually the institutionalization of this struggle through time and space—globalization is the negation of political competition through the negation of politics and the political itself. Where in universalism intellectuals could engage in violent confrontation from different ideological standpoints, conventional ideological differences are meaningless in globalization.

Most importantly, however, the ideological content previously framed within the implicit frame of universalistic claims is mutated by the new and similarly implicit terms of a single corporate ideology. What is the meaning of *égalité* beyond the reach of personal acquaintances if not a standardization device? What is the meaning of *fraternité* beyond the limits of the familiar, if not a normative constitution of a community "imagined" by an authority engaged in expansionist efforts? And what does *liberté* look like when practiced independently of a shared framework of values and unwritten norms? What Baudrillard adds to this is his view that not only the global negates the political—in terms of conventional ideological struggle—but it also effaces universalism as an intellectual possibility, and the values associated with it.

The situation is becoming radicalized as universal values lose their authority and legitimacy. So long as they could assert themselves as mediating values, they succeeded in integrating singularities as differences into a universal culture of difference. But they can no longer do this now, as triumphant globalization has swept away all differences and all values, bringing into being a culture of indifference.

Once the universal has disappeared, all that remains is the all-powerful global technostructure, set over against singularities that are now returned to the wild and left to themselves.

(Baudrillard, *The Spirit* 91)

With universalism gone, and the struggle for alternative ideological values deprived of meaning, intellectuals have lost both the reason to fight their ideological battles and the intellectual ground to fight them. And now the intellectual itself is at risk: not challenged but merely ignored or mutated into a plethora of subjugated profiles— "consultant," "expert," "adviser," and so on—fed in captivity and allowed to reproduce itself in the breeding ground of universities increasingly dependent on corporate funding for mere survival. And still very few even nowadays dare to see the ideological roots of this general disarray.

And that is why terrorism, the new "international" terrorism that followed the decade of humanitarian wars, appears the distinctive form of violence at this stage of globalization. This is the "sovereign hypothesis" that Baudrillard formulates as follows:

> The sovereign hypothesis is the one that conceives terrorism, beyond its particular violence, beyond Islam and America, as the emergence of radical antagonism at the very heart of the process of globalization, of a force irreducible to this integral technical and mental realization of the world, irreducible to this inexorable movement towards completed global order.
> (Baudrillard, *The Spirit* 57–8)

What Baudrillard suggests is the conceptual possibility that resistance to globalization is part of, rather than antithetical to, universalism as an intellectual project.

THE MEANING OF VIOLENCE

According to René Girard, the distinction between legitimate and illegitimate violence is distinctively modern. In the classical age, violence was considered as "impure" whatever the uses and the goals it was supposed to serve (Girard 44–5). The modern legal system is based instead on a notion of legitimacy that is essentially hypocritical: the agent who makes the most effective use of violence establishes its own legitimacy and claims an unconditional and unlimited right to repression. This logic, which is the birthmark of the modern state and dynamic element in the shift from the medieval "anarchy" to the post-Westphalia "order," is based on the idea that the one who is strong is good because he is strong and will be good as long as he remains strong. This essential principle regulates the use of violence in Western modernity. The same logic and hypocrisy has been transferred to the globalized world while the "violence of globalization" remains still largely unappreciated (a notable exception is McKinley).

If one follows Baudrillard, one possible explanation for this state of affairs is that the cold war had detrimental effects on an entire generation of intellectuals. As Baudrillard observed, the "balance of terror is the terror of balance...the best system of control that has never existed" (Baudrillard, *The Spirit* 33). The relevant political consequence of this system was the impossibility of conflict on a planetary scale and, therefore, the impossibility of even thinking of the role of organized violence in relation to political change. In Baudrillard"s words:

> A gigantic involution that makes every conflict, every finality, every confrontation contract in proportion to this blackmail that interrupts, neutralizes, freezes them all. No longer can any revolt, any story be deployed according to its own logic because it risks annihilation. No strategy is possible any longer, and escalation is only a puerile game given over to the military. The political stake is dead. Only simulacra of conflicts and carefully circumscribed stakes remain.
>
> (Baudrillard, *The Spirit* 33–4)

But Baudrillard elaborated on what Marcuse, 30 years earlier, had already identified as a formidable challenge to the practical possibility of political freedom in his *One Dimensional Man*:

> Does not the threat of an atomic catastrophe which could wipe out the human race also serve to protect the very forces which perpetuate this danger? The efforts to prevent such a catastrophe overshadow the search for its potential causes in contemporary industrial society. These causes remain unidentified, unexposed, unattacked by the public because they recede before the all too obvious threat from without—to the West from the East, to the East from the West. Equally obvious is the need for being prepared, for living on the brink, for facing the challenge. We submit to the peaceful production of the means of destruction, to the perfection of waste, to being educated for a defence which deforms the defenders and that which they defend.
>
> (Marcuse: xxxix)

The political efficacy of nuclear weapons consisted of making not only war but also political change almost impossible: in "freezing" the potential for change that is intrinsic to violence—and to organized violence in particular—but also the mere idea that violence can be a tool to bring about political change. The impotence of intellectuals consisted of the impossibility of addressing the political role of violence while avoiding two conceptual "traps": the "nuclear catastrophe" and the "apology" of terrorism.

In the conditions dictated by the nuclear logic of the cold war, socialism and capitalism were institutionalized in their bipolar form and pitted against each other as the only relevant—and fundamentally misleading—ideological antagonism. There were no other "enemies" besides the Communists and no other "friends" besides the supporters of (the one and only form of) capitalism—each with its own exclusive meaning of freedom, equality, justice, and so on.

In a political system where large-scale violence is impossible, the conceptualization of nonincremental change is related to terror—or even "terroristic"—because it implies the breakdown of an established order and the return to the possibility of nonincremental change. In a system like this, there is no need for the political, since the competition for the distribution of values in society has been resolved once and for all. And there is no need for intellectuals since the idea of looking beyond convention was a subversive one. The same conditions, however, were favorable to the growth of "security" experts of all sorts: individuals that applied their intellectual skills to help preserve these conventions rather than to see beyond them and overcome them.

Eventually the cold war ended, but in those 50 years of intellectual ice age an entire generation was lost. Or was it? According to many, political postmodernism emerged as a result of the disenchantment of the Left—those intellectuals in the West who did not have to fear the persecutions of their colleagues in the East, only the inadequacy of their beliefs concerning the "necessary" demise of Western capitalism.

The intellectuals who dare to engage in discussions on the political role of violence are too few to make a difference and to effectively counter the legions of "experts" deployed to channel opinion making within mainstream terms. Too many among these few, however, misconstrued this role after the cold war, in what Mary Kaldor described as "the decade of humanitarian wars" (17–72). They did that, in my view, in good faith: pursuing the genuine belief that the military power of the West, and in particular that of the United States, could be turned to good use. However, they underestimated the ambivalence of organized violence.

Why did so many intellectuals, even Left-leaning or liberal, endorse the "humanitarian" wars of the West? At least two interpretations are worth citing here. First, because they believed that was an effective way of enforcing ideals of freedom, justice, and human rights, and so on, which had to be sacrificed to the logic of nuclear balance. Second, because once the rhetoric of the "end of history" had been taken seriously, alternatives once more came in a binary mode: military intervention of the West—mostly the United States and the United Kingdom—to preserve the post–cold war "new world" order, or the idea that a chaos that would ultimately threaten the "vital interests" of the West itself. Once in command, the West would simply *have to* rule the world.

The decade of military intervention after the end of the cold war has been interpreted as a result of an ideological vacuum afflicting Western political systems after the decline of the Left deprived the Right of its atavistic enemy, and its main *raison d'être* (Hammond 37–58).

As a consequence, "humanitarian wars" were expected to fill in the ideological vacuum of the West. As Hammond put it,

> [I]t was precisely because the old framework of Left and Right no longer made sense, either in domestic politics or as a justification for international action, that humanitarianism and human rights were called on to provide a new sense of purpose. Indeed, to a great extent the attraction of this discourse lay in the fact that it was anti-political. Putting morality above *realpolitik* and vested interests, it appealed directly to no interest, and addressed itself to no particular constituency.
>
> (Hammond 57)

In practice, this thesis suggests that humanitarian wars were a source of legitimization for that "mature capitalism" whose legitimization crisis was anticipated by Habermas in the 1980s. These wars were not about international but domestic politics, not a way to promote fundamental changes abroad but rather to *avoid* ideological challenges at home.

And this is why, after all, the political problem afflicting a "world without meaning," to use Zaki Laïdi's expression, does not seem to be an ideological *vacuum*, but rather, the ideological *saturation*: a step further from the Gramscian "hegemony" in which not only a few ideas become dominant, but in this case even the mere conception of ideological alternatives became practically impossible. McKinley (12–57) cites as a reason the deeply saturated logic of Western—mostly U.S.- military commitment from World War II to 9/11—emphasizing the economic dimension of the use of organized violence in international politics. He, as many others, however, forget the symbolical dimension. Globalization is not only about allowing the exploitation of people, but it is also about convincing everyone that this is the way it should be. If self-respect and not only wealth are at stake in the spread of neoliberal dogmas, in the homogenizing force of globalization, in the "violence" of the global, then Baudrillard is right in saying that the goal of the terrorist attacks on 9/11 was humiliation:

> To understand the rest of the world's hatred of the West, we have to overturn all our usual ways of seeing. It is not the hatred of those from whom we have taken everything and given nothing back; it is the hatred of those to whom we have given everything without their being able to give it back. It is

not, then, the hatred bred of deprivation and exploitation, but of humiliation. And it is to humiliation that the terrorism of September 11 was a response: one humiliation for another.

(Baudrillard, *The Spirit* 100)

The argument that the humanitarian wars of the West were originated by an ideological vacuum is dangerous, because it cannot be proved wrong within the ideological consensus of globalization. It could be argued that it undermines the understanding of the violence of the global by reproducing this ideological saturation,

the violence of a system that hounds out any form of negativity or singularity, including that ultimate form of singularity that is death itself. It is the violence of a society in which conflict is virtually banned and death forbidden. It is a violence which, in a sense, puts an end to violence itself, and works to set in place a world freed from any natural order, whether it be that of the body, sex, birth or death. It is more than violence indeed; we should speak of virulence. This violence is viral: it operates by contagion, by chain reaction, and it gradually destroys all our immunities and our power to resist.

(Baudrillard, *The Spirit* 94)

If the violence of the global is not acknowledged, the political meaning of terrorist violence cannot be understood, in which case the political implications of the "war on terror" are also dramatically misconstrued. Result? The idea of "innocent civilians," for example, is challenged not by some terrorist leaders but by Western academics. In an interesting article following 9/11, and on the eve of the invasion of Iraq, Barry Buzan asked—and answered—the important question "Who may we bomb?"

The idea that in war, peoples and their governments should be treated separately, has recently become something of a Western fetish, a way of asserting the West's claim to be civilized.... The distinction between combatants and civilians has solid and valuable legal standing in the Geneva Convention on the laws of war. But that distinction should not lead to the assumption, now becoming a centrepiece of the Western way of war, that all civilians are innocent and that only evil leaderships are the enemy... To delink people from their governments, when they are in fact closely linked, is to undermine the political point of resorting to war in the first place. *In the end war is about changing people's mind about what sort of government they want.*

(Buzan 85–91, emphasis added)

This idea legitimizes terrorist strategy. In fact, bombing people in order to change "people's mind about what sort of government they want" (91) is what both the U.S. government *and* terrorists are doing. By the same logic, once the government of the United States has endorsed the idea that support for local government is the reason for bombing, on which ground U.S. citizens can be still considered "innocent" by those who are bombed?.

Furthermore, Buzan argues,

[B]ut if people do deserve the government they get, and if that government is in gross breach of standards of civilization, then, as in the Second World War, the war should be against both government and people. (93)

While a war against a government has capitulation as its goal, a war against people has extermination as the only rational objective. The idea of a "war against the people," however, is not as repulsive as that of the "standards of civilization" that should allegedly justify the extermination.

But Buzan is not alone. By the same token, Fukuyama advances the point that political ideas do not win by their intrinsic quality but need to be supported by bombing—a point that any terrorist leader could easily endorse. As he put it,

despite the events since September 11: modernity, as represented by the United States and other developed democracies, will remain the dominant force in world politics, and the institutions embodying the West's underlying principles of freedom and equality will continue to spread around the world. The September 11 attacks represent a desperate backlash against the modern world, which appears to be a speeding freight train to those unwilling to get on board...Much as people would like to believe that ideas live or die as a result of their inner moral rectitude, power matters a great deal. German fascism didn't collapse because of its internal moral contradictions; it died because Germany was bombed to rubble and occupied by Allied armies.

(Fukuyama 27–34)

As obvious as it is, this idea not only debunks the modern myth of legitimate violence but, more interestingly, legitimizes the violent opposition to globalization. Contained in the ideas of the "defence of civilization" and the march of the "freight train" of progress is an enormous violence that can remain invisible because its effect—death—affects only Alter, that is, all that cannot be reduced to the narcissistic Ego of globalization. But it is the enormous tragedy of death that makes violence a formidable political tool. To remove death from the process of globalization—"our" death through technological distance and "their" death by denial—is to pretend that the exercise of violence has nothing to do with politics, that it is a "technical" matter, a sanitary operation like disinfecting or debugging, or empty, fanatical madness. To deny the intimate relationship between violence, death, and politics is to deny the existence of an irreducible antagonism. It is to deny that there is an Other, a dialogical Alter to the globalizing Ego, a form of humanity that is irreducible to "global" order.

Today, ten years after that dramatic turning point, the confrontation between the West—impersonated by the United States and its allies—and (Islamic) terrorism is still misconstrued. Influential economist Alan B. Krueger, for example, believes that the effects of terrorism would be negligible if it were not for the media—that amplifies fear and visibility "propagating the fear of terrorism beyond the immediate area in which the attack takes place" (Krueger 131).

Finally, Kenneth Waltz and Baudrillard may agree on one point: terrorism is not a credible (military) threat to the (military) power of the United States—let alone the West (Waltz 350–51, Baudrillard, *The Spirit* 17). But Baudrillard saw clearly the fundamental implication of terrorism's symbolic dimension, the most political aspect of organized violence: humiliation, not "defeat," was the goal of 9/11. And humiliation is a symbolical "gift" that neither the United States nor its allies can return.

> Never attack the system in terms of relations of force... But shift the struggle into the symbolic sphere, where the rule is that of challenge, reversion and outbidding. So that death can be met only by equal or greater death. Defy the system by a gift to which it cannot respond except by its own death and its own collapse.
>
> (Baudrillard, *The Spirit* 17)

Truth and Sacrifice

When the quotation in the beginning of this chapter was published, Baudrillard actually "performed" an intellectual role of subversion or "scandal" (derived from a Greek word that also means entrapment, temptation, and offence) that has been waiting to be performed for too long. He wrote words that went far beyond the conventions. He did so at his own risk and independently from any of the interests involved. These words are literally unbearable within the widely accepted conceptual framework that distinguishes "good" and "bad" violence in relation to the identity of the killers.

Depending on the interests at stake, war is now conceived as a crime, spectacle, murder, execution, entertainment, business, and so on. Intellectuals, however, should be able to tell a society what the political meaning of organized violence is. Baudrillard suggested that the United States—and its allies—cannot win the "war on terror" because they cannot "return" the humiliation inflicted on 9/11 (*The Spirit* 100). Rather, they are setting the conditions for more humiliations to come. The presumed capacity of the West to export death with unmatched efficiency gives terrorists a reason to live for and especially to die for (Reuter 1–18).

While experts and professionals have to serve the master—and serve themselves while doing it—the intellectual has to serve his or her imagined community: an ideal group of people that exists only for those who believe in forms of social bonding that the ideas of "risk aversion" and "performativity" are fatally undermining. Intellectuals as "truth seekers" may not have a constituency anymore: no one seems to have any use for truths that are not dependent on specific interests and are not suitable for "strategic" communication.

What is then the political role of intellectuals in the age of the political without truth? This is a dilemma because intellectual discourse needs and depends on some sort of truth. Is intellectual discourse doomed to political irrelevance because of its "enchantment" with and attachment to the truth? Is the age of incredulity the end of the intellectual as a politically relevant actor? Is there any alternative to hegemony and irrelevance?

If Baudrillard is right, and sacrifice is indeed the "gift,"[3] that the system cannot return, then sacrifice may also be the way of the intellectual. But the first step in this direction is to rediscover the political meaning of violence. Intellectuals have to equip themselves with the capacity to see power at work *and* to experience the "will to opposition" by perceiving the presence of a dominant power as an unbearable condition, a form of premature and unnatural death to be resisted even, sometimes, at the cost of one's life.

The unconscious self-inhibitions that make us refuse to see what we fear to see hide the lethal emancipatory power of violence. But to rediscover the "political" and to practice the "will to opposition," intellectuals must rediscover their role as parrhesiastes: bearers of a moral truth that, to be credible, must be subversive and therefore potentially dangerous for the one who speaks it, since *parrhesia* is the only form of truth left for intellectuals today. This truth does not depend on the correspondence between utterance and reality—how could that be after the "perfect" crime of the substitution of the real with its representation?—but on the moral authority of its author. In this sense, it is not performative and, therefore, it cannot reproduce reality according to the wishes of the hegemonic power (Lyotard 45–8). If this is accepted, then the possibility of truth is not dead in the postmodern condition, but more risky and potentially dangerous for those who are committed to it.

To be valuable, the knowledge of the intellectual has to make its author vulnerable. If Baudrillard is right and sacrifice is the only "weapon" against the system because sacrifice is the only thing that the system cannot produce, perform, implement, or exchange, then it is presumably within the logic of the sacrifice that would-be critical political actors and intellectuals can find the source of their relevance. It is within the boundaries of this logic that a new form of legitimization—one still credibly associated with authority and from there with the power of discourse—can be found in support of the political role of the intellectual.

NOTES

1. For a review of the reactions to Baudrillard's essay, "The Spirit of Terrorism," see (Merrin 105–06).
2. See Shaw 32–4 for a critique of RMA.
3. I should add that Baudrillard was not alone in this and René Girard made this point as well. Thanks to Silvia Nagy-Zekmi to point this out.

WORKS CITED

Anderson, Terry H. *Protest in America from Greensboro to Wounded Knee*. Oxford: Oxford UP, May 16, 1996.

Baudrillard, Jean. *Simulacra and Simulation*. Trans. Sheila Faria Glaser. Ann Arbor, Michigan: Michigan UP, 1994.

——*The Gulf War Did Not Take Place*. Bloomington: Indiana UP Paris, 1995.

——*The Spirit of Terrorism and Other Essays*. Trans. Chris Turner. London: Verso, 2003.

——*Forget Foucault*. Los Angeles: Semiotext(e), 2007.

Buzan, Barry. "Who May We Bomb?" *World in Collision. Terror and the Future of Global Order*. New York: Palgrave MacMillan, 2002. 85–94.

Coser, L. A. *Men of Ideas: A Sociologist's View*. New York: The Free Press, 1965.

Elliott, G. *Ends in Sight. Marx/Fukuyama/Hobsbawm/Anderson*. London: Pluto Press, 2008.

Eyerman, Ron. *Between Culture and Politics: Intellectuals in Modern Society*. Cambridge: Polity Press, 1994.

Foucault, Michel. "Discourse and Truth: the Problematization of *Parrhesia*." Transcript from lectures given at the University of California at Berkeley.

October-November 1983. Web. January 9, 2011. http://foucault.info/documents/parrhesia/
Fromm, Eric. *To Have or To Be?* London: Jonathan Cape, 1978.
Fukayama, Francis. *The End of History and the Last Man.* New York: Free Press, 2006.
Furedi, Frank. *Where Have all the Intellectuals Gone? Confronting 21st Century Philistinism.* London: Continuum, 2004.
Giddens, Anthony. *The Consequences of Modernity.* Cambridge: Polity, 1990.
Girard, René. *Violence and the Sacred.* London: Continuum, 2005.
Habermas, Jürgen. *Moral Consciousness and Communicative Action.* Oxford: Blackwell, 1992.
——*The Theory of Communicative Action*, Vol. 1. Cambridge: Polity, 1986.
Hammond, Philip. *Media, War and Postmodernity.* London: Routledge, 2007.
Huntington, Samuel P. *The Clash of Civilizations and the Remaking of World Order.* New York: Simon and Schuster, 1998.
Kaldor, Mary. *Human Security.* London: Polity, 2007.
Krueger, Alan B. *What Makes a Terrorist.* Princeton: Princeton UP, 2007.
Laïdi, Zaki. *A World without Meaning. The Crisis of Meaning in International Politics.* Trans. June Burnham and Jenny Coulon. London: Routledge, 1998.
Lyotard, Jean-Françoise. "Introduction." *The Postmodern Condition: A Report on Knowledge.* Trans. Geoff Bennington and Brian Massumi. Minneapolis: Minnesota UP, 1982.
Marcuse, Herbert. "The Paralysis of Criticism: Society without Opposition." *One-dimensional Man. Studies in the Ideology of Advanced Industrial Society.* London: Routledge, 2002, xxxix–xlviii.
McKinley, Michael. *Economic Globalization as Religious War. Tragic Convergence.* London: Routledge, 2007.
Merrin William. *Baudrillard and the Media: A Critical Introduction.* Cambridge: Polity, 2005.
Moses and Knutsen. *Ways of Knowing. Competing Methodologies in Social and Political Research.* New York: Palgrave MacMillan, 2007.
Reuter, Christopher. *My Life Is a Weapon. A Modern History of Suicide Bombing.* Princeton: Princeton UP, 2004.
Said, Edward. *Representations of the Intellectual.* London: Vintage, 1994.
Schmitt, Carl. *The Concept of the Political.* Chicago: The U of Chicago P, 2007 (1932).
Shaw, Martin. *The Western Way of War.* Cambridge: Polity, 2005.
Waltz, Kenneth N. "The Continuity of International Politics." *Worlds in Collision, Terror and the Future of Global Order.* Eds. Ken Booth and Tim Dunne. London: Palgrave MacMillan, 2002. 348–53.

Chapter 7

Far Out! Exile, Hipsterism, and the Existential Situation of the African American Public Intellectual

Adebe DeRango-Adem

> White people invented Black people to give White people identity.
>
> James Baldwin and Nikki Giovanni, *A Dialogue*

> There is a zone of non-being, an extraordinary sterile and arid region,
> an utterly naked declivity where an authentic upheaval can be born.
>
> Frantz Fanon, *Black Skin, White Masks*

African American intellectuals have always been in crisis—from the contentious relationship between Black versus White standards and traditions of American scholarship, to the legacies of racism that made "Black" and "American" incommensurable forms of identification, the state of Black intellectualism bears an inherently existential impetus. Black intellectuals have extensively fought against the real ("material") "situation" of Blackness as, paradoxically, an abstract gauge of difference through which an authentic American identity could solidify itself. These themes, though expressed in somewhat oppositional terms, are made vivid in Norman Mailer's 1957 essay "The White Negro" and James Baldwin's 1955 collection of essays *Notes of a Native Son*. Each of the works forward particular ways of theorizing Blackness as both a fiction of pure abstract difference and necessary, if not tragic, identification. Documenting Black intellectual history thus requires a peculiar awareness of absences, of "race" whose mark is bodily negation on par with the almost metronomic regularity of racial oppression in America. As such, the assessment of Black intellectual history always requires what C. L. R. James has called "fill[ing] up certain gaps" (51). In an analysis of texts written by Mailer and Baldwin, coupled with the theoretical works of Alain Locke, Robert Cruse, and Cornel West amongst a myriad others, it becomes apparent that the documentation of Black intellectual production is a sort of management of uncertainty, requiring not merely the displacement of the marginal to the center, but honest critical engagement with the outskirts: the impossibility for the Black intellectual to be Black, American, and intellectual at once. While all Black intellectual production is a venture in part determined by a demand for political membership and public recognition, whose legacy of struggle might find elaboration on the existential plane, Black discourses in America almost always refuse to abandon the political register: as Locke notes, Black intellectuals in America have always been "forced radicals" (11). This paper argues that the "crisis" of the Black public intellectual is thus not in his relation or negation from White institutions of power, but in his thwarted ability to "know himself and be known for precisely what he is" in a way that does not invoke a rhetoric of crisis from the outset (Locke 8). Despite the discursive limitations of a male-centric model of Black intellectual discourse, this paper focuses on a particular inventory of Black intellectual thought that embodies a sense of critique and resistance applicable to the cultural history of Black communities in general and a coterie of Black male thinkers in particular.

Harlem was known as both the space and symbol for Black America, whose assemblage of writers, artists, and public intellectuals saw themselves as the bearers not only of the "New Negro" but, in many ways, of the American culture. For Alain Locke the Harlem Renaissance was a literal movement that led to larger American metamorphoses, affecting a new mode and attitude toward Black cultural production, as well as a renewed sense of Black (i.e., "Negro") identity as a category that could bring about endless discursive possibilities. Whereas once "the Negro" made his intellectual contribution "through a sort of protective social mimicry forced upon him by the adverse circumstances of dependence," the new ethos inaugurated by the Harlem intellectuals brought about a new, self-authored, politicized aesthetic (Locke 3). Yet this ethos was still profoundly underscored by the specters of racism and exploitation, in which the Black subject was made to "see himself in the distorted perspective of a social problem" (Locke 4). Several Harlem writers of the 1920s took up this dilemma in hopes of not merely repairing a damaged Black consciousness, but constructing this consciousness anew, in order to move beyond "the peasant matrix of that section of America which has most undervalued him" and long obstructed his achievement (Locke 15).

C. L. R. James surveys patterns of modern (early twentieth-century) social organization in an America under threat of nuclear war with the rising cultural need for individualist self-expression. These conflicting sentiments contributed to the rise of the American public intellectual who, positioned against all forms of bureaucracy, became representative of the American struggle to resist mass culture hegemony while also becoming a figure "dependent upon the mass audience for their success" (36). The American public intellectual is, for James, always involved in a critique of the *ideal* conditions for bourgeois individualism, is ultimately a proponent of "the free individual" capable of "expressing himself fully in industry or in adventure on the seas seeking trade" (James 48). Caught in a modus operandi hauntingly similar to the economic patterns of the colonial enterprise, when public intellectuals emerged as a class, they were thought to be socially distinct from "Negroes [and] women" (James 199). The public intellectual is not a part of the mass but can somehow be substituted for it as a spokesperson from the edges. This reflects a dynamic whose totalitarian conditions James critiques for having marked the impossibility of a Black intellectual class from the outset. James cites Richard Wright as one of the first who brought this predicament to the public eye who, in spite of his affiliation with the French existentialists, remained exclusively concerned with the totality of political and psychic constraints experienced by American Blacks in particular. James considers Wright's famous proposition—that "Negroes are the metaphor for America"—as highlighting the fundamental crux of the possibility of Black intellectual scholarship: that the "Negro question" was never other than "a question of human relations" (James 202). In James' estimation, the insurgent power of the existential tradition followed by intellectuals such as Wright was not to be found in its literary manifestations but in its ability to express the register of Black negation, the particular Black experience of Blacks as to some extent *always already exiled*. The Black existential dilemma was not a matter of renewing a sense of authenticity but attempting to forge a self from the ground up, the ground being a place called America (the United States, that is), where absurd racialism had for centuries demanded Black self-cancelation (Locke 11).

According to George Cotkin, the existential "attitude" was central in the formation of American culture and for writers such as Norman Mailer whose essay on "The White Negro" (1957) led literary and cultural historians to rethink America's "demands on the courage of men," and prompted alternative ways of being, in particular, a life of "Hip" as espoused by the "Negro...[who] ha[d] been living on the margin between totalitarianism and democracy for two centuries" (3). Mailer's essay offers a critique of the antibourgeois individualists who longed to be known as the American manifestation of willful exiles and renegades: the hipsters (and by extension, the Beats). In a refusal to enter into institutions, accept the shell-shocked values and domesticated male models of postwar America, or plainly live in one place too long, hipster New York—bred writers such as Jack Kerouac and Allen Ginsberg fought against the conformity of the Eisenhower era using a radical poetics they hoped would hit a nerve in the cultural nexus and take the literary citadel by storm. For Mailer, these forms of bohemian libertarianism were symptomatic of America's larger existential dilemmas of "self" and the "crisis" of American (White) identification. Forwarded by an assemblage of primarily White participants who could largely afford the vanguard lifestyle in their search for alternatives, hipsters "were promiscuous consumers of both high and popular culture and vernacular strains of subordinate groups in the Americas" as well as "pluralists and also great talkers" who transmitted the diverse sources of their inspiration "through their own speech of imitation, parody, and pastiche—sometimes erroneous, sometimes offensive, and at other times incisive" (Whaley 4).

The White appropriation of Black idioms was not a new American phenomenon with the rise of the hipster; historical traditions of minstrelsy and White patronage of the Black arts long offered White artists and intellectuals a way out of "Victorian principles" and a "return to the alienated personality that machine-age modernity had taken away, nature...the primitive" (Whaley 29). In *Love and Theft: Blackface Minstrelsy and the American Working Class,* Eric Lott complicates the legacy of Blackness as an American cultural attraction (and source of repulsion) by suggesting that critics think of Blackface "as less a *repetition* of power relations than a *signifier* for them, a distorted mirror, reflecting displacements and condensations and discontinuities between which and the social field there exist lags, unevenness, multiple determinations" (8). This mirror is perhaps akin to Fanon's *Black Skin, White Masks,* which the author himself hoped would serve as "a mirror with a progressive infrastructure, in which it will be possible to discern the Negro on the road to disalienation" (184). For the Black American intellectual, this "on the road" project of "disalienation" was not a matter of *masking* his uncertainties in bourgeois preoccupations but *uncovering* the conspiracy at work in America to make Black liberation a dream deferred.

Mailer's "White Negro" hipster was a fictional American icon born out of a spiritual fatigue masked by narcissistic detachment by day and a desire to channel African American idioms by night–idioms based on the Negro as both abstract mediation and corporeal excess, whose strange and estranged configuration enables—nearly calls for—appropriation. Mailer mentions that while Blacks indeed formed the American cultural dowry, their intellectual lack was what turned the White hipster into a psychopathic personality, unable to reasonably work through his own existential crisis of *being Black*—granted that the Negro, "hated from the outside and therefore hating himself" is always already on the margins of civilized life and who has survived only by "relinquishing the pleasures of the mind for the more obligatory pleasures of the body" (Mailer 4). In speculating on the essay's racialist tones, it is not surprising that the publication of the essay emerged in the wake of the Civil Rights era and the affirmation of Black power. Nor is it difficult to read the essay as yet another effort to thwart this power, as an almost pathological text that in part reveals its own idiosyncrasies as a critique of White inauthenticity based on an imagined Black authenticity that is pure minstrel performance. The source of doubt for Mailer is perhaps, then, not the Black body (which he essentializes), or Black ways of being (which he praises), but the degree to which the White body, being, and ego can continue to exist authentically in America once the Black body is given a fully accountable presence. Though taking on a Black "soul" and "situation" might offer a way out of the blocked options of postwar America, the anxious irresponsibility of the "White Negro" will inevitably, in Mailer's estimation, bring (White) America into great intellectual debt. Mailer's hipster underscores the underlying tension between American intellectual development and the tyrannical mechanizations of modern life within a simplistic relation between the White and the Negro, with an ambiguous force of "Blackness" as both the problem and antidote to the sterility of the status quo. Christopher Lasch makes the keen observation that while the Black power movement underscoring

Mailer's writing promised a type of "moral rehabilitation," it failed to free itself from the self-destructiveness and "romantic anarchism" of the New Left in its preference for rhetoric and gesture over practical politics (127–8). Mailer's crisis becomes apparent in his exploiting the relation between the legacy of systematic Black degradation and the relatively modern, existential concern for White anxiety around modernization and commercial culture.

The "White Negro" is an invention representative of the sense of frustration and impotence of the White American male who absorbed the existentialist synapses of the Negro only to exorcize him altogether. For all its breathless panegyrics, the essay effectively draws attention to the quiet erosion of White America in fearfully revealing the possibility that Whiteness and White identities have only ever existed by relegating blackness to the status of nonidentity. While seeming to elude racial binaries, the "White Negro" is indeed a statement on Whiteness as an endangered species in America. In *Advertisements for Myself*, Mailer offers yet another narcissistic set of shorthand "evaluations" that seem promising, such as "[Whites'] experience is not as real as the experience of the Negro"—but ends up making gravely embarrassing speculations, such as his critique of Ralph Ellison's *Invisible Man* as a novel whose "thesis which could not be more absurd, for the Negro is the least invisible of all people in America" and the greater challenge would be to explore "the difficult and conceivably more awful invisibility of the White man" (432). The prologue of Ellison's famous novel states the following: "I am invisible, understand, simply because people refuse to see me...I have been surrounded by mirrors of hard distorting glass" (3). Blindness toward racism as a play of optics between hypervisibility and invisibility requires, perhaps, a mirror that might make visible what has always been a blind spot in the American intellectual tradition and White imaginary: the Black mind.

James Baldwin's *Notes of a Native Son* (1955) offers commentary on American race relations as well as the role, responsibility, and life of the Black intellectual mind as both a claiming and resistance of one's heritage. Spoken in the rhythm of apocalypse, through the arrhythmias of the rising civil rights era, and in using Richard Wright's *Native Son* (1940) as his point of departure, Baldwin explores the difficulty with which Blacks can emancipate themselves from their antecedents, and intimates how the constitution of an "American" identity has been a direct product of Black degradation. Baldwin suggests that there is something that has been activated in the American imagination to negate the Black presence in literature and life, to brand it as both sinfully corporeal and an almost theological terror to be exorcized, exiled, and erased—to indeed turn Black presence into absence whenever possible. It is against this eternal struggle of erasure that Baldwin picks up his pen in 1955, and then again in 1984, where he writes a new preface to the reprinted edition of *Notes*. The preface opens with the premise that his writing always had

> [s]omething to do... with what I was trying to discover and, also, trying to avoid. If I was trying to discover myself—on the whole, when examined, a somewhat dubious notion, since I was also trying to avoid myself—there was, certainly, between that self and me, the accumulated rock of ages. This rock scarred the hand, and all tools broke against it. Yet, there was a *me*, somewhere: I could feel it, stirring within and against captivity. The hope of salvation—identity—depended on whether or not one would be able to decipher and describe the rock.
>
> (xi)

Between this rock and a hard place, between the silence of the Black intellectual and the necessity to find an idiom capable of expressing his situation, is the question of identity as salvation. Denouncing his authorial voice as the grounding anchor for his work, the rock becomes a microcosm of Langston Hughes's racial mountain, bringing about larger questions of what, perhaps, all Black intellectuals inherit: a sense of one's identity as somehow already determined yet nonexistent, always in the throes of a spiritual crusade against desiring Whiteness, desiring "to be as little Negro and as much American as possible" (55). Baldwin fights against the assumption that Blackness is a synonym for oppression using a self-consciously apocalyptic voice. Though written two years before Mailer's "White Negro," Baldwin's text prophetically anticipates the kind of terror Blacks would inspire within White heterosexual American discourse with the rise of Black intellectuals committed to revealing how "the Savage [could], now, describe the Civilized" (xiv). Later, Baldwin mentions that while history "has made some changes in the Negro face, nothing has succeeded in making it exactly like *our* own" (25, my emphasis). Here Baldwin slyly refuses to speak as a *Black* intellectual, desiring to speak as an American intellectual instead. His use of "we" in several of the essays is, nonetheless, a rhetorical strategy that slips back and forth across the color line, aligning himself as African American only to view them from a distance, then embodying the same desire to be less Black and more American, and finally obscuring the difference between the two. Baldwin complicates the frame of reference that has given value to being American in a way that almost directly addresses Norman Mailer. In the essay "Many Thousands Gone," Baldwin writes,

> The ways in which the Negro has affected the American psychology are betrayed in our popular culture and in our morality; in our estrangement from him is the depth of our estrangement from ourselves... we cannot ask: what do we really feel about him—such a question merely opens the gates on chaos. What we really feel about him is involved with all that we feel about everything, about everyone, about ourselves.
>
> (65)

In narrating the death of his father in the title section, "Notes of a Native Son," Baldwin enunciates the difficulty of claiming a birthright and establishing himself in relation to a past that is American only because it springs from "depthless alienation from oneself and one's people" (123). Upon his father's death and just prior to the funeral, Baldwin makes a point of describing his crisis of finding something "Black" to wear. This is not Baldwin's deference of his pain; it is the crisis of the Black man who must learn to dress his part or be the "native son" forever. His father is that "native" threat that Baldwin fears will throw him into anonymity—the fear, perhaps, of all public intellectuals at large—as well as a reminder of his Blackness in particular that might add up not to an identity, but "a substitution that is also a gravestone" (Cheng 178).

Cornel West writes about the Black existential impetus in his prolific *Race Matters,* where he notes—or, rather, in the intellectual style of the "native son," *deeply* engages with—the basic issue of Black America as being "the nihilistic threat to its very existence" (19). This nihilism, West continues, goes further back in history to

> the first African encounter with the New World [which] was an encounter with a distinctive form of the Absurd. The initial Black struggle against degradation and devaluation in the enslaved circumstances of the New World was, in part, a struggle against nihilism... that is, loss of hope and absence of meaning."
>
> (West 23)

West attributes the continued resonance of the nihilistic threat with two key factors: market forces and a crisis of Black intellectual leadership. Self-erasure becomes the Black intellectual's response to a corporate market environment within which he or she must contend with the general issues of academic bureaucratization on the one hand and the trap of having to join a community composed of either "race-distancing elitists, race-embracing rebels, [or] race-transcending prophets" on the other (West 64–5). No matter how much the Black intellectual fights for the famous existential credo *existence precedes essence*, his struggle against nihilism is always a struggle against those outside forces that, from the American context, situate him as the credo in reverse. Granted, Harold Cruse's *The Crisis of the Negro Intellectual* (1967), a prolific documentation of the estranged relationship between American Blacks and American public intellectuals, is still hauntingly significant. Reviewing Black intellectual life from the Harlem Renaissance through the 1960s, Cruse attributes the failure of the Black intellectual in America to the legacy of racism that brought "Americanness" into focus vis-à-vis various forms of sensationalist Black abstraction. The Black public intellectual was to free his community from cultural degeneracy but did not yet know how to free himself.

This dilemma, combined with the lack of a strong intellectual community and Black institutional channels to sustain their intellectual accomplishments, Black intellectuals, according to West, eventually fell into one of four models: "The Bourgeois Model: Black Intellectual as Humanist," "The Marxist Model: Black Intellectual as Revolutionary," "The Foucauldian Model: Black Intellectual as Postmodern Skeptic," or, most promising but also the most rare, "The Insurgency Model: Black Intellectual as Critical Organic Catalyst." The first model, in an appeal to White academic institutions and intellectual traditions, always places

Black intellectuals on the defensive: there is always the need to assert and defend the humanity of Black people, including their ability and capacity to reason logically, think coherently, and write lucidly... Black intellectual life remains largely preoccupied with such defensiveness, with "successful" Black intellectuals often proud of their White approval and "unsuccessful" ones usually scornful of their rejection.

(West 62)

West scorns this "post-1968" model as "existentially debilitating" but sadly inescapable given that "most of the important and illuminating discourses in the country take place in White bourgeois academic institutions" and "Black intellectuals must pass through the White bourgeois academy" (West 63).

Hailing Du Bois, C. L. R. James, and Harold Cruse as exceptions to the rule, West considers the Marxist model to be equally debilitating for Black intellectuals "because the cathartic needs it satisfies tend to stifle the further development of Black critical consciousness and attitudes" in its drive—albeit using a rearview mirror—toward lofty future solutions rather than attentiveness to the structural problems of Black social crises (West 64). Nor is the "Foucauldian Model" attentive to these crises as a contemporary model attuned to the structural predicaments of discursive power relations for Blacks in particular—the focus on micropolitical truth regimes ends up amounting to little more than "a sophisticated excuse for ideological and social distance from insurgent Black movements for liberation" (West 64). What is truly "left" then, is what West calls "the Insurgency Model," which vies for a Black intelligentsia that can use an institutionalized critical consciousness to direct Black intellectual energies into insurgent programs of meaningful resistance rather than anxieties over "Whitening... as the very condition of becoming a Black intellectual" (Posnock 334).

Richard Posner claims that Cornel West's insurgent model is itself somewhat sophisticated, given that its political program is written by "a full professor at Harvard after many years as a full professor at Princeton," and that while "West wants to help his fellow Black Americans... it is apparent from his writings that he is much more comfortable talking about Hegel, Gramsci, Lyotard, Jameson, and other intellectual notables unknown to non-academic people of any color than formulating or articulating social reforms that might help such people" (59). What Posner does not consider is the viability and scope of Black intellectual commitment that is, in most cases, not merely a "talking about Hegel" but a necessary "talking back." He also does not fully consider the revolutionary instance of being Black and educated, a necessary gesture should Black intellectuals be regarded for the range and depth of their ideas.

Unlike the "White Negro" who chooses to fight against his alienation with the appropriation of new bodily norms, or Edward Said's intellectual who speaks the truth to power from the sidelines, the situation of African American alienation is always created by circumstances not of their own choosing, in that "the choice of becoming a Black intellectual is an act of self-imposed marginality" (West "Dilemma" 59). Indeed, to be a double outsider, to be doubly conscious, to have "Black intellectual" as a double entendre instead of critical enterprise, is precisely what the Black intellectual has fought against in wading through the psychological, cultural, and moral matrix of the color line that has haunted African American discourse with the question: must Blackness be anathema to Americanness?

The fight for an accountable self, as opposed to an authentic self, is where Black existentialism must finally abandon its European antecedent. Required by the Black intellectual tradition is not the addition of more critical or theoretical "tools" for analysis, but rather a more critical, recognizable—and recognizably critical—inventory. As Gramsci delineates in *The Prison Notebooks*, "The starting-point of critical elaboration is consciousness of what one really is...is 'knowing thyself' as a product of the historical process to date which has deposited in [us] an infinity of traces, without leaving an inventory. Such an inventory must, therefore, be made at the outset" (324). Baldwin's inventory of traces advances from a particular dismantling impulse committed not to exposing new forms of knowledge but betraying the very power/knowledge nexus as it has served the will to mastery in the Western metaphysical tradition. Just as Baldwin's essays are "notes," an inventory of Black public intellectual production is an unfinished business, in part because we continue to believe this business to be a solely Black concern. West believes that Black intellectual leadership is a matter of transcendence, of transcending one's race to "critique the powers that be" and "[put]forward a vision of fundamental social change for all who suffer from socially induced misery" (West "Matters" 70).

In a 2007 interview, when asked about the future of Black intellectuals—and in particular the "insurgent" Black intellectual's ability to respond to future social misery—West responded with the following:

> What it really means is to be a jazz man in the life of the mind and a blues man in the world of ideas. A jazz man is someone who tries to find his or her own voice. This is crucial. To find your own voice means you have to have enough courage to discover who you are, what your own vocation is, so the vocation is never to be reduced to your profession, your calling's never to be reduced to your career. But you don't find your voice unless you bounce it up against other voices.
>
> (Judaken and Geddes 85)

"Jazz man" is a far cry from "Black Intellectual as Critical Organic Catalyst," and yet a fetishistic focus on racial authenticity within the African American intellectual milieu ignores the creative, often self-reflexive inventiveness and irony of Black intellectual production. Invention is a power strategy of the Black intellectual, one that opens uncertainties about race—an inventiveness perhaps part of Mailer's approach or West's image of the jazz man—in a way that also addresses the uncertainty of the Black intellectual's place by way of a "leap...[from] invention into existence" (Fanon 229). It remains difficult to ascertain whether the mediocrity of the hipster was an effect of Black inheritance or White appropriation. What does become apparent is that the suspicion and criticism the Beats incited for their arrogance and bohemianism was a way for White intellectuals to curtail the larger issue of Black nihilism against the Whiteness of America that always was, to quote Richard Dyer, "everything and nothing," a curious existential positioning of its own (142). As a key player cast in Mailer's therapeutic project, the "White Negro" haunts the American racial imaginary as a work of fiction and reminder of the stark reality of Black intellectual negation as a viable force in American culture—a force that made Black intellectualism seem like it was "happening," but not here to stay. From the distorted mirror of minstrelsy, to Fanon's work as a "mirror" on the road to "disalienation," the tower of Black intellectualism is a hall of mirrors. The question raised is whether, in the end, we can "see" the Black intellectual at all, or if he will always be a distorted reflection of a tradition that has erased his image.

Black intellectual production is always a political and spiritual striving, never hermetically sealed from questions of the ethical. As West argues, the invention of new models of Black intellectual production will only ever be forwarded by "an affirmation fuelled by the concern of others" given that "a love ethic must be at the center" ("Matters" 29). Even Mailer admits that, "[a]t bottom, the drama of the psychopath is that he seeks love" ("White" 8). Indeed, what unites the logic of the Negro, existentialist, and psychopath with "the saint and the bullfighter and the lover" is that each of them bears a "burning consciousness" (Mailer "White" 5). If we then add the third term of the performative, so that we see the Black public intellectual as potentially performing the existentialist, psychopath, saint, and so on, then the possibility of new scripts, audiences, and players in the Black intellectual arena are all the more profound. Invention is indeed the ethical appeal of Black intellectual production, is what allows it to move beyond the discourse of authenticity by suggesting social change to arrive not in an exchange of racial subject positions—with Whites becoming "White negroes" or Blacks passing for White—no matter how creative the bodily performance, but in recognizing that White and Black identities are predicated on each other. The "jazz man" knows that his program must be left radically unfinished as an inventive play between unity and dissonance, a multiplicity of routes and citations in which America is merely one point of departure, and an idiom whose roots are rhizomes, growing scattershot into the ages, confounding all attempts to essentialize it.

WORKS CITED

Baldwin, James. *Notes of a Native Son*. [1955] Boston: Beacon Press, 1984.
―― and Nikki Giovanni. *A Dialogue*. Philadelphia: Lippincott, 1975.
Balfour, Lawrie. *The Evidence of Things Not Said: James Baldwin and the Promise of American Democracy*. Ithaca: Cornell UP, 2001.
―― " 'A Most Disagreeable Mirror': Race Consciousness as Double Consciousness." *Political Theory* 26.3 (1998): 346–69.
Bell, Bernard. *The Afro-American Novel and Its Tradition*. Amherst: U of Massachusetts P, 1987.
Benn Michaels, Walter. "Race into Culture: A Critical Genealogy of Cultural Identity." *Critical Inquiry* 18.4 (1992): 655–85.
Cheng, Anne. *The Melancholy of Race: Psychoanalysis, Assimilation, and Hidden Grief*. London: Oxford UP, 2000.
C.L.R. James. *American Civilization*. Cambridge: Blackwell Publishers, 1993.
Cotkin, George. *Existential America*. Baltimore: Johns Hopkins UP, 2003.
Cruse, Harold. *The Crisis of the Negro Intellectual from its Origins to the Present*. New York: William Morrow and Co., 1967.
Dyer, Richard. *White: Essays on Race and Culture*. Routledge: London, 1997.
Ellison, Ralph. *The Invisible Man*. New York: Vintage, 1972.
Evans, Nicholas M. *Writing Jazz: Race, Nationalism, and Modern Culture in the 1920s*. New York: Garland Publishing, 2000.
Fanon, Frantz. *Black Skin, White Masks*. Trans. Charles Lam Markmann. New York: Grove Press, 1968.
Gordon, Lewis R. *Existentia Africana: Understanding Africana Existential Thought*. London: Routledge, 2000.
Gramsci, Antonio. *The Prison Notebooks*. Trans. Quintin Hoare. London: Lawrence and Wishart, 1971.
Hebdige, Dick. *Subculture: The Meaning of Style*. New York: Methuen, 1979.
Hofstadter, Richard. *Anti-intellectualism in American Life*. New York: Knopf, 1963.
Judaken, Jonathan and Jennifer L. Geddes. "Black Intellectuals in America: A Conversation with Cornel West." *The Hedgehog Review* 9.1 (2007): 81–91.
Lasch, Christopher. "Black Power: Cultural Nationalism as Politics." *The Agony of the American Left*. New York: Vintage, 1969. 127–8.
Locke, Alain. Ed. *The New Negro: Voices of the Harlem Renaissance*. New York: Oxford UP, 1992.
Lott, Eric. *Love and Theft: Blackface Minstrelsy and the American Working Class*. New York: Oxford UP, 1993.
Mailer, Norman. "Evaluations. Quick and Expensive Comments on the Talent in the Room." *Advertisements for Myself*. 1959. Cambridge, MA: Harvard UP, First Edition, September 15, 1992.
―― *The White Negro*. 1957. San Francisco: City Lights Books, 1967.

Maxwell, William J. *New Negro, Old Left: African-American Writing and Communism*. New York: Columbia UP, 1999.

Posner, Richard A. *Public Intellectuals: A Study of Decline*. Cambridge: Harvard UP, 2001.

Posnock, Ross. "How It Feels to Be a Problem: Du Bois, Fanon, and the 'Impossible Life' of the Black Intellectual." *Critical Inquiry* 23 (1997): 323–49.

Said, Edward. *Representations of the Intellectual*. New York: Vintage Books, 1994.

Wald, Alan M. *The Responsibility of Intellectuals. Selected Essay on Marxist Traditions in Cultural Commitment*. Atlantic Highlands, NJ: Humanities Press International, 1992.

Wenke, Joseph. *Mailer's America*. Hanover, NH: UP of New England, 1987.

West, Cornel. "The Dilemma of the Black Intellectual." *The Journal of Blacks in Higher Education* 2 (1993/94): 59–67.

——*Race Matters*. 1993. New York: Vintage, 2001.

Whaley, Jr., Preston. *Blows Like a Horn: Beat Writing, Jazz, Style, and Markets in the Transformation of U.S. Culture*. Cambridge: Harvard UP, 2004.

Chapter 8

Language and Limitations: Toward a New Praxis of Public Intellectualism

Kathryn Comer and Tim Jensen

We first became invested in debates about public intellectualism during the creation of *Harlot: A Revealing Look at the Arts of Persuasion,* a digital journal and web forum dedicated to fostering public conversations about everyday rhetoric.[1] Frustrated by the systemic isolation of scholarly publication and its exclusionary language, we found inspiration in calls for the public intellectual, one who seeks communion with a broader audience with the aim of raising the collective, critical consciousness. We were energized by Edward Said's fierce spirit and speech about public intellectualism, especially the particular brand of vitriol he reserved for academics that retreat into the insularity of "special private languages of criticism" (Viswanathan 176). *Harlot: A Revealing Look at the Arts of Persuasion* was our effort to resist the temptations and pressures of what Said labeled a "cult of professionalism" ("Response" 373). The fashionable academic stance of being misunderstood held no glory; to choose this way of life is to avoid, as Henry Giroux puts it, "the vocabulary for understanding and questioning how dominant authority worked through and on institutions, social relations, and individuals" (5). The public intellectual strives against this detachment, Said argued, by confronting injustice and the "normalized quiet of unseen power" wherever it may exist, in a vernacular that reaches beyond a circle of specialist peers ("Public").

From its inception, a primary goal of the *Harlot* project has been to challenge the conventions of academic discourse and its resulting mystique in public spheres. Specifically, *Harlot* aims to reveal the subtle and powerful ways we are influenced through communication, illuminating how truth and knowledge are inextricable from and intertwined with rhetoric. The title derives from pejorative references to rhetoric as "the harlot of the arts," an expression from antiquity that was meant to cast rhetoric as suspect and even potentially sordid, distinct from truth and knowledge but able to " 'dress it up' so as to communicate it more effectively" (Lucaites and Condit 6). Acknowledging such prevalent negative connotations instead of ignoring their power, *Harlot* provides a space for bridging rhetorical scholarship and public discourse.

To create the conditions for such collaborative investigations, and the potential Said and Giroux suggest they hold for social justice, however, we need to ask how the phrase "public intellectual" itself exercises an unseen power. Our aim in this essay is to examine how the language of public intellectualism frames scholarly debates about and attitudes toward social change and, consequently, academics' participation in public-oriented scholarship. The power of the label—evidenced by its use in the mass media, numerous academic forums, and indeed, this very collection—leads us to ask: What frames of understanding are triggered by such a phrase? What narratives are invoked, assumed, and reinforced by its usage? This examination is grounded in a particular project that highlights what is at stake when the term is used to label, rally others to action, or draw boundaries between groups. Reflecting on *Harlot: A Revealing Look at the Arts of Persuasion,* a project that aspires to a new praxis of public intellectualism, we examine the assumptions of engagement that are tacitly propagated by debates centered on the term "public intellectual." Limitations in the language, we argue, misdirect the swells of creative energy found within these debates, and so we conclude by calling for *projects* of collective critical inquiry as part of the developing movement toward a scholarship of engagement.

Our concern with ongoing negotiations of public intellectualism is rooted in a particular experience: the creation of an inclusive online space for rhetorical criticism. The project's origin can be traced back to a particular conversation about calls within contemporary rhetorical theory to shift "from criticism as method to critique as practice" (McKerrow 108). There was lively debate about critique as transformative practice and rhetorical analysis as a special tool for demystifying how power conceals and reveals itself through discourse.

The conversation, however invigorating in its acknowledgment that power circulates through everyday social practice, was utterly devoid of material contextualization. It occurred to us that all of these bold claims about the stakes of rhetorical criticism become moot when such criticism is circulated only among academics. Where is the value, we wondered, in proclaiming the need for a citizenry sensitized to rhetorical forces and calling for change, when that call is heard only amongst those whom already agree? How can we make such bold claims about criticism's potency when it only reaches a handful of academics? From our perspective, the very integrity of the field was at stake. And so we set out to create a space for critical—but inclusive and informal—conversations about rhetoric's role in everyday lives, designed to influence participants' beliefs and behaviors. In short, we wanted to take accessible, relevant criticism to the streets. Several years later, *Harlot* is in full operation as a peer-reviewed journal and open web forum, listed in the *MLA International Bibliography* and steadily growing its community of web visitors.

During *Harlot*'s nascent stages, we sought practical wisdom in theoretical examinations of public engagement. Like any conditioned academics, we first turned to the scholarship. Naturally, we began by trying to define the expression as well as we could. The majority of treatments, we found, are loosely structured around three points: first, the label of "intellectual" is used to signify an identity that is, by and large, both individual and based on academic credentials. Although there are exceptions, this observation aligns with Russell Jacoby's argument in *The Last Intellectuals*, which suggests that the critical, independent, nonspecialist thinkers of the 1950s, who wielded great influence through magazines and small-scale publishers, were eventually absorbed into the university system. It is understandable, then, that the term now seems sutured to academia; it was Jacoby's book in 1987 that helped usher in a popularization of the phrase "public intellectual" (see figure 8.1).

Second, the intellectual in question addresses an audience considerably larger than his or her immediate circle of specialist peers, ideally the broadly conceived "public sphere." And, finally, the intellectual is placed in a position of authority in relation to a public in need of enlightenment. A few examples demonstrate these commonalities: The public intellectual is a "critical commentator addressing a non-specialist audience on matters of broad public concern" (Posner 5); "someone who takes as his or her subject matters of public concern, and *has the public's attention*" (Fish 118); "someone who brings academic expertise to bear on important topics of the day in a language

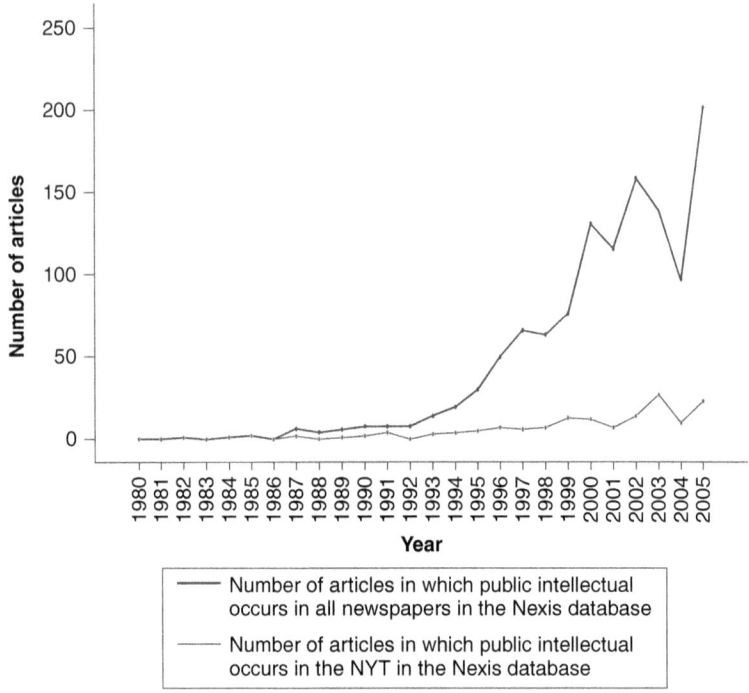

Figure 8.1 Frequency of use of "public intellectual" in print media, 1980–2005, "Major Papers," Nexis Database. Courtesy of Springer and *The American Sociologist* journal, volume 37.3, 2006, pp. 39–66, "The Public Intellectual Trope in the United States," Eleanor Townsley, figure 1

that can be understood by the public" (Wolfe B20). There are, of course, exceptions to be found, as in the work of Cornel West and Ellen Cushman, who include community-oriented local activists among public intellectuals. Despite such ongoing efforts to expand the terms of the conversation, however, most definitions hinge upon an individual, educated specialist passing along knowledge to general audiences.

To point out that "public intellectual" is a trope centered on the individual is hardly a noteworthy announcement. Our point, rather, is that the consequences of these assumptions have escaped critical attention. The very definite article so often applied in scholarship—*the* public intellectual—posits a sort of platonic ideal, an essential identity that forecloses alternatives. As a result, certain assumptions have been cultivated and normalized that shape the conversation in subtle but profound ways. Our own experience provides some evidence; although our true concern was with the *process* and *exercise* of intellectual inquiry in public fora, we found ourselves caught up in Posner-like taxonomies, trying to discover models of "successful" public intellectuals. The association between individual identity and the intellectual implicitly hinges upon one's qualifications for the role, namely, those earned by education and privileged position. Both Said and Chomsky base their calls for public intellectualism on the premise that with great power comes great responsibility:

> For a privileged minority, Western democracy provides the leisure, the facilities, and the training to seek the truth lying hidden behind the veil of distortion and misrepresentation, ideology and class interest, through which the events of current history are presented to us. The responsibilities of intellectuals, then, are much deeper than what Macdonald calls the "responsibility of people," given the unique privileges that intellectuals enjoy.
>
> (Chomsky 2)

According to these foundational arguments, public intellectuals are held distinct from average citizens, simultaneously elevated above and beholden to everyday people.

In this light it also becomes apparent that although intellectualism is treated as an identity, it is not an occupation. Intellectuals have day jobs, and "[n]owadays the term 'public intellectual' merely refers to an academic in his capacity as a moon-lighter" (Crain). Even Stephen Mailloux and John Michael, who parse distinctions between different types of intellectuals, focus their attention on academic incarnations. The very spaces of these conversations locate them as an academic concern; rarely do we see these debates rehearsed in public discourse. The "trivial repetition and dull, daily reinforcement" (Burke 26) of these discursive elisions assign the label of intellectual only to those with advanced academic degrees. Obviously, yoking intellectual identity to the academy effectively obstructs the possibility of labeling those outside the academy as intellectuals in their own right. Consequently, the emphasis on the individual intellectual locates and awards power to that figure, not the public. The unspoken logic at work in many calls for more public intellectuals is the long-debunked narrative of smashing false consciousness, as if to suggest that it is just a matter of getting knowledge out to the public and that social change will naturally follow. Given these associations, we should not be surprised to find both publics and intellectuals bristling at the label.

Most problematic of all are the verbs and directional prepositions that position the public as an object to be acted upon. For example,

Mailloux's hybrid academic/public intellectuals are assigned verbs that establish a one-way transfer of knowledge: the translators "provide," the commentators and inventors "present," and the metacritics "comment on" issues and ideas. Similarly, rhetoricians "can produce [analyses] *for* various audiences" (144, emphasis added). Even Said describes public intellectuals as individuals "endowed with a faculty for representing, embodying, articulating a message, a view, an attitude, philosophy or opinion *to*, as well as *for*, a public" (*Role* 11, emphasis added). This kind of phrasing evokes what Nathan Crick identifies as an Enlightenment mentality in which "timeless truths" are presented for "passive absorption" by public audiences (130). Such a unidirectional approach seems fundamentally self-defeating. We are also uneasy with speaking *for* a public so confidently; politics of representation suggest that we should be creating possibilities for those public voices to represent themselves, inviting interaction without positioning the audience as student and the intellectual as authoritative teacher. Any project that seeks to raise the collective consciousness on an ongoing basis, we argue, must be done in collaboration: critical intellectuals should speak *with* other audiences, not just *to* them. But here, again, we must resist a syntactical objectification that implies a stable or unified public sphere. Critical scholars like Warner, Fraser, Kluge, and Hauser, for all their differences, have roundly refuted any idealized, impossible whole in favor of complex negotiations among multiple, shifting counter- and micropublics. It is no longer possible, especially in an age where media fragment and converge in new ways every day, to conceive of a single, locatable polis in which "the public" can be addressed as a mass, and yet reaching "the masses" seems to remain a cornerstone of public intellectualism.

By normalizing a one-way transfer of knowledge by an authoritative individual, academic discourses run the risk of normalizing the alienation that frequently occurs as a result. If we are to foster real, systemic change, public intellectualism must seek above all to engage audiences in active, mutual conversation. Though admirable in its willingness to speak tough truths, Said's brand of public intellectualism is decidedly confrontational: "Least of all should an intellectual be there to make his/her audiences feel good: the whole point is to be embarrassing, contrary, even unpleasant" (*Role* 12). Though less obvious, the same oppositional stance is embedded in the language of "intervention" in public affairs. Even Henry Giroux, whose calls for engagement we find particularly inspiring, at times endorses a dynamic that is ultimately at odds with the projects he encourages. He writes, for instance, that "democracy also demands a pedagogical intervention organized around the need to create the conditions for educating citizens" (4). Elsewhere, when describing Said's opprobrium for insulated academics, Giroux suggests that we need to fight against the "the tendency to ignore questions of intervention and degenerate into scholasticism, formalism, or career opportunism" (6). Though we appreciate the urgency and conviction the term brings with it, "intervention" presupposes opposition between parties. We respectfully disagree with Said and Giroux on this point, and suggest that a transformative and sustainable public intellectualism is one that ultimately encourages its audience to engage in intellectual work on their own terms and to act on their own behalf. This is not, to be clear, a call to simply tone down the language for fear that we might scare off the timid. Our suggestion, rather, is to take the spirit and conviction motivating the antagonistic language and translate it into a discourse that prompts collaborative intellectual inquiry, fosters conversation and collective action, and empowers rather than embarrasses participants.

Thus, even as we were energized by these arguments for the potential influence of public intellectuals, we realized that these approaches would not teach us how to perform the type of public intellectualism for which we saw a real need. Although our project sought to enact the noble goals espoused by Said and others, we could not locate *Harlot* in these conversations. We were not an individual, nor did we want to speak to other audiences from an assumed position of authority, nor did we aspire to reach some vast, abstract public. We were a collective, seeking to build an open, accessible space for critique and intellectual play among invested participants from diverse communities. It was this goal that brought to light for us the counterproductive subtexts of dominant models. The discomfort our explorations engendered has proven incredibly useful as *Harlot* progressed from concept toward reality. Our identification of the major points of tension within scholarly treatments of public intellectualism—problematic assumptions about the intellectual, the public, and the relationship between them—served as both warning and inspiration. If *Harlot* were to enact a new praxis of public intellectualism, we would have to be just as critical about our technologies as our theories; we aimed to subject our tools to the same scrutiny as our language.

The name of the journal, of course, was a major consideration as well as an early negotiation that presaged many of those to come. Around the same time that we began talking about the project, we happened across the phrase "harlot of the arts" as a pejorative reference to rhetoric's ability to play fast and loose with meaning and laughingly noted its rich potential. Our initial misgivings about raised eyebrows and rolled eyes were mitigated, however, when we dug into the word's etymology. According to the *Oxford English Dictionary*, the term has varied greatly in its usage over the centuries, referring to both men and women and carrying both positive and negative associations. The key definition, for our purposes, is that of "an itinerant jester, buffoon, or juggler; one who tells or does something to raise a laugh." This neglected denotation evokes the harlot's ability to speak irreverent truths in the face of complacency, to voice critique with a smile and (usually) without reprisal. The *American Heritage Dictionary* highlights the word' s association with a lack of fixed occupation, what we like to think of as a fluid professional identity in line with Said's figure of the "traveler" who abandons fixed positions in favor of "a multiplicity of disguises, masks, and rhetorics" (qtd. in Howe). Even in its contemporary associations with prostitution, the harlot figure is one who circumvents, reverses, or flattens the various boundaries and controls enforced by social and political norms. And so to us, the harlot is a gender-neutral trickster figure who encourages the carnivalesque overturning of traditional hierarchies, even if just for a moment. *Harlot: A Revealing Look at the Arts of Persuasion* refers to the goal of promiscuous—inclusive, informal, and accessible—intellectual play.

This figure of the shape-shifting harlot has proven helpful for working against dominant fixed positions or individualistic ideologies. From that first debate and throughout the planning stages and our first years of publication, *Harlot* has been a collaborative effort that resists a version of public intellectualism as an individual enterprise. Indeed, the whole premise of the project is that academic isolation is counterproductive. As teachers and thinkers, we understand that the process of sharing and creating knowledge is enhanced by a diversity of voices and perspectives interacting in a variety of places and modes, each combination of which constitutes a space for mutual learning. And there was plenty of learning to be done, learning that would require team building within and beyond academic settings. To that end, we recruited colleagues and institutional sponsors who could foster multidimensional growth. The reassuring ease with which we gained the material and moral support of our peers reaffirmed our sense that many academics are looking for new ways to play in public. These experiences, especially the invaluable technological expertise and training offered by the Ohio State University community, confirmed the importance of developing strong ties among intellectuals and the institutional administrators who have the knowledge and (often) the funds to bring their ambitious ideas to fruition. Of course, as Deborah Brandt wisely reminds us, sponsorship always comes with strings; this push and pull is an unavoidable factor of institutional support, one that requires careful negotiation of ideologies and economics. Nevertheless, as scholars look for new ways to work together, such resources should be recognized and mobilized en route to productive collective action.

With the "intellectual" reconstituted as a community, we turned our attention to the idea of "public" as a factor of two considerations: the public space and the public body. From the outset, *Harlot* was conceived not as an *act of* communication but rather as a *space for* communication, an arena in which participants would engage the issues and ideas that mattered in their daily lives. But before we could determine where or how *Harlot*'s space would materialize, the question became: who was our public? If it was not some abstract mass, how could we locate, or rather create, an alternative discursive community? In those early conversations, we used the phrase "popular audiences" as shorthand to signify those curious and engaged citizens interested in thinking critically together; each of the editors had his or her own image of friends, family, and colleagues who fit the bill. This language, of course, was soon dismissed on account of its own implicit distinction between "elite" and "common" participants in "high" and "low" culture. In fact, we have yet to settle on an appropriate terminology for *Harlot*'s target audiences, an indeterminacy with which we have become comfortable. This ambiguity remains bound up with our rejection of the outdated assumption that any such public can be approached as a whole.

Such a version of "the public" as a coherent, identifiable mass is not just a theoretical fallacy; in practice, it can have a paralyzing or disheartening effect. We cannot all be Stanley Fish, reaching millions through the *New York Times,* nor achieve Henry Louis Gates's level of recognition and influence. But that kind of exposure does not have to be the goal of an alternative version of public intellectualism. As the late great Howard Zinn reminds us, "We don't have to engage in grand, heroic actions to participate in the process of change. Small acts, when multiplied by millions of people, can transform the world." Our modest goal was simply to create a space in which individuals came together to engage in a form of intellectual exchange that can participate in—influence and be influenced by—public discourse. But that does not necessarily equate to addressing or engaging some elusive "public as a whole." Instead, we formulated our public as *a* public "both larger in meaning but more local in scope" than *the* public

(Farmer 204), simply those who wanted to play with rhetoric, with dual emphasis on fluidity and activity. We would invite these public participants in much the way we engaged academic participants at the local level of connection, whether that meant physical proximity, personal relationship, or online access.

What these revisions of the public and the intellectual brought to the fore was the relationship between them, the dynamic of public intellectualism. Theoretically, *Harlot*'s ideal was to foster reciprocal conversations among diverse, interested public players. Practically, then, our task became "to join others in creating a space within which such matters can be articulated publicly and debated critically" (Jacoby 3). We quickly understood that the form of this space would irrevocably determine the dynamics within it, and any early considerations of print media were swiftly rejected. The obvious objections (prohibitive cost and declining circulation) paled in comparison to those arising from our philosophic commitments. Conventional print publication would rehearse the linear, one-to-many dynamic we wanted to challenge; it simply cannot offer the community and responsivity we imagined for *Harlot*. To create that kind of interactivity, we needed the affordances of the Internet, with its shared discursive spaces and the exchanges they enable. This is not to suggest that the Internet has unified definitions of the public sphere, nor simplified debates about its liberatory capabilities. Issues of access and equity remain paramount, and as scholars like Irene Ward caution, it would be naive to assume that the Internet constitutes a democratic public sphere. Nevertheless, the qualified optimism of Susan Kates and Siva Vaidhyanathan, each of whom approvingly notes new options for online intellectualism, is infectious. The Internet makes possible multiple shape-shifting public spaces that can foster critical thought and conscious action on a micro scale or local level. This kind of activity, in turn, has the potential to create pockets of conversation that can web outward and offline, influencing the everyday lives and practices of users.

Again, the hope for active collaboration dictated our practical decisions, leading us to embrace the inclusive, dynamic spirit of Web 2.0. Just as the World Wide Web has irrevocably complicated old notions of the public sphere as based on physical spaces and direct influence, Web 2.0 fostered new patterns of interaction that have fundamentally challenged the top-down model of disseminating knowledge in favor of lateral connections among "users" actively seeking and creating new knowledge. Richard MacManus's explanation speaks to fresh opportunities for a new public intellectualism: "the philosophy of Web 2.0

is to let go of control, share ideas and code, build on what others have built, free your data." In this light *Harlot* seeks to free academic rhetorical criticism and its multiplicity of analytical tools, allowing rhetorical resources to be generated, debated, and edited by a wide range of users. With the addition of blogs, wikis, and commenting functions, along with complementary activity on social networking sites, *Harlot* is designed to resemble a virtual playground for genuine, open-ended encounters. Of course, we also want to encourage a level of critical and thoughtful participation, an intellectual rigor that leaves *Harlot*'s users feeling invigorated in the face of the rhetorical forces all around us. To that end, we have tweaked the traditional academic peer review system, heeding Crick's reminder that professional intellectuals' contributions to public discourse are "no more or less significant than those of the 'average citizen' " (136). In *Harlot*'s public, peers are equal participants, experts of everyday rhetoric working alongside experts in the field of rhetoric, all engaged in the same task of fostering productive dialogue.

Harlot's modified review system—in which each submission is vetted by at least one academic and one reviewer who does not self-identify as a professional scholar—has validated itself repeatedly. What initially felt like a necessary capitulation to gate-keeping academic publishing standards has become essential to *Harlot*'s integrity. From one angle, our decision to implement a version of peer review constitutes an act of inclusion for some of *Harlot*'s public; when professional academics are able to situate alternative work within their institutional reward structures, they are far more likely to play along. Meanwhile, the review process has held academic contributors to high standards of relevance and accessibility that consistently challenge conventional scholarly performances. More importantly, the resulting collaboration between editors, reviewers, and authors constitutes its own participatory space within our open-source online journal management system. Users actively participate at every stage of the editorial process, creating encounters that have become one of the most satisfying aspects of the project for all involved, leading to heightened levels of participation in and enthusiasm for other areas. The result, we hope, is increased rhetorical consciousness and critical practice for all of *Harlot*'s publics; we can certainly attest to these results in our own experiences.

Playing across these borders, as *Harlot* has shown its editors and contributors, offers opportunities to hone our rhetorical awareness and resources of strategic communication. These exercises train us to become the kinds of travelers called for by Said. So whether the role we perform is that of the professional academic supporting systematic reform, the local community activist, or the digital trickster, we can do so with greater flexibility and facility. Given the challenges faced by academics and academia more generally, we will need all the acumen we can develop. As we have hinted, a major hurdle to academics' active participation in projects like *Harlot* is the dominant reward system built around "too narrow a definition of scholarship and too limited a range of instruction" (Lynton and Elman 7). No one reading this volume needs reminding of the "publish or perish" mentality that demands increasing amounts of scholarship in the face of diminishing audiences and budgets, nor of the negative consequences of such limited notions of academic work or success. This does not mean, of course, that we dismiss the value of sharing knowledge with other specialists; we do not wish to downplay or discredit the significant accomplishments achieved through such models. We do, however, suggest that our definitions of *professional* intellectualism may well merit the same kind of reconsiderations as *public* intellectualism if we are to see our current position as one of opportunity rather than adversity.

Indeed, there is increasing evidence that some long-awaited changes are in process. In the 20 years since the highly influential Carnegie study *Scholarship Reconsidered: Priorities of the Professoriate* was released, the four-part model of scholarship Earnest Boyer suggested, in which alternative forms of intellectual labor merit recognition and reward, has facilitated broad conversations and local institutional change. These negotiations highlight the practical value of tweaking our terminology, as well as the stakes of those choices. For example, Boyer originally designated community-oriented work as "scholarship of application"; quickly detecting the implications of a one-way dissemination of academic wisdom, he soon rephrased such work as "scholarship of engagement." As R. Eugene Rice observes, this language change rejects "the 'expert' model" in favor of one that "emphasizes genuine *collaboration:* that the learning and the teaching be multidirectional and the expertise shared" (28). These ideas coincide with "the public turn" in rhetoric and composition studies, in which teachers, students, and researchers reconsider the standard assumptions of writing in/as academic discourse, increasingly looking outside of academic settings to address issues with real-world exigencies. Such ongoing redefinitions, and the traction they are gaining, hold the promise for increased participation of academics in alternative projects and spheres as we continually revise assumptions regarding the priorities of intellectual work.

As this narrative attests, this process of revision, literally seeing anew, necessitates turning a critical eye on our language choices as well as the behaviors they inscribe. If scholars truly hope to pursue public intellectualism in action as well as in theory, we must excavate this underlying logic in order to move in more productive directions. But this is not simply a matter of finding a better term, the "right" phrase. Rather, we call for an ongoing process of discovering language that works for *your* particular project, that impels *your* particular public to action and inquiry, and expands—rather than consolidates—conversations about intellectualism. *Harlot: A Revealing Look at the Arts of Persuasion* is just one example of reimagining academic discourse in the twenty-first century, one step toward a new praxis of public intellectualism. Negotiation between the change we wish to see and the current structures calls forth our trickster capacities to challenge the status quo with a disarming smile instead of a clenched fist. A harlot of the arts, like the trickster, "is many things, and is no thing as well. Ambivalent, androgynous, anti-definitional, the trickster is slippery and constantly mutable" (Powell 9). In an age marked by both the consolidation of power and the proliferation of communicative resources, such dynamic potential becomes intellectuals' greatest asset.

Note

1. *Harlot* can be accessed at www.HarlotoftheArts.org.

Works Cited

Boyer, Ernest L. *Scholarship Reconsidered: Priorities of the Professoriate.* New York: Carnegie Foundation for the Advancement of Teaching, 1990.

Burke, Kenneth. *A Rhetoric of Motives.* Berkeley: U of California P, 1969.

Chomsky, Noam. "The Responsibility of Intellectuals." *The New York Review of Books.* February 23, 1967. *Chomsky.info.* Web. Jan. 20, 2010.

Crain, Caleb. "License to Ink." *The Nation* Feb. 11, 2002. Web. Jan. 20, 2010.

Crick, Nathan. "Rhetoric, Philosophy, and the Public Intellectual." *Philosophy and Rhetoric* 39.2 (2006): 127–39.

Farmer, Frank. "Community Intellectuals [Review]." *College English* 65.2 (2002): 202–10.

Fish, Stanley. *Professional Correctness: Literary Studies and Political Change.* New York: Clarendon, 1995.

Giroux, Henry A. "Democracy's Promise and the Politics of Worldliness: Implications for Public Intellectuals." *Afterimage* 33.6 (2006): 20–25.

Hauser, Gerard A. *Vernacular Voices: The Rhetoric of Publics and Public Spheres.* Columbia: U of South Carolina P, 1999.
Howe, Stephen. "Edward Said: The Traveller and the Exile." *OpenDemocracy* Oct. 1, 2003. Web. Jan. 13, 2010.
Jacoby, Russell. "The Future of the Public Intellectual: A Forum" *The Nation* Jan. 25, 2001. Web. Aug. 7, 2009.
Kates, Susan. "Emerging Technologies and the Public Intellectual." *Literature Interpretation Theory* 16.4 (2005): 381–88.
Lucaites, John Louis, and Celeste Michelle Condit. "Introduction." *Contemporary Rhetorical Theory.* Ed. John Louis Lucaites, Celeste Michelle Condit, and Sally Caudill. New York: Guilford, 1999. 1–18.
Lynton, Ernest A. and Sandra E. Elman. *New Priorities for the University.* San Francisco: Jossey-Bass, 1987.
MacManus, Richard. "Web as Platform Mash-ups." *ReadWriteWeb.* Aug. 17, 2005. Web. Sept. 14, 2009.
Mailloux, Stephen. "Thinking in Public with Rhetoric." *Philosophy and Rhetoric* 39.2 (2006): 140–46.
McKerrow, Raymie E. "Critical Rhetoric: Theory and Praxis." *Communication Monographs* 56 (1989): 91–111.
Michael, John. *Anxious Intellects: Academic Professionals, Public Intellectuals, and Enlightenment Values.* Durham, NC: Duke UP, 2000.
Powell, Malea. "Blood and Scholarship: One Mixed-Blood's Story." *Race, Rhetoric and Composition.* Ed. Keith Gilyard. Portsmouth: Heinneman, Boyton/Cook, 1999. 1–16.
Rice, R. Eugene. " 'Scholarship Reconsidered': History and Context." *Faculty Priorities Reconsidered: Rewarding Multiple Forums of Scholarship.* Ed. KerryAnn O'Meara and R. Eugene Rice. San Francisco: Jossey Bass, 2005. 303–12.
Said, Edward. "The Public Role of Writers and Intellectuals." *The Nation* Sept. 17, 2001. Web. Jan. 12, 2010.
——*Representations of the Intellectual: The 1993 Reith Lectures.* New York: Vintage Press, 1996.
——"Response to Stanley Fish." *Critical Inquiry.* 10.2 (1983): 371–73.
Townsley, Eleanor. "The Public Intellectual Trope in the United States." *The American Sociologist.* 37.3 (2006): 39–66.
Vaidhyanathan, Siva. "The Lessons of Juan Cole: Can Blogging Derail Your Career?" *The Chronicle Review* 52.47 (2006): B6. Web. Jan. 18, 2010.
Viswanathan, Gauri. ed. *Power, Politics, and Culture: Interviews with Edward Said.* New York: Vintage Press, 2001.
Warner, Michael. "Publics and Counterpublics." *Public Culture* 14.1 (2002): 49–90.
Wolfe, Alan. "The Calling of the Public Intellectual." *Chronicle of Higher Education* May 25, 2001: B20. Web. Jan. 12, 2010.
Zinn, Howard. "The Optimism of Uncertainty." *The Nation* Sept. 2, 2004. Web. Jan. 17, 2010.

Part II

Case Studies

Chapter 9

Should Philosophers Become Public Intellectuals?

Samuel C. Rickless

The public intellectual has come under heavy fire in the last 25 years.[1] Academic professionals, particularly tenured university professors, who engage in public commentary on matters of broad social, political, or legal concern in venues with wide readership or viewership, such as newspapers, magazines, popular blogs, and televised programs devoted to analysis of the news of the day, have been pilloried for their lack of accountability and for their intellectual irresponsibility. Some of these criticisms are warranted; others not. My purpose here is to consider whether, and if so how, these criticisms properly apply to professional philosophers who venture outside the groves of academe to pronounce on issues of public policy. I am particularly interested in whether something about academic philosophers renders them *intrinsically* unfit to wade into the public sphere, or whether the shortcomings of their public intellectual output, such as they are, derive from purely *contingent* factors. For if it is the former, then the obvious conclusion is that professional philosophers should stick to their discipline and avoid inducements to venture outside the ivory tower, whereas if it is the latter, then the right approach would be to find and correct for those factors that conduce to mistaken public pronouncements on the part of philosophy professors.

I will be focusing on Richard Posner's criticisms of the public intellectual output of academic philosophers in his *Public Intellectuals:*

A Study in Decline. I do this partly for reasons of space, partly because Posner's attacks are thought provoking and representative, and partly because they are likely to reinforce the widely shared but mistaken public perception that philosophers have their heads in the clouds and are, therefore, signally incapable of contributing much of value to public political discourse.

Most of Posner's criticisms are directed at a small number of academic philosophers, notably Martha Nussbaum, Richard Rorty, Thomas Nagel, and Ronald Dworkin, among other academics that fall outside of the inquiry of this chapter. I believe that some of these criticisms are accurate, and my main purpose will not be to defend each of these targets against Posner's attacks. I will discuss, instead, Posner's disagreements with some of the details of their public pronouncements in the service of deriving general morals about whether philosophers should be welcomed to the public policy table.

The first of Posner's charges is that philosophers lack the kind of experience that makes it possible or desirable for the nonphilosophical public to take their proposals seriously. Posner praises the nonphilosopher (and nonacademic) George Orwell for his eloquent denunciation of W. H. Auden's blithe acceptance of "necessary murder" as a means to achieving justice (in the form of communist revolution) (84). As Posner sees it, what gave Orwell the moral authority to criticize Auden was the fact that, unlike Auden, Orwell had "not led a sheltered, academic life"; rather, Orwell "had been a policeman in Burma and so knew murder at first hand,... had fought in Spain with the anarchists, had been seriously wounded, and had narrowly escaped being killed by the Stalinists" (84). By contrast, Posner criticizes the law professor Laurence Tribe for his way of "splitting the difference" between supporters and opponents of abortion rights, largely on the grounds that Tribe was

> too little informed about the ethical, scientific, and legal arguments of opponents of abortion to be able to explain them, too unacquainted with pro-life people to understand their motivations or address their concerns, [and] too committed to his own perspective to see things through the eyes of the other side.
>
> (91, quoting Michael W. McConnell)

This criticism will surely strike a chord with those of us who have experienced suffering firsthand, for there are surely facts that those with firsthand knowledge can understand and appreciate in ways that those with secondhand knowledge cannot. Nevertheless, Posner's criticism is wrong-headed. One need not have been an Auschwitz prisoner or a victim of the Gulag or a witness to the Cambodian killing fields in order to see the moral atrocities of Nazism, Stalinism, and Khmerism for what they are. The fact that murder in the service of an abstract goal is a moral abomination is something that all humans—no matter their upbringing or circumstances—can appreciate, and it insults the common moral sense of humanity to suggest otherwise. There is no doubt that the fact that Orwell experienced bloodshed firsthand *added* moral authority to his condemnation of political murder; but it does not in the least follow from this that one's relative *lack* of experience *detracts* from the moral authority of one's refusal to accept that the end justifies such means.

Indeed, Posner does not see the potential flip side of a harrowing experience. Repeated exposure to atrocities can just as easily deaden the moral sense as it can enliven it. For those who experience human suffering daily, it can begin to seem like the fact of suffering is a part of the human condition, something to which it is appropriate to become inured, rather than something it is incumbent on them to condemn. When Israelis die in a restaurant or bus bombing, some Palestinians feel no revulsion, in part because they experience suffering on a daily basis. And when Palestinians die in the crossfire between Israeli reservists and militants, some Israelis feel nothing, in part because they think that Palestinians have brought this on themselves. Sometimes only those who are not in the middle of the fray can see the true costs of violence, precisely because they do not experience the distorting effects of anger, hatred, and other negative passions. Indeed, one of the reasons Orwell is so much to be admired is that he did not allow his political sympathies and other passions to interfere with his objective evaluation of the facts. And objectivity being one of the virtues most prized by philosophers, one would expect them to *aim* at true, unfiltered understanding of moral wrongs.

The philosopher's quest for objective truth also explains why it is simple-minded to upbraid a legal theorist like Tribe for his failure to understand pro-life motivations from the inside. Many in the pro-life movement rest their evaluation of the morality of abortion on religious dogma, assumptions accepted on faith rather than reason or evidence. The Catholic Church teaches (though it has not always taught) that the human fetus acquires a soul at conception, but offers no evidence that could possibly convince an atheist of the truth of this particular theory of ensoulment. Were Tribe to do what Posner recommends, he would have to understand "from the inside" what a certain kind of faith is; that is, he would have to become a Christian fundamentalist. But this is absurd. In order to find a middle way between extremes, it is neither possible nor desirable to "see things through the eyes of the other side" (91). What we want of our legal theorists is to look at the situation *objectively*, without finding themselves tossed this way and that through identification with the motivations of one side or the other. Again, because philosophers at least *aim* at objectivity, it makes sense for all of us to turn to them, perhaps more than anyone else, for enlightenment.

The second of Posner's charges is that when philosophers attempt to communicate with the general public about matters of public policy, they *ipso facto* range inappropriately outside their own narrow fields of expertise. When they do this, philosophers make mistakes born of ignorance, and these mistakes are *necessary*, and not merely contingent, consequences of their ventures outside university walls.

Exhibit number one in defense of this charge is Posner's allegation that philosophers such as Martha Nussbaum are wrong to suggest, in his view blithely, that males and females should be treated equally in Third World countries. The thesis of equal treatment is a consequence of Nussbaum's "capabilities" approach to public policy, a view according to which justice requires the equal distribution of basic capabilities, including the ability to form a conception of the good life and make plans in furtherance of that conception. But, as Posner opines, "[I]t is useless and even mischievous to advocate equal rights for women in a Third World nation on the basis of general principles without considering the practical entailments of such rights in the specific circumstances of that nation" (345). Posner continues:

> Consider the question whether to require that girls be guaranteed the same amount of education as boys. Such a guaranty would increase the cost of the educational system... and responsible analysis would have to consider how large the additional cost would be and where the resources would be taken from to defray the cost and what would be lost by this diversion of resources. The likely impact of additional education on women's lives would also have to be considered... Its positive impact [in terms of the lowering of the birth rate] would have to be balanced against the cost. In a society in which few occupations are open to women except the bearing and rearing of children, female education is apt to be less productive than male education. And if girls are needed to work in or outside the home, they may not be able to take advantage of the schooling opportunities that are offered to them. Religious and customary obstacles to female education have to be considered, and the costs and benefits of overcoming them assayed too.
>
> (345–6)

Exhibit number two is Posner's claim that philosophers such as Thomas Nagel—who in public fora criticized the impeachment of

President Clinton on the grounds that people are entitled to sexual privacy—did not understand "the issue that had prompted the investigation and the impeachment inquiry: the issue of obstruction of justice" (109). The charge here is that philosophers who are not themselves experts on the law of impeachment should not make public pronouncements on the issue, because they are likely to make mistakes of legal fact, mistakes that there are no public intellectual gatekeepers to correct and no pecuniary or other incentives to avoid.

Now I readily admit that there are occasions when philosophers intemperately pronounce on matters concerning which they have no expertise. In this they are surely to be faulted, as would anyone whose judgments are not grounded in the relevant facts. But there is nothing about philosophers per se that makes it more likely that they will make these sorts of mistakes, and, indeed, I would contend that their knowledge and experience make it *less*, rather than more, likely. To establish this, I will first consider the examples of Nussbaum and Nagel, and then move on to more general remarks about the sort of public issues that philosophers are particularly competent to discuss.

Is Nussbaum naive about the costs of implementing a system of education in Third World countries that treats boys and girls equally? And does this kind of naivete derive from the fact that she is a philosopher concerned with theory over practice? Surely not. Nussbaum would be the first to point out that the pursuit of equality is hardly ever costless. But even supposing that the costs of implementation outweighed the benefits (by some measure or other), this would not prove that she is Panglossian. Nussbaum's political philosophy (like many nonutilitarian, nonconsequentialist political theories) is guided by the claim that justice is worth pursuing even when the costs of doing so outweigh the benefits. So pointing out that the cost of educating girls in Third World countries outweighs the benefits of doing so merely begs the question against her.

And, indeed, there are good reasons to reject the utilitarian approach that underlies Posner's charge of naivete. To see this, one need only transpose Posner's remarks about the education of girls to the case of the education of African Americans at the time of *Brown v. Board of Education*. Looking back at *Brown*, should we think of the U.S. Supreme Court as having been naive in its endorsement of the proposition that African Americans have a right to equal opportunity in education? After all, didn't the need to accommodate African Americans on equal terms impose serious costs on the educational system of the United States, and weren't there customary obstacles to the employment of African Americans in a wide variety of economic sectors? Merely considering these questions shows that the answers to them should not be taken to determine public policy in this area. It is not that costs do not matter: it is that justice trumps a poor cost/benefit ratio. Equalizing educational opportunity is the right thing to do *even if* the costs of doing so outweigh the benefits, and this is no less true regarding the education of boys and girls in the Third World than it is true regarding the education of blacks and whites in the United States.[2]

To his credit, Posner himself *supports* "allocating more resources to the education of girls" in the Third World, but "not because of any philosophical arguments in favor of the capabilities approach"; Posner's rather tepid support for this policy derives from his "guess, for what little it is worth" that "the most certain consequence of an increase in the female educational level" would be a reduction in the birth rate (346). But are we to say that the policy of racial equality endorsed by *Brown* is justified only because more professions were open to African Americans in 1954 than are open to women in India now? The very notion is absurd. One need not endorse Nussbaum's "capabilities approach" to recognize that women have a fundamental right to equality that encompasses educational opportunity. A society that denies them this right is fundamentally unjust, so unjust, in fact, that only a serious risk of total anarchy or social implosion would justify such a denial.[3]

On the question of President Clinton's impeachment, the policy question is far more complex than Posner acknowledges. It is true, as Posner claims, that the charge of obstruction of justice is far more serious than the charge of sexual infidelity. The impeachment was ostensibly designed to punish Clinton for a public, rather than a merely private, transgression. But if Clinton obstructed justice, it was obviously to prevent the public (including his political opponents) from knowing the truth about his private life, for what were clearly both private and political reasons. So it is of the utmost importance whether citizens were entitled to know that Clinton was being unfaithful to his wife. And the signal fact here, as Nagel pointed out in both academic and nonacademic venues, is that they were not so entitled. This is precisely what Clinton's having a right to privacy entails. Clinton's problem was that he had fallen into a political and legal trap that Kenneth W. Starr, the independent prosecutor whose work led to impeachment proceedings, had no right to spring on him: either reveal lurid details of his private infidelities or lie under oath. If Clinton committed obstruction of justice, it may have been in order to prevent the general public from knowing what they had no right to know in the first place. So there is no call for Posner to criticize philosophers such as Nagel for missing the point on the impeachment question.[4]

So much for Posner's charge that Nussbaum and Nagel committed serious errors of fact when they ventured outside of philosophy proper to make public policy recommendations about the education of women and the impeachment of presidents. But what of his more general charge that philosophers who venture beyond university walls inevitably err in ways that bring their public policy recommendations into disrepute? The charge is, in a word, baseless. To see this, it is sufficient to make two points.

The first is that philosophers are well placed to help those of us who are enmeshed in the details of some issue see the forest for the trees. As long as they keep to what they have learned in the course of their professional studies, they have a great deal to teach us. Nussbaum's public policy recommendations rest on a philosophical conception of the right to equality, and Nagel's public policy recommendations rest on a philosophical conception of the right to privacy. Like many philosophical theories, Nussbaum's and Nagel's positions have *practical* consequences. This is no accident. For philosophy is not a purely academic exercise, limited to an examination of the nature of reality and the possibility of knowledge. Moral philosophy in particular is the search for fundamental moral truths and an examination of their theoretical and practical consequences. So when Nussbaum and Nagel pronounced in the way they did, it was only because they were applying what they had learned in their fields to the particular facts in front of their noses. Indeed, this is something that philosophers do *routinely*, and there are even academic journals almost wholly devoted to the investigation of the practical consequences of normative ethical theories, such as *Philosophy and Public Affairs, the Journal of Social Philosophy, Social Theory and Practice, Social Philosophy and Policy,* and *Ethical Theory and Moral Practice*. The topics touched on in these journals include abortion, euthanasia, assisted suicide, torture, lying, promise breaking, juvenile detention, secession, the targeting of innocent civilians in war, terrorism, self-defense, the death penalty, the moral status of nonhuman animals, genetic screening and enhancement, privacy, and property. This is as it should be, and it puts paid to Posner's absurd charge that philosophers do not know enough to speak confidently on issues of general public concern.

The second is that the professional discipline of philosophy is concerned, above almost all else, with rigor and logical consistency. Philosophers receive extensive training in logic and the detection of fallacies. This training puts them in a great position to recognize errors of reasoning in *any* area of general concern. When public intellectuals confuse euthanasia and assisted suicide (as it often happens), self-defensive war and pre-emptive war, deductive proof and inductive evidence (for, say, Darwin's theory of evolution), socialism and fascism (as in the recent debate over health insurance legislation), it is perfectly appropriate for philosophers to step in and hold them to account. Indeed, there are no persons inside (or, for that matter, outside) the academy better able to detect and correct common and pernicious logical fallacies than philosophers. If they do not stand up and speak their piece, then we are all the worse for it.

The third of Posner's main charges is that philosophers are intrinsically incapable of persuading anyone, whether they appeal to authority or to their own theories. On the issue of authority, Posner chides Nussbaum in particular for relying on Aristotle for inspiration on a wide variety of issues. He is concerned to make three points. The first is that appeal to the authority of Aristotle for a liberal conception of justice is a "two-edged sword" because Aristotle's articulation of a worldly conception of human flourishing runs hand in glove with his approval of slavery and the subjection of women (332). The second is that appeal to the authority of Aristotle "suggests anxiety that [one's] arguments . . . are not compelling in themselves without regard to their provenance" (333). And the third is that philosophers such as Aristotle "have little resonance for modern Americans, even of the educated class," and hence appeal to philosophical authority is "the wrong strategy for an aspiring public intellectual" (334).

What should we make of these criticisms? Not much. To say that we should not appeal to Aristotle for inspiration when developing a theory of justice because Aristotle took the institution of slavery for granted and treated women as inferior is like saying that we should not appeal to John Stuart Mill's harm principle (as Posner himself does) because Mill was more worried about the tyranny of public opinion than he was about governmental coercion of the citizenry. What matters is whether Aristotle's theory of justice is *inherently* sexist or *inherently* inegalitarian, not whether Aristotle made mistakes in the course of *applying* his theory to the facts as he (mistakenly) saw them. And what matters is whether Mill's principles are *essentially* designed to protect equally against governmental coercion and the tyranny of public opinion, not whether Mill was right to worry about the latter more than the former. Further, the idea that philosophers, such as Nussbaum, appeal to Aristotle out of some sort of anxiety that their arguments would not be compelling in themselves is, quite frankly, laughable. Nussbaum references Aristotle, not because she worries that her arguments do not stand on their own, but because she believes that he is right about very important matters and (rightly) believes in giving credit where credit is due. Finally, the claim that Plato, Aristotle, Locke, Mill, Kant, and their ilk have little resonance for educated Americans is silly. Why else would Posner himself appeal to Mill's *On Liberty* as "the best starting point for a public philosophy" (355)? And why else would thousands upon thousands of students at universities across the country go out of their way to study the works of long dead philosophers? At the University of California, San Diego, where I teach, courses on Plato, Aristotle, Hellenistic Philosophy, Seventeenth Century Rationalism, Kant, Nietzsche, and Existentialism are routinely oversubscribed. This is no accident. Educated Americans know that there is a great deal to be learned about the human condition from the philosophical giants of the past.

But what of Posner's charge that philosophers' appeal to their own theories is, of its very nature, rhetorically useless? Posner writes:

There is no intellectual procedure for arguing with someone who would prefer a society dedicated to martial glory or aesthetic or spiritual perfection or radical egalitarianism out of his preference. Only a lack of imagination makes us unshakably convinced that our values are really the best and that we can prove this.

(334)

This, I think, is really the nub of most attacks on the potential resonance of philosophy on matters of general public concern. The charge is based on a hidden and particularly insidious brand of philosophical relativism, and simply begs the question against philosophical objectivists. The claim that there is no *possible* way to argue someone out of his particular political preferences rests on the view that it is impossible for philosophical arguments to sway those who do not share one's own philosophical premises. And this view itself rests on the claim that which philosophical premises one chooses to accept is essentially a matter of personal preference: what is right is merely what seems right *to me*. Ironically, as Posner himself rightly recognizes, relativism "is vulnerable to serious criticisms, such as that the relativist is disabled from arguing that relativism is true; he can say only that it is true for him" (329).[5]

The basic fact of the matter is that there is nothing intrinsic to philosophy as a discipline that should disable its academic practitioners from speaking publicly, knowledgeably, and intelligently about important issues of public policy. Of course some philosophers who are lucky enough to be given a public platform will make mistakes of fact, some will appeal to mistaken philosophical theories, and others will distort or simplify the truth in order to make their writings more widely accessible. Some may even fall in love with their own celebrity, develop hubristic tendencies, and opine where they should withhold judgment. But the best of them (such as Nussbaum and Nagel), as befits their profession, will pronounce wisely and temperately, distinguishing between what they are and what they are not in a position to know, keeping their own desire for widespread acclaim in check in the service of truth. They will do this because they have received the education and training to do so, because they are signally aware of the pitfalls of not doing so, and because the very nature of their discipline enables them to avoid self-congratulation and self-aggrandizement. We very badly need philosophers to help us see our prejudices and irrational proclivities for what they are; they, more than others, are likely to view matters objectively, without passion but with understanding. It is a remarkable irony that Posner's favorite public intellectual, John Stuart Mill, is well ensconced in the philosophical pantheon. May we continue to heed Mill's pronouncements, as well as the pronouncements of his intellectual ancestors and progenitors, despite the naysayings of his own misguided intellectual supporters.[6]

Notes

1. See Russell Jacoby, *The Last Intellectuals: American Culture in the Age of Academe*; and *The End of Utopia: Politics and Culture in an Age of Apathy*; Paul Johnson, *Intellectuals*; and Richard A. Posner, *Public Intellectuals: A Study of Decline*.
2. It would also be wrong to suggest that the reason for favoring equal educational opportunity across the races in the United States is that the benefits of equality outweigh the costs *in the long run*. No one knows enough about the long run to make this judgment, which renders it completely irrelevant in deciding questions of public policy.
3. Consider also that one of the most important reasons why preferences and customs run *against* the education of girls in the Third World when they do is that girls and women are not sufficiently well educated to *realize* that they have a right to an education! To his credit, Posner recognizes the existence of "adaptive and inauthentic preferences," that is, preferences that do not reflect what is all things considered good for the people who have them (327). But when push comes to shove, he is more than happy to take existing preferences as fixed, suggesting that public policies be crafted in such a way as to accommodate them. This is a practical contradiction, and it infects the entirety of Posner's analysis of female education in the Third World.

4. I leave aside the question whether Clinton lied about his sexual liaisons in order to avoid prosecution for abuse of power. This kind of obstruction of justice may be impeachable. My point is that it is simple-minded of Posner to suggest that obstruction of justice per se is impeachable.
5. It should also be noted that, even if it is true, relativism puts philosophers at no greater disadvantage than anyone else who chooses to pronounce in the public square.
6. I would like to thank Sarah Baker for suggesting that I contribute to this volume, and I would also like to thank Silvia Nagy-Zekmi for her welcome advice and editorial suggestions.

WORKS CITED

Jacoby, Russell. *The Last Intellectuals: American Culture in the Age of Academe*. New York: Basic Books, 1987.

——*The End of Utopia: Politics and Culture in an Age of Apathy*. New York: Basic Books, 1999.

Johnson, Paul. *Intellectuals: From Marx and Tolstoy to Sartre and Chomsky*. New York: Harper and Row, 1988.

Mill, John Stuart. *On Liberty*. London: Penguin Books, 1985.

Posner, Richard A. *Public Intellectuals: A Study of Decline*. Cambridge, MA: Harvard UP, 2001.

CHAPTER 10

THE ETHICS OF PUBLIC
INTELLECTUAL WORK

David Beard

This essay explores the distinctions between the legal and professional constraints on public intellectual work and the ethical obligations that arise from that work. It is occasioned by the highly controversial tenure case of political scientist Norman Finkelstein. On June 8, 2007, the president of DePaul University refused Finkelstein tenure in the Political Science Department (a department that had voted 9–3 in favor of tenuring Finkelstein). Finkelstein has made an academic career of chasing the biggest prey in academic and popular discussion of U.S. affairs, Israeli and Palestinian policies and politics. From his first monograph, in which he criticized Joan Peters' history of Palestine prior to Israeli occupation (*From Time Immemorial*, critiqued in Finkelstein's *Image and Reality of the Israel-Palestine Conflict*), through his role in bringing Daniel Goldhagen's controversial history of German citizens in the Holocaust to scrutiny (*Hitler's Willing Executioners (HWE)*, critiqued in Finkelstein's coauthored *A Nation on Trial*), Finkelstein approached specific influential texts with the laser precision of a scholar seeking historical truth.

After *A Nation on Trial*, however, Finkelstein began to move into a broader mode of cultural criticism. Instead of targeting specific works by specific scholars for the commission of specific historical errors, Finkelstein moved into criticism of "the Holocaust Industry" as that industry was responsible for reshaping American cultural life and justifying American foreign policy. That set of criticisms extended through two monographs (*The Holocaust Industry* and *Beyond Chutzpah*). The second monograph addressed American popular understandings of Israel more broadly. As Finkelstein's writing addressed works more immediately germane to contemporary policy debates—so he moved toward becoming a public intellectual.

Most controversial in his tenure case were the intellectual character of his work and his persona as a public intellectual, as discussed in the letter from Rev. Holtschneider. The yoking together of the academic work and the public intellectual persona is important; taken together, Holtschneider describes Finkelstein's work as shifting "toward advocacy and away from scholarship." Advocacy, unlike scholarship, is susceptible to claims of libel. Alan Dershowitz wrote to Niels Hooper, acquisitions editor of the University of California Press, that "Finkelstein's book, as presently written, contains defamatory material that is actionable not only in America, but in many other countries in which this book will be distributed" (qtd. in Dershowitz et al. 87).[1]

Finkelstein is a prolific author and orator in both public outlets and scholarly venues. The distinction between the academic and the public in Finkelstein's work is a difficult one to parse. Notably, the president of DePaul synthesized his public and disciplinary writings into a single entity—Finkelstein's "work." That collective body of work was the basis for overturning the tenure case, and it begs investigation (then) of the relationship between the narrowly disciplinary and the broadly public writings of a scholar.

This essay looks at Finkelstein's work in two contexts: the academic forum and the public intellectual forum. We typically believe that each forum is unique and can be understood on its own terms. Finkelstein's late career work crosses those boundaries and engages a kind of double-voicedness, speaking both to the academic community and to the public.

It is the claim of this chapter that appealing to issues of academic freedom in discussing Finkelstein's case helps us understand his tenure decision while complicating his work as a public intellectual. Using notions of *parrhesia* (the speaking of truth to power) in Foucault and using the description of the work of the intellectual (as described in the writings of both Julien Benda and Edward Said), I determine, in the end, that if Finkelstein's work is protected under academic freedom, it no longer constitutes the intellectual work of *parrhesia*. Finkelstein (and every member of the professoriate in the age of global academe) must instead learn to ethically and responsibly negotiate a third voice in his writing, one that addresses a complex ethical relationship to his reading, listening, and learning audiences. The Finkelstein tenure case raises this challenge for all of us.

The Purposes and Conventions of Scholarship in the Academic Field

Finkelstein has a degree in Politics from Princeton and has the pedigree of an outstanding academic. Our standard understanding of the language of the academic is as old as the sociological research of Gouldner, who claims that the mark of the academic is mastery of a lingua franca to address issues within a "culture of critical discourse" (qtd. in Said 9). Edward Said summarizes Gouldner's position succinctly:

> Each intellectual...speaks and deals in a language that has become specialized and usable by other members of the same field, specialized experts addressing other specialized experts in a lingua franca largely unintelligible to unspecialized people.
>
> (9)

This kind of research is typified by knowledge claims, research methods to justify those knowledge claims, and a strong sense of the disciplinary community to whom those claims and methods matter. "Relevance," outside the academic world, is an afterthought, if not an impossibility because the outsiders lack access to the language of the academy.[2]

Finkelstein has engaged in this kind of substantive academic debate. His career began with a devastating analysis of Joan Peters' polemical history of Israel, *From Time Immemorial*, giving Finkelstein the opportunity to meditate in *Image and Reality of the Israel-Palestine Conflict* and *The Rise and Fall of Palestine*.

Finkelstein's early work makes traditional academic contributions to our understanding of the historical record of the Israel-Palestine conflict. In the *Journal of Palestinian Studies*, Finkelstein debated Benny Morris on the historical facts of the 1948 expulsion of the Palestinians. Always pushing to discover the facts of the case, Finkelstein argues that Morris offers a "new myth" ("Myths Old and New" 67). Morris, in turn, argues for the validity of his own historical account ("Response to Finkelstein and Masalha"). Finkelstein has also contributed directly to the historical record through his own accounts of "Bayut Sahur in Year II of the Intifada: A Personal Account" expanded in "The Ordinary, the Awful, and the Sublime: Bayut Sahur in Year II of the Intifada." He has added to our historical knowledge of the Israeli-Palestinian conflict.

When Finkelstein engages Daniel Goldhagen's *HWE*, a popular history book that argues that German actions in the Holocaust were motivated by "eliminationist anti-Semitism," he does so primarily through the vehicle of correcting the historical record. He reads Goldhagen's secondary-source texts (as Goldhagen was not a historian and conducted little original historical research of his own) for his misreadings, minimizations, and distorting interpretations of the historical record. In that sense, his essay was well-paired with archivist Ruth Bettina Birn's on archival method to constitute the book, *A Nation on Trial*. Both Birn and Goldhagen participate in the academic discourse of historians in correcting Goldhagen's historical account, which they see as flawed.

To demonstrate the coolness, the level headedness of Finkelstein's critique of Goldhagen, we can observe the lines of argument he uses to engage critique. Notably, he takes the role of the skeptic, stating that Goldhagen's claims are limited because they take only partial evidence into account and that he overreaches in the implications of his claims.

Goldhagen's use of partial evidence fuels Finkelstein's critiques. Goldhagen's claims about a broadly determinist anti-Semitism in *HWE* are undermined because "Goldhagen's monochromatic thumbnail sketch also completely omits the remarkable successes registered by German Jews" (Finkelstein, *A Nation on Trial* 27). His claims about the broad popularity of Nazism as the party manifesting anti-Semitic principles are undermined by the evidence of the electorate: "Even as late as 1928," Finkelstein claims, only 2.8 percent of the German electorate cast ballots for the Nazi party" (32). (He offers a table outlining Goldhagen's errors in a schema: errors of only tacit admission, of minimization, and of misrepresentation.) Finkelstein is careful here to make an academic, historical argument from a skeptical perspective—not making a powerful counterhistory, but simply a scrutiny of the historical claims made in Goldhagen's book.

Finkelstein is also careful to critique the implications of Goldhagen's work. Goldhagen believes that his take on German anti-Semitism explains the psychodynamics of the Holocaust. And that German anti-Semitism is potentially unique, historically because "alleged indifference in the face of mass slaughter is a 'virtual psychological impossibility,' " in Goldhagen's terms (54). That impossibility, Finkelstein argues, is not unique: "how differently did ordinary Americans react to the slaughter of four million Indochinese, ordinary French to the slaughter of one million Algerians" (54). After demonstrating that Goldhagen's use of evidence is profoundly incomplete (and so results in a flawed history), he then pulls apart the claims for explanatory power. Though *A Nation on Trial* had national popular distribution in the book trade, it is clear Finkelstein is an academic taking a radically skeptical perspective on Goldhagen's historical work.

It is clear that Finkelstein can read archival and historical documentation and that he does both: he critiques false histories and he attempts to construct useful histories. This is the work of the academy. When readers of Finkelstein's later work express their disappointment, they express it in terms of its failure to meet these standards of academic work. Marc Saperstein notes that *Beyond Chutzpah* adds nothing to our knowledge of the issues pertaining to anti-Semitism or to our understanding of the Arab-Israeli conflict. In his review, he argues that it presents no new sources and applies no new methodology of analysis." Finkelstein's later monographs, like *Beyond Chutzpah*, are, by genre and intent, radically different from his work in earlier books and articles. They try to speak, double-voicedly, to the scholar as well as the popular reader.

THE PURPOSES OF SCHOLARSHIP IN THE PUBLIC FIELD

The complexity in assessing Finkelstein's later work begins when he makes two moves simultaneously: he seeks to *analyze* popular works as symptomatic of larger cultural trends and he seeks to *engage* popular figures directly. As a result, Finkelstein moves from the academic work of offering us insight into the history, representation, and structures of the Israeli-Palestinian conflict into the work of the public intellectual: speaking directly to American popular and political cultures. This is a complex and powerful, double-voiced gesture that makes assessing his work complicated.

Often, controversial academic works are explained away as controversial because they are interdisciplinary. It is a misunderstanding to read *Nation on Trial, Holocaust Industry,* and *Beyond Chutzpah* as merely interdisciplinary adventures of a scholar trained in the study of the Middle East. Such descriptions tame the texts. The statement of the University of California Press upon the publication of *Beyond Chutzpah* attempts to redescribe Finkelstein's controversial work in this way: they assert that "we are respected for attracting authors whose work transcends traditional academic boundaries" (Dershowitz et al. 86). But the real complexity is not the double-voicedness of interdisciplinarity, but the double-voicedness of both *critiquing* and *addressing* popular texts.

We can see that double-voicedness in part when we look at the publication history of his works. Much of the contents of *The Holocaust Industry* were published in *The Guardian* and in *The London Review of Books*. Further, Finkelstein writes "the Occupation's Spillover Effect" in *Tikkun*, an essay "adapted" from *Beyond Chutzpah*—clearly indicating that Finkelstein aspires to both a popular and scholarly readership. Some explication of that double-voicedness follows.

Voice #1: The Academic Analyzing the Popular Phenomenon

There is no doubt that the authors of the texts that Finkelstein takes to task (Goldhagen's *HWE*, Dershowitz's *The Case for Israel* and, to a lesser extent, Peter Novick's *The Holocaust in American Life*) have academic credentials. But these texts, in their prose style and in the way they are marketed, are popular texts crafted by scholars. As Tanweer Akram noted in the Letters to the Editor in the *Chronicle of Higher Education* of September 2, 2005, "Finkelstein's book is directed against spurious work that manages to pass itself off as scholarship" (A95). Akram is not alone in assessing Dershowitz, Goldhagen, and others writers of mass market, rather than scholarly monographs.

Finkelstein confirms other critics' views of Dershowitz's books as a popular phenomenon by stating that *The Case for Israel* was "reportedly earmarked...for every Jewish high school graduate" (*Beyond Chutzpah* 90). Clearly, Finkelstein is dissecting a popular media phenomenon, work he has done throughout his career. In "Myths Old and New," Finkelstein engages a provocative criticism of the *New York Times* coverage of Iraq against similar coverage of Israel. His essay in *A Nation on Trial* ends with an analysis of the "Goldhagen phenomenon," his assessment of why Goldhagen's belief in a cognitive structure called eliminationist anti-Semitism appealed to the American reading public. And the book that made Finkelstein an international celebrity, *The Holocaust Industry*, begins with the claim that "'the Holocaust Industry' is an ideological representation of the Nazi holocaust" (3), and that ideological representation is advanced as much by scholars as by popular literary figures like Elie Wiesel (45), Jerzy Kosinski (55), and the fraudulent memoirist Binjamin Wilkomirski (57). As Finkelstein puts it in his analysis of "the popular image of the Holocaust," "Elie Wiesel *is* the Holocaust" (55). If Finkelstein's early career centered primarily on the issues of the historical truth of the Israeli-Palestinian conflict, his later career investigated the popular manifestations of the Israeli-Palestinian politics (inextricably bound to the American Jewish experience of the Holocaust) in American public life.

But unlike a media critic, Finkelstein is not content to merely critique the ideological representations he found in Wiesel, Dershowitz, Goldhagen and others in coolly written, peer-reviewed articles in scholarly journals. Finkelstein engages these popular authors directly in the public media outlets. He takes on Dershowitz, Novick, and Goldhagen in the popular publishing outlets.

Voice #2: The Intellectual Addressing the Popular Figures Directly

A direct intervention in the contemporary scene has become a second goal of Finkelstein's career. The final section of *The Holocaust Industry* addresses the "shakedown" of Switzerland, Germany, and Eastern Europe in the name of restitution to Holocaust victims (130), here Finkelstein moves to impact foreign policy by demonstrating that the threat of U.S. economic sanctions is the weapon used to enforce restitutions from foreign governments (133). Finkelstein takes the leap to speak outside the university in the public sphere, and he recognizes the risk: In "Civility and Academic Life," Finkelstein claims that "the most urgent problems regarding liberty of speech arise not from what can and can't be said within the university but what can and can't be said outside it" (726), and his megaphone is aimed outside the university. He also argues that the United States invokes the Holocaust selectively: "Crimes of official enemies... recall the Holocaust; crimes in which the U.S. is complicit do not" (*Holocaust Industry* 146). The conclusion of the *Holocaust Industry* is an impassioned plea to correct U.S. foreign policy and to respond more fully to our own history of violence within our own borders.

Finkelstein's advocacy aim has been recognized by his enemies and his advocates. According to the University of California Press peer reviewer Avi Shlaim, "Above all, [*Beyond Chutzpah*] is a devastating indictment of Alan Dershowitz, *The Case for Israel* (2003)... I have never come across a more thorough and comprehensive demolition job" (qtd. in Dershowitz et al. 89). Similarly, a less friendly reader—Cambridge-educated historian Benny Morris—described Finkelstein's earlier research of the 1948 Exodus as a project to "find culprits and lay blame" ("Response to Finkelstein and Masalha" 103). Jay Rayner, writing in a feature for the *Observer*, declares that Finkelstein is on a "personal pogrom" (par. 6). These gestures (demolition, indictment, finding culprits, engaging a personal pogrom) move perception of Finkelstein's work outside the cool detachments of ideological or media critique into the realm of direct political intervention.

This indictment is more significant than the media critic's analysis of the gender implication of a movie or the literary critic's analysis of the Marxist implications of the Oprah bestsellers. In *those* texts, the primary goal is the analysis and critique of the mechanisms of a text. Finkelstein's work, on the other hand, enters into discourse with his subjects: policymakers and popular figures. In the case of Dershowitz, Finkelstein does not hide this, at all: "Alan Dershowitz has concocted a threadbare hoax" (*Beyond Chutzpah* 91). You can feel the finger pointing, if not the fingers around the throat. Finkelstein is not only interested in explaining Dershowitz's effects on the American public and political cultures; he is interested in decentering Dershowitz's writings within those cultures by demolishing his work, even going so far as to suggest that Dershowitz plagiarizes his work. This is work beyond the norm in academic circles; in his essay "Civility and Academic Life," Finkelstein claims that "academia is a relatively freewheeling place so long as one's opinions and carryings-on are kept within university confines" (725), and Finkelstein intentionally steps outside those confines.

Such interventionist impulses earn Finkelstein accolades as well as criticisms. Omer Bartov hyperbolically calls Finkelstein "a lone ranger with a holy mission" in *The New York Times* (par. 2). Jonathan Freedland notes that "Finkelstein likes to cast himself as the brave prophet, nobly confronting his wayward people with a truth only he dare tell." Evidently, Freedland finds that "truth" uncompelling (par. 2). On this account, Finkelstein's double-voiced discourse manages to be both scholarly and political. It speaks truth to his colleagues in the academy, and it speaks truth to power.

The Consequences of Speaking Truth to Power in the Context of Academic Freedom

There is a long tradition of viewing the role of the intellectual in relation to speaking truth to power. Said describes the work of the intellectual as "disputing the images, official narratives, justifications of power circulated by an increasingly powerful media" (22). Said calls upon the intellectual to "unearth the forgotten, to make connections that were denied, to cite alternative courses of action" (22). His position is directly related to the classical notion of *parrhesia*.

Truth telling, or *parrhesia*, is defined by five characteristics in Foucault's *Fearless Speech*.

1. Truthfulness is a necessary quality of *parrhesia*.
2. *Parrhesia* entails frankness: the truth which the subjects tell is the truth as they know it, and as they can speak it without restraint. Without restraint, Foucault notes, can mean a kind of "chattering," a usage found in Plato's *Republic, Phaedrus,* and *Laws* and consonant with discussions of *athuroglossos* in Plutarch (63). But more commonly, Foucault identifies a usage that sets out that "the *parrhesiastes* says what is true because he knows that it is true, and he knows that it is true because it is true" (14).
3. Proof of the sincerity of the *parrhesiastes* lies in the fact that his words are uttered in conditions of danger (the third characteristic): conditions such that uttering the truth might mean risking the *parrhesiastes*' life. The example Foucault first cites is that of the philosopher, telling the tyrant that his rules of governing are incompatible with justice (16). This example illustrates both the risk to the speaker and the fourth characteristic.
4. Criticism: Foucault clearly states that "*parrhesia* is a form of criticism [in which] the *parrhesiastes* is always less powerful than the one with whom he speaks" (17–18).
5. Finally, *parrhesia* entails a fifth characteristic: duty. No one compels the philosopher to critique the tyrant, yet he does, from a sense of duty.

There can be no doubt that Finkelstein speaks truth to power. He does so in a spirit of criticism and always from a sense of duty (inspired by his parents' experience of the Holocaust). While his critics may describe his speech acts as "chatter," we know that he speaks sincerely and of a truth that he is confident of. His work easily meets four of the five criteria for *parrhesia*.

As for the fifth criterion (speech despite a context of risk), Finkelstein's academic career shows that he has faced risk and paid for his unapologetic position. Finkelstein, himself, makes this risk clear in his own reflective essay on academic freedom, where he claims that

> academic freedom is not quite so liberating as it might appear prima facie. Insofar as your colleagues decide your competence, you won't survive very long the academic vetting process if they are of the decided opinion that your speculations, however copiously documented and compellingly advanced, lack scholarly merit.
> ("Civility and Academic Life" 724)

Colleagues do not reward the risk of the *parrhesiastes*. In a letter to *The Guardian,* William Dalrymple calls Finkelstein and others (like

Avi Shlaim, Noam Chomsky, and Benny Morris) scholars who have "suffered much abuse in their attempt to re-examine the foundation myth of Israel" ("Letter: Finkelstein: The Row Rumbles on" 19 par. 1). The tenure dispute at DePaul, then, becomes Finkelstein's latest and perhaps final moment as *parrhesiastes*. Denial of tenure would have been the consequence for speaking truth to power, especially if that denial was a consequence of the intervention of Dershowitz and others. But whether Finkelstein can any longer meet the criteria for the *parrhesiastes* is an open question. To the extent that claims of academic freedom led to the reversal of this tenure decision in Finkelstein's favor, it can be argued that academic freedom shielded Finkelstein from the consequences of speaking truth to power.

Because his work is entangled in questions of academic freedom, we can dispute whether Finkelstein constitutes a contemporary parrhesiastes. There is a tension between academic freedom (defined as the institutional shielding of the intellectual from consequences following from his professional speaking and writing) and the claim found in Foucault that the *parrhesiastes* speaks in condition of danger. If Julien Benda is right, and "real intellectuals...are supposed to risk being burned at the stake, ostracized or crucified" (summarized in Said 7), the shield of academic freedom may convert the tenured Finkelstein from one of the *parrhesiastes* into an instigator. At the very least, he will need to develop a third voice for his discourse.

From Speaking Truth to Power to Speaking Truth to the Powerless

As a tenured faculty member, Finkelstein is guaranteed a job for life (barring grossly illegal misconduct). No matter what he writes or speaks from this day forward, there will be no serious economic consequences to him. The situation is best described by Jacques Berlinerblau:

> To be an academic heretic is a peculiar privilege...He is securely and permanently employed. As far as his research is concerned, he is subject only to his own whims. Tenured and in good standing...the author is entitled to speak his heresy. That he is still around to tell his story, still employed and still publishing is a state of affairs that should stand as Exhibit A in any coming defense of the institution of tenure.
>
> (186)

Whatever its creature comforts, tenure places Finkelstein in a complex ethical position. The listeners and readers, the students and others whom Finkelstein will address in the future, do not share these protections.

The ethical risk is a real one. The University Board on Promotion and Tenure at DePaul noted that Finkelstein is "an excellent teacher, popular with his students and effective in the classroom" (cited by Holtschneider, from www.normanfinkelstein.com). Finkelstein recognizes the special burden of responsibility his role as an educator places upon him: "because students often defer to the moral authority of a professor and because the title of professor carries unique moral prestige, a professor ought to acquit himself in a morally responsible fashion" ("Civility and Academic Life" 729).

His students do feel a call to action. Finkelstein is a powerful rhetor in print and may be even more powerful in person in the classroom context. When his tenure controversy flared, DePaul students, faculty, and alumni conducted a sit-in to protest the denial of tenure. The consequences for students of civil disobedience loom larger than for faculty. Even untenured faculty face consequences: Finkelstein's colleague Mehene Larudee, also denied tenure at DePaul, believed that "her defense of Mr. Finkelstein derailed her career" (Millman A12). At this juncture, before he earned tenure, Finkelstein and the students and Larudee shared in the role of *parrhesiastes*, for they shared equally in the risks of speaking truth to power.

After tenure, however, Finkelstein's share in the risks of speaking truth to power will always be proportionally smaller. As long as he does not go beyond writing based on documented and verifiable information targeting Wiesel, Goldhagen, or Dershowitz (and so avoid slander), a tenured Finkelstein will be gainfully employed by a university. Students and untenured colleagues, on the other hand, will always run the risk of economic consequences should they take up his cause and join in his project to speak truth to power. Can Finkelstein speak to students in the same way that he speaks to Dershowitz, with all the rhetorical power he musters in *Beyond Chutzpah*? Or is the use of that "second voice" potentially an unethical call to incite others to take a risk he does not share?

Implications for Global Academe

The larger issues raised by Finkelstein's tenure case are not those of the definition of academic freedom or the relationship between academic freedom, politics, and the tenure process. Those are the questions that animate the *Chronicle* and academic listservs. Philosopher Sidney Hook defined academic freedom, as derived from the

German intellectual tradition, as "the freedom to inquire, discover, publish, and teach the truth as they see it in the field of their competence...freedom to teach and freedom to learn" (34). If anything, Finkelstein's case affirms this traditional definition of academic freedom. Academic freedom is a professional issue; this volume on *Global Academe* has a larger agenda at its core.

Most tenured faculty members are tenured because they learn to speak one voice well: the voice of the professional academic. They may also be civically engaged: they may work a soup kitchen or write letters to the editor for the local newspaper or do any of a thousand possible good works in their community. But their civic engagement and their professional work are separated. Other academics engage, actively, in consulting work for corporations. Therein, they, too, learn to speak with another voice, one distinct from their academic voice. And many, many of the scholars cited in this essay use these strategies to discover a third voice: Novick, Goldhagen, Dershowitz—each of them speaks with a different voice when they address the public. And they are not the only ones: think of Stanley Fish's unique power to write for the public via the *New York Times* in a voice that echoes but does not match identically his voice in his literary criticism. Think, too, of the legions of academic bloggers active today—attempting to reach an audience wider than the 500 readers of a journal by using a new platform and a new voice.

The tenure controversy of Norman Finkelstein shows us that a skilled rhetor can use a single voice to negotiate multiple audiences: to speak truth to their colleagues in the profession, to their students, and to the public. In that sense, Finkelstein demonstrates a sophistication that few academics reach. With all the power, the prestige, the certainty, and the rhetorical force that a member of the university can muster, he promises to speak the truth where his opponents speak myths and distortions. In fact, Finkelstein's very promise to speak the truth, to offer "reality" in opposition to "image" in the most pertinent political questions of our age, gives his rhetoric an edge, a bite that echoes the premises of the Sokal hoax: the left cannot retreat into the language of postmodern discourse to destabilize the languages of power. Finkelstein is as modern a scholar as anyone can imagine, promising to reveal what is real, and this starting point helps make his rhetoric persuasive in a public sphere that values certainty (whether scientific or religious) over skepticism. In that sense, Finkelstein represents a strong counter to the popular writings of conservative scholars like Mary Lefkowitz, Dinesh D'Souza, and others—the academics who speak on behalf of power.

The question that Finkelstein (and every tenured academic) must face involves whether the same voice that they use to speak truth to *power* (inside or outside their discipline, or both) can ethically be used to speak truth to the *powerless,* if that truth might cause greater consequences for the powerless than for the faculty member themselves. The question is not of Finkelstein's freedom to teach and research and write, but of his ethical responsibilities while teaching these highly controversial topics to young adults. We are called upon, more and more, to bring powerful issues of the day into our classrooms (through service learning, through civic engagement, and through the demand that we revise our curriculum to engage questions of diversity, of internationalization, of sustainability, and more). We must reflect on the rhetoric we employ as we do so.

The Finkelstein case raises the question: must we develop a third voice, speaking truth to the powerless who are our students? And if so, what would the rhetorical features of this third voice look like? How do we differentiate the act of speaking truth to power from the act of encouraging our students to speak truth to power, knowing that they lack our institutional protections? That is the challenge that faces global academics in the twenty first century.

NOTES

1. In response to the threats of libel lawsuits, the University of California Press reported that the Press secured the help of "American and British legal experts" to review the manuscript in light of differing American and British libel laws (Dershowitz et al. 98).
2. It is notable that common discussion of academic freedom and the typical features of academic work often include peer review. But surviving the process of peer review does not ensure that the text in question is an example of academic work. Jon Wiener describes the peer review process at the University of California Press prior to the publication of Finkelstein's *Beyond Chutzpah*: "The manuscript was sent out for peer review by six leading scholars in the field; then, publication was recommended by a committee of 20 UC faculty members. The manuscript was also reviewed by several libel attorneys" (Dershowitz et al. 96). Despite this process, it is clear that some critics do not agree that *Beyond Chutzpah* is academic work, as Gouldner defines it.

WORKS CITED

Akram, Tanweer. "A Battle between Authors over a New Book." Letter. *Chronicle of Higher Education* 52.2 (2005): A95.

Bartov, Omer. "A Tale of Two Holocausts." Review of *Reflections on the Exploitation of Jewish Suffering*. Ed. Norman G. Finkelstein. *The New York Times* August 6, 2000: n.p. Web. July 6, 2010.

Benda, Julien. *The Treason of the Intellectuals*. Trans. Richard Aldington. New Brunswick, NJ: Transaction Publishers, Rutgers, 2007.

Berlinerblau, Jacques. *Heresy in the University: The Black Athena Controversy and the Responsibilities of American Intellectuals*. New Brunswick: Rutgers UP, 1999.

Birn, Ruth Bettina. "Revising the Holocaust." *The Historical Journal of Cambridge* 40.1 (1997): 195–215. Rprt. *A Nation on Trial: The Goldhagen Thesis and Historical Truth*. Ed. Norman G. Finkelstein and Ruth Bettina Birn. New York: Metropolitan Books, 1998. 101–48.

Dalrymple, William. "Finkelstein: The Row Rumbles On." Letter. *The Guardian* July 19, 2000, n.p. Guardian.co.uk. Web. July 6, 2010.

Dershowitz, Alan. *The Case for Israel*. Hoboken: John Wiley & Sons, 2003.

——Letter. *Tikkun* 20.4 (2005): 3–4.

——et al. "Academic Freedom and Palestine Israel: The Case of 'Beyond Chutzpah.' " *Journal of Palestine Studies* 35.2 (2006): 85–99.

Farmer, Stephanie. Review of *Chutzpah: On the Misuse of Anti-Semitism and the Abuse of History* Ed. Norman G. Finkelstein. *Arab Studies Quarterly* 28.1 (2006): 59–62.

Finkelstein, Norman G. *Beyond Chutzpah: On the Misuse of Anti-Semitism and the Abuse of History*. Berkeley: U of California P, 2005.

——"Civility and Academic Life." *South Atlantic Quarterly* 108.4 (2009): 723–40.

——*The Holocaust Industry: Reflection on the Exploitation of Jewish Suffering*. London: Verso, 2000.

——"How the Arab-Israeli War of 1967 Gave Birth to a Memorial Industry." Rev. of *The Holocaust in American Life* by Peter Novick. *London Review of Books* 22.1 (2000): 33–36. Web. July 6, 2010.

——*Image and Reality of the Israel-Palestine Conflict*. London: Verso, 2003.

——"Myths Old and New." *Journal of Palestinian Studies* 21.1 (1991): 66–89.

——"The Occupation's Spillover Effect." *Tikkun* 20.2 (2005): 13–14.

——"The Ordinary, the Awful, and the Sublime: Beit Sahur in Year II of the Intifada." *Social Text* 24 (1990): 3–30.

——*The Rise and Fall of Palestine*. Minneapolis: U of Minnesota P, 1996.

Finkelstein, Norman G. and Ruth Bettina Birn. *A Nation on Trial: The Goldhagen Thesis and Historical Truth*. New York: Metropolitan Books, 1998.

Foucault, Michel. *Fearless Speech*. Trans. Joseph Pearson. Los Angeles: Semiotext(e), 2001.

Freedland, Jonathan. "An Enemy of the People." *The Guardian* July 14, 2000: n.p. Guardian.co.uk. Web. July 6, 2010.

Goldhagen, Daniel. *Hitler's Willing Executioners: Ordinary Germans and the Holocaust*. New York: Knopf, 1996.
Holtschneider, Dennis H. Letter. Norman Finkelstein's website. Jerzy http://www.normanfinkelstein.com/aaup-v-father-holtschneider-of-depaul/
Hook, Sidney. *Academic Freedom and Academic Anarchy*. New York: Cowles Book Co, 1970.
Millman, Sierra. "Students Protest Tenure Denials at DePaul U." *Chronicle of Higher Education* 53.42 (2007): A12.
Morris, Benny. "Response to Finkelstein and Masalha." *Journal of Palestine Studies* 21.1 (1991): 98–114.
"News for Educational Workers." *Radical Teacher* 80 (2007): 46–48.
Novick, Peter. *The Holocaust in American Life*. Boson: Houghton Mifflin, 1999.
Peters, Joan. *From Time Immemorial: The Origins of the Arab-Jewish Conflict over Palestine*. New York: Harper & Row, 1984.
Quill, Elizabeth. "Finkelstein Supporters Stage Protest at DePaul U's Convocation." *The Chronicle of Higher Education* August 31, 2007: n.p. *Chronicle.com*. Web. July 6, 2010.
Rayner, Jay. "Finkelstein's List." *The Observer* July 16, 2000: n.p. *Guardian.co.uk*. Web. July 6, 2010.
Said, Edward. *Representations of the Intellectual: The 1993 Reith Lectures*. New York: Pantheon Books, 1994.
Saperstein, Marc. Rev. of *Beyond Chutzpah: On the Misuse of Anti-Semitism and the Abuse of History* Ed. Norman G. Finkelstein. *Middle East Journal* 60.1 (2006): 183–85.
Sokal, Alan and Jean Bricmont. *Intellectual Impostures*. London: Profile Books, 1998.

Chapter 11

Multilingual Academics in a Global World and the Burden of Responsibility

Lahcen E. Ezzaher

I was born and raised in Morocco, a rich contact zone crisscrossed for centuries by Arab, Berber, African, and European travelers through linguistic and cultural lines. I grew up speaking Arabic and French, which, at first, resulted in an intense moment of displacement not only at the levels of phonology, lexis, syntax, and graphology, but also in terms of values and worldviews. However, I must admit that—as the French language gradually made its way into my intellectual consciousness, like a *pharmakon*—things began to take a different dimension. When I was eight, the fables of La Fontaine already occupied a good part of my memory and a few years later, the works of Victor Hugo, Emile Zola, Honoré de Balzac, Molière, Racine, Camus, and Sartre firmly expanded the French linguistic and cultural territory in my imagination and made the Arabic literary tradition, the Koran, and the sayings of Prophet Muhammad look sadly outdated in an emerging modern Morocco. Little by little, I started to drift away from the folk wisdom of my mother and grandparents, which seemed more and more remote and archaic, and soon found myself moving away from the narrow alleys, the squares, and the marketplaces in my hometown Fes to imaginary places in Paris.

In college I developed a keen sense of awareness of the difficult historical circumstances that made me part of a universal colonial project that gave itself the authority to name and "civilize" its colonial subjects in Africa, Asia, and South America. Most of the colonial literary works that I studied in college, like E. M. Forster's *A Passage to India,* Rudyard Kipling's *Kim,* or Conrad's *Heart of Darkness* portrayed the colonial subjects of Europe as foxy, untrustworthy children or lazy, unreliable savages showing a gruesome drive for cannibalism. I felt I was not alone, for there were other people from various parts of the world who were dragged into this messy and shameful colonial enterprise that deprived them of their land and dignity and distorted their histories.

With this already hybrid, non-Western identity, I came to seek out American English and fell in love with the language of Thoreau, Emerson, Walt Whitman, Emily Dickinson, Flannery O'Connor, Eugene O'Neil, and other American writers, several of whom I had studied in Morocco. In addition to the thirst for more knowledge that I had brought with me from the old country and to a handful of books in Arabic, French, and English that I had packed in my suitcase, I had especially treasured in my heart Walt Whitman's concept of identification with fellow humans from all walks of life. I was particularly captivated by the poet's fascination with himself as a member of the human carnival, a theme I saw working as a unifying thread throughout *Leaves of Grass.* I still have vivid memories of the first time I was rocketed in a matter of a few hours from Casablanca airport to JFK in 1990. When I saw the crowds in New York, the opening lines in Whitman's poem "Song of Myself" rushed into my mind:

> I celebrate myself;
> And what I assume you shall assume;
> For every atom belonging to me, as good belongs to you.
> (61)

I decided then that every sound of the English language that belonged to all Americans also belonged to me, since Whitman's poetry had already given me an extraordinary sense of openness of form and theme. Whitman's poetry was as large as life and therefore it created for me a large intellectual space that, as a freshly established immigrant, I inhabited with hope for tolerance and acceptance. Today much as Whitman imagined a cosmic unity with me and for me, a fusion of poet and subject, a multilingual voice to celebrate, he must stand aside and be at once a part of me and apart from me. When he is apart from me, I put the accent on difference and detach myself from America to nurse this persistent guilt toward my family that I had to leave in order to become who I am today. What compounds this sense of guilt is the vague feeling that in leaving those loved ones, I had left my Third Worldness behind as well, in order to end up in a space that is neither Third World nor First World, a world in between, an uneasy, imaginary homeland.

Twenty years after my first encounter with America, I still experience a deep feeling of sadness perhaps peculiar to immigrants; a sense of being cast in a strange, vast world where the rules are such that it is actually not easy for me to observe them without an overwhelming self-consciousness. For example, although the statement, "your English is excellent," is often meant to be a compliment by people I meet outside of academe, it still puts me right on the other side of the English language. Knowing that there is nothing necessarily strange or frightening about being on the other side, I welcome the compliment with a smile, but the smile is usually mixed with slight unease. To be on the other side implies that I have to be constantly watchful for what I say, which can be extremely exhausting. A mispronunciation of a word or a grammatical error brings me utter discomfort. When such blunders happen, I feel like a guest who is inadvertently knocking things over at his hosts' home. And this feeling of embarrassment is distressing, especially when I sense that my peers are watching and that I am an outsider who is breaking rules of a language that has a long history behind it. Every moment I enter this risky order of discourse in English, anxiety sets in, because I am fully aware of the social materiality of academic language, the production of which is, as Michel Foucault put it, "at once controlled, selected, organized, and redistributed by a certain number of procedures" (216).

However, in my attempt to be part of Whitman's America, to belong more specifically to the academic culture in the United States, I bring my Third World accent with me. That is, I bring views and a sensibility with me only to see them grate against the Western rationality of the First World. The arena in which these worldviews collide is now my new home, which is a rich and complex borderland that hosts the green-card holder, the *alien*(!) resident, and all categories of fellow immigrants who are fingerprinted, numbered, labeled, and classified. Every time I am thrown into the marginality of the borderland, into what Gloria Anzaldúa calls "the constant state of transition" I experience a deep sense of frustration. When I get comments like "You don't have to stay, if you don't like it here. You can always go back home." True, I dream about the old country, the old self, the old me. True, as often as I can, I surrender to the magnetic pull of home and make the journey back even for a second to make sure the places, the faces, and the memories I left behind are still there. But every time I actually go back even for a short visit, I feel the urge to return to the borderland. I have never realized that homecoming is another form of departure. The fear of going back to the old country, of opening old wounds of oppression and persecution, or simply the fear of not being taken back, not being accepted eats the soul of every immigrant. It is that same fear that gave me the guts to get out and seek refuge in the borderland.

In this borderland, the fusion of Arabic with French and English has significantly created a complex zone of contact for me where—as Mary Louise Pratt puts it—"disparate cultures meet, clash, and grapple with each other, often in highly asymmetrical relations of domination and subordination" (4). Contact zones can oftentimes cause a severe form of epistemological displacement which, to put it in Arif Dirlik's words, " 'decenters' intellectuals... who, as it were, learn to live in two cultural worlds without belonging in either one completely" (413). But contact zones also allow for debates to be staged, for unique perspectives to materialize, and for new accents to fall differently from those of old. For example, in the American university, I find myself pulled into an arena where serious debates are staged over burning issues of race, class, gender, sexual orientation, ethnicity, and other social and cultural categories. In these debates, language and education are definitely not neutral or innocent and I certainly cannot afford to stand by and watch. Since I carry the Arabic-Muslim tradition with me and in me, I find myself engaged in the process of translation introducing this cultural tradition, which has been either demonized or completely ignored in the Western public sphere until the tragic events of 9/11. I bring this tradition to my new academic community and, in this way, serve as a conduit between East and West.

Translation is traditionally defined as an operation that takes place in the realm of equivalence, but this operation becomes even more fascinating when it announces the play of difference at the threshold of untranslatability. Translation allows the translator to construct an open frame of reference, open cultural spaces, and open systems of thought. If a translation traditionally seeks to be a copy of the source language text, if it attempts to become the other by achieving proximity to and similarity with the primary text, it consciously or unconsciously works as a strategy that generates difference and meaning. In this perspective, translation opens up the source language text to an outside world teeming with multiple views and values. In this way, a translation is not reduced to a mere task of communicating information, nor is it considered a secondary reading that is subservient to the primary text; rather it is an act of creativity inside and between languages and cultures.

Through a process of transformation and renewal of signs, translation also allows the primary text to live longer, for it generates a debate over the primary text, which over the years constitutes a sort of history of ideas. Moreover, in translation, the target language undergoes significant changes, since it has to accommodate the source language text in its cultural space. As George Steiner appropriately observes, translations enrich the target language by allowing the source language to penetrate it and modify it (65). That is, when a translation takes place, ideas and views from the target language and culture have to be shuffled and reshuffled to give room to new ideas from the source language and culture. Today translation continues to be a working metaphor in my academic career, since it allows me to constantly define my role as an academic worker. To be an academic worker is to activate a kind of translation in such a manner as to introduce change not only in the thinking of those I interact with in the classroom, but also in my own thinking. To be an academic worker is to get to think other things than the ones I used to think before. It is to engage myself in a complex dialogue with the members of the academic discourse community over the nature of language and culture.

To undermine the higher mode of Western consciousness and rationality, to do away with duality upon which this Western rationality is based, I put the accent, especially in my teaching of writing and literature, on the principle of discourse community as an arena in which multiple local social groups clamor for attention. As Ira Shor explains, "all of us emerge from local cultures set in global contexts where languages from multiple sources shape us" (2). In this sense, the academic discursive community and, by extension, the larger public emits a polyphonic discourse in which every cultural sign is a prism that is constructed by multiple conflicting views, all of which are manifest and all are having a claim to truth. In the context of colonial discourse and postcolonial criticism, the postcolonial critics operate in a unique space, generating knowledge. This gesture comes with a unique tone and attitude toward the consequences of the colonial condition. For example, Aimé Césaire opens his political essay *Discourse on Colonialism* by sending a chilling warning to former European colonial powers when he writes:

A civilization that proves incapable of solving the problems it creates is a decadent civilization. A civilization that chooses to close its eyes to its most crucial problems is a stricken civilization. A civilization that uses its principles for trickery and deceit is a dying civilization.

(9)

Césaire explains that colonization "dehumanizes even the most civilized man" because it is based "on contempt for the native and justified by that contempt" (20).

Although the essay was originally published in 1955, the warning is still relevant and appropriate, for Europe, which during the course of the last century either abandoned or was forced out of most of its colonies, has joined forces with the so-called industrialized countries in the Western hemisphere to move into a new phase of economic domination by creating an overpowering force of globalization that has sucked in the rest of the world. In the late 1950s and early 1960s, the dark(er)-skinned colonial subjects in Africa, Latin America, and Asia took upon themselves the difficult task of solving the social, political, and economic problems that Europe had created for them, and of exposing the principles of trickery and deceit that Europe had used for decades to keep them under the yoke of colonialism. The intellectuals participating in this task were mostly bilingual and today the bilingual or multilingual academics are still engaged in decolonization, although they face new challenges and have to address new questions about the global situation: "Have I used the wrong language to write?" "What does it sound like when I express the thoughts that I am thinking now in my mother tongue into the foreign language that has adopted me and that I am also adopting?"

The questions become even more complex when one realizes that there is no exact symmetry between the mother tongue and the foreign language, that there is only the shifting ground in which one language leans on the other. I call that shifting ground "accent." So the academic worker speaks, reads, and writes with an accent. Put in the context of bilingualism, accent, as a unique perspective of seeing, derives pleasure from its own being, for it gives the bilingual speaking subjects the right to want to see things differently in the richness of language; it gives them the rare opportunity to compose a rhythmic pulse of otherness that reflects not only an individual characteristic, but also a regional, social, and cultural history. Additionally, at the confluence of two or more cultural streams, particularly at the level of text production, with linguistic signs constantly crossing over, accent, rather than resulting in an inferior text product, provides a fruitful, mutable, and more malleable corpus with a rich pool of cultural signs.

The intellectual workers living in a foreign land usually leave behind "home." This home is generally distraught by the colonial experience. North African writers Assia Djebar, Kateb Yacine, and Abdelkebir Khatibi acknowledge in their work a violent process of acculturation advanced actively by French colonial school system. In his novel *Le polygone étoilé*, Kateb Yacine equates his educational experience with being thrust into "la gueule du loup" (the jaws of the wolf, 181). Moroccan writer Abdelkébir Khatibi uses autobiographical fragments combined with poetry and parable in his works *La mémoire tatouée* and *Amour bilingue* to express his uneasy alliance with the French language and culture. Algerian writer Assia Djebar admits that the process of Western cultural intervention, resulting in her mastery of the colonizer's language and access to European readership, excluded her from many aspects of traditional women's world. Her works, especially *Women of Algiers in Their Apartment*, constitute a serious intellectual effort to reclaim that space through the French language. In this sense, writing in the foreign language becomes a liberating factor and an opportunity for empowerment. In his book *In the Name of Identity: Violence and the Need to Belong*, Francophone Lebanese writer Amin Maalouf identifies two extreme ideas in matters of writing and immigration that he judges "unrealistic, sterile, and harmful" (39). The first one, Maalouf explains, occurs when the migrant subject "regards the host country as a blank sheet of paper on which everyone can write whatever he pleases, or, worse as a wasteland where everyone can set up house with all his impedimenta without making any changes in his habits or behavior" (40). The other attitude considers "the host country as a page already written and printed, a land where the laws, values, beliefs, and other human and cultural characteristics have been fixed once and for all, and where all that immigrants can do is conform to them" (39–40). Maalouf comes to the conclusion that a host country is "neither a tabula rasa, nor a fait accompli, but a page in the process of being written" (40) and proceeds to set up two equations: "The more you steep yourself in the culture of the host country, the more you will be able to steep yourself in your own....; the more an immigrant feels that his own culture is respected, the more open he will be to the culture of the host country" (40). This, Maalouf concludes, is "a moral contract" (40).

This moral contract can be safely extended to include a global context. Globalization, in this sense, presents itself as a collective ethos and a complex amalgam of social and cultural practices by means of which people display a rhetoric of belonging to a place that has wider historical and geographical landmarks. One has to come to terms with the global condition and turn it into an intellectual mission whose purpose is to make one see life, and express it through language, not as a commodity but as a new way of being. The burden of responsibility of the multilingual academic workers, in this context, is to claim a specific discursive space in which they discover, maintain, and strengthen bridges with other languages and hence identify with their countries of origin, with their host countries, and also with the global world. They can learn to carry different allegiances in them, without fear of being accused of treason. It is true that sometimes, at first sight, allegiances to different languages and cultures collide with one another. For example, the 9/11 attack and the war on Iraq pulled me into two different directions. My heart and mind were torn between two poles to the point that I couldn't even afford to make choices, take sides or even stand by and watch because there weren't any choices to be made. There was only pain and anger at the malicious character of human beings.

In the context of globalization, the first step is for academics to see this new phenomenon not necessarily as exclusively American. As Maalouf appropriately explains, "[E]verybody must be able to recognize himself in it, to identify with it a little. No one must be made to think that it is irremediably alien and, therefore, hostile to him" (120). The question that one must ask is, "What contribution can I make to the ever expanding global culture?" because as Maalouf puts it "[the world] belongs to all those who want to make a place for themselves in it" (124). The role of academic workers, then, is to cement the cultural encounter between themselves and the "other," first by acknowledging and highlighting universality of values and second by appreciating "otherness" as part of human growth and diversity. Put differently, the burden of responsibility of academic workers is to forge links and correct misconceptions.

What I am learning more and more throughout this journey into the complex realm of language and culture is that, in theory as well as in practice, culture does not exist in a vacuum. Equally important, I realize more and more that my students bring to the classroom their worldviews only to see them grate against firmly established discursive conventions in academe. They, just like me, bring their own accent to the classroom and end up speaking, reading, and writing with an accent, which makes every student a potentially marginal voice trying to find a niche in the academy. In this context, my responsibility as a teacher is to enable students to acknowledge the social nature of discourse, to criticize and question its rhetorical moves, and, more important perhaps, to formulate a counterdiscourse. And this means to encourage them to accept historical responsibility and to acknowledge the political and social relation between themselves and the world around them.

I started this essay out of nostalgia for home, my first linguistic and cultural space that hosts memories, friends, and loved ones. But every time I go to Morocco to visit, after a few weeks, I start missing my other home in the United States, which is another important space that hosts memories, friends, and loved ones. The same longing pulls me in two opposite directions. To come to terms with this constant pull, I imagine myself in another dimension of language, in many places at once, and I watch the words bubbling out of people's mouths, creating a sweet confusion. Some may ask what it is that drives me away from the old country. I say "oppression." Others may ask what it is that makes me escape, even through dreams, the harsh reality of being an immigrant in the United States. I say "oppression." Others still ask me in what language I dream. Instead of answering this question, let me say what I dream of. I dream of what Min-Zhan Lu characterizes as "an ideal literate self" working in the context of social justice. Lu defines literacy as that which "might bring us hope and courage as well as vision and analysis for negotiating the crucial crossroad in the history of this nation" (173).

Works Cited

Anzaldúa, Gloria. *Borderlands/La Frontera: The New Mestiza*. San Francisco, CA: Aunt Lute Books, 1987.

Césaire, Aimé. *Discourse on Colonialism,* trans. Joan Pinkham. New York: Monthly Review Press, 1972.

Dirlik, Arif. "Culturalism as Hegemonic Ideology and Liberating Practice." *The Nature and Context of Minority Discourse*. Ed. JanMohamed, Abdul R. and David Lloyd. New York: Oxford UP, 1990. 394–431.

Djebar, Assia. *Women of Algiers in Their Apartment*. Trans. Marjolijn de Jager. Charlottesville, VA: U of Virginia P, 1992.

Foucault, Michel. "The Discourse on Language," *The Archeology of Language,* trans. M. Sheridan Smith. New York: Pantheon, 1972.

Kateb, Yacine. *Le polygone étoilé*. Paris: Seuil, 1986.

Khatibi, Abdelkébir. *La mémoire tatouée*. Paris: Denoël, Lettres Nouvelles, 1971.

——*Amour bilingue* Montpellier: Fata Morgana, 1983.

Lu, Min-Zahn. "Redefining the Literate Self: The Politics of Critical Affirmation." *College Composition and Communication* 51.2 (December 1999): 172–94.

Maalouf, Amin. *In the Name of Identity: Violence and the Need to Belong.* Trans. Barbara Bray. New York: Arcade Publishing, 2001.

Pratt, Mary Louise. *Imperial Eyes: Travel Writing and Transculturation.* London: Routledge, 1992.

Shor, Ira. "What Is Critical Literacy?" *Critical Literacy in Action: Writing Words, Changing Worlds. A Tribute to the Teachings of Paulo Freire.* Ed. Ira Shor and Caroline Pari. Portsmouth, NH: Boynton/Cook Publishers, 1999. 1–30.

Whitman, Walt. *Leaves of Grass. The Portable Walt Whitman.* Ed. Mark Van Doren. New York: The Viking Press, 1972.

Chapter 12

International Perspectives on Speaking Truth to Power

D. Ray Heisey and Ehsan Shaghasemi

This chapter presents an intercultural dialogue about speaking truth to power from the international perspective of two colleagues in university contexts—an American and an Iranian. The two have worked together on previous research projects, and in the spirit of collaborative inquiry they have undertaken a dialogical work from the cultural context of their own personal situations. This chapter presents the result of their collaboration. In the first section, author D. Ray Heisey discusses his American experience and in the next section coauthor Ehsan Shaghasemi responds to Heisey; in the sections that follow the authors pose questions to each other and answer them. The conclusion section sums up their findings.

The American Experience—by D. Ray Heisey

My story begins with a youthful decision not to participate in the war against Vietnam. This action became my first public opposition to my government's military engagements. I grew up in a religious denomination much like the historic peace churches: the Quakers and Mennonites. After the completion of my M.A. degree in 1955, because of the military draft, I was expected to register with the Selective Service System. I filed as a conscientious objector and was classified as 1-W, according to the U.S. government's provision for such persons. I was assigned to teach for two years in a private college as my alternate service. This was my first public protest to the government's policy of going to war with the proclaimed aim of solving international problems.

After I began teaching at Kent State University in 1966, I was invited to speak at a public meeting in the Methodist church pastored by one of my former students, LeRoy Tyson. I decided to speak about my opposition to the Vietnam War. I argued that the government's policy of going to war was unjustified, unwise, and morally wrong. In the Question and Answer session, a local gentleman in the congregation stood up and confronted me in a hostile manner, saying, "How can you, a liberal professor, stand here and argue against our government for wanting to stop Communism in that part of the world?" I replied by standing my ground before going on to another question.

Another personal example of taking a public stand against the Vietnam War relates to the case of four students killed on May 4, 1970, by the National Guard on the campus of Kent State University where I was teaching and serving on the Faculty Senate. In the wake of that terrible tragedy, the Faculty Senate held numerous meetings to discuss what position the faculty should take on the issue. At one of the Senate meetings following the shootings, I stood up and spoke of the importance of faculty members taking a stand for freedom of speech and against the government's policy in Vietnam, as well as to the university administration's acquiescence to the governor's decision to take over the campus.

A few days later, I received a phone call from Dr. Martin Nurmi, the chairman of the Faculty Senate, inviting me to become a member of the Faculty Senate Executive Committee for the upcoming year. As a result of my involvement in the Faculty Senate Executive Committee, and becoming its secretary, I was later invited to be a member of a Faculty Senate Committee, along with Ken Calkins and Daniel Jones, that analyzed the published Report of the Ohio Special Grand Jury on the May 4 shootings and also to be on the search committee to select the next president following Dr. White's retirement the year following these events. Our analysis of the Ohio Special Grand Jury Report, which refused to indict any members of the National Guard, took a strong position against the government's representation of what had happened on May 4. It raised "serious questions about both the competence and the intentions of the Grand Jury" (O'Neil et al. 139) when it called the faculty action "irresponsible" (140), and concluded, "The length to which the Grand Jury Report goes to develop its case suggests the one-sided nature of its investigation" (142). Our committee's analysis was adopted as the official position of the Kent State University Faculty Senate. Parts of it were later published in Robert O'Neil's book *No Heroes, No Villains: New Perspectives on Kent State and Jackson State*.

Another follow-up event of the May 4 shootings was a study my colleague Carl Moore and I completed on challenging James Michener's book *Kent State: What Happened and Why*, which was proclaimed one of the leading authoritative documents of the Kent State events. Michener claimed that his book was based on numerous interviews and that there was "not a great deal of error" in his work. My colleague and I asked our class of students studying argumentation to send a questionnaire to the interviewees and found that many of them had been misquoted or not fairly represented by Michener (cf. Eszterhas 35–40). Based on Michener's study, we later wrote a paper, "Not a Great Deal of Error...?" in 1972. It was accepted by the *Columbia Journalism Review*, but later it was mysteriously pulled back and not published.

In these examples of my speaking truth to power, my goal was to use my intellectual and research skills to communicate a perspective not usually heard in the public media or accepted by the majority attitudes at the time.

THE IRANIAN EXPERIENCE—BY EHSAN SHAGHASEMI

The history of power in the East more or less reveals the nature of contact between intellectuals and rulers (Karimi-Hakkak 189); the king holds the power and concentrates it in his court as much as possible. Consequently, punishment was an effective means to show the people who is in control. Persian literary mysticism has always provided a space to express the lack of freedom of speech by telling the truth to power for hundreds of years. On the one hand, poets told the truth to power, and on the other, mysticism allowed for other interpretations, sometimes in complete contradiction to the first. Rashid Vatvat, a Persian[1] poet from the thirteenth century writes, "Oh my lord, darkness becomes light by your face." In Persian, it could be interpreted as "Oh my lord, your face illuminates darkness" or, "Oh my lord, your face darkens light." Both could be equally acceptable interpretations (Shamisa 109). Although Vatvat was in the court of cruel Mongol occupiers, he got no punishment for the possible insult.

But, in the wake of new media, Iranians can now experience an alternative approach. According to Internetworldstats.com, at the beginning of 2011, there were more than 33 million Internet users in Iran. The perceived anonymity of the Internet has helped Iranians to speak truth to power. Nevertheless, the traditional ways of using mysticism in talk and image are still used when action is needed, both at the individual and at the collective level. I present here three examples of my own experiences of speaking truth to power in Iran.

After getting my B.A. degree in Mechanics of Agricultural Machinery in June 2003, I joined the Iranian army to complete my two years of mandatory military service, after which I planned to continue my studies in Communications. I passed the primary training in Tehran, and then I was transferred to Broujerd to become an expert in explosion and mine neutralization. But, after five months of training and becoming a second lieutenant, they informed me that I was to serve in the Politics and Beliefs section of the Army.[2]

In spite of my wishes, I had become part of the Politics and Beliefs section in November 2003. I thanked them for choosing me but told them that I did not want to serve in their section. A colonel asked me, "Don't you believe in our sacred work of keeping the Iranian Army clean?" I said, "Yes, of course I do, but I think the person who wants to work in such a sacred place should be above reproach himself. I think I can be more useful if you send me to an operational zone."

He looked at me angrily and wrote something in my file. Then he introduced me to the Beliefs Evaluation section. This part was the strictest section of Politics and Beliefs. I asked, "Why do you do this?" He said, "There is no 'why' in the army. Everybody wishes to serve in this section. But, a 'stupid guy' like you is trying to go to the front." So, I presented myself to the Beliefs Evaluation section. There were two colonels there. I said, "Sir, I don't like to serve here." They looked at me with surprise and said, "So, why did you come here?" I said "because they sent me!" They called back the same colonel, and after a small consultation they told me I had two choices, one was to stay there and serve as a loyal soldier and the second was to be exiled to the Iraq border. I chose the second option. They said, "You will regret this." I said nothing. They ordered Human Resources Management to send me to the Iraq border.

On November 4, 2009, on the anniversary of the American embassy U.S. hostage incident, a government-sponsored rally was held. The Green Movement took this opportunity to hold a demonstration. Out of curiosity, I participated in this demonstration accompanied by two female classmates from the University of Tehran. In the morning I warned them that there would be much danger there. They said they were the voices for Iranian women, and they have to be seen on the streets.

Near the Haft-e-Tir square we saw thousands of plain clothes *Basij* militia[3] with batons and clubs. On a playground, several people were arrested and handcuffed, captured by the *Basij*. When people saw that all the streets to Haft-e-Tir Square were closed, they tried to reach Vali-Asr square, a mile away and started to chant "Death to the dictator!" "Obama, Obama, you are either with us or with them!" "Russia, China, shame on you, leave my country!" "No Gaza, No Lebanon, my life would be dedicated to Iran!" and so on. They were trying not to reference a specific person, so that it would not provoke the police and *Basij* militias. In fact, only a "dictator" will react to hearing "death to the dictator."

Nevertheless, the guards attacked the demonstrators. I wanted to run, but I remembered the girls left behind. Some antiriot guards had cornered them while beating them with batons. I ran back and shouted, "Leave them alone, they are girls!" They pulled back for a while. Perhaps my seriousness had given them the impression that I was a security agent in plain clothes. The girls escaped, but the guards suddenly turned on me. I was able to escape somehow, and fortunately I did not suffer serious injury. It was a bad scene in one of the most beautiful parts of Tehran: tear gas, violence and fire. Then we went to the Fathi-Shaghaghi Junction until the gathering ended.

On December 7, 2009, students at the University of Tehran held a ceremony for Student's Day anniversary.[4] Students have held this ceremony for many years, but 2009 was different. At least 2,000 *Basij* militia members entered the campus with invitation cards issued by the University of Tehran's administration and attacked the students. After disbanding the students, they held some gatherings. One leader was speaking for his fellow *Basijis,* saying that the students were being influenced by Western media. I stepped forward and said "I am one of you. I think like you. But, I have a question." He said, "My brother, ask your question." I said, "I do accept that these students are influenced by Western ideals, but can we make them aware by beating them?" He said, "Nobody has beaten them." I said, "I saw it with my own eyes." He said, "They were trying to beat us, and we were just defending ourselves." I wanted to ask him how many of them were injured in comparison to the numerous injured students, but I decided not to continue this line of arguing. Instead, I tried to argue from another direction and asked: "When we shut down the domestic media, how could we expect the students not to seek out Western media outlets?" He replied, "The domestic newspapers were the home of the enemy; just name one of them that promoted Islamic values." I said. "*Farasoo* is one." He said, "The *Farasoo* newspaper was among the most aggressive newspapers directed against our supreme leader. The most corrupt articles were published in it. How can you call it a pro-Islamic newspaper?" I replied, "There has never been a newspaper named *Farasoo*. How can you tell a lie being a Muslim?" He was shocked for a while. Other *Basij* members tried to help him by testifying that, indeed, there was a newspaper called *Farasoo* during the Khatami administration!

D. Ray Heisey's Questions followed by Ehsan Shaghasemi's Response

D.R.H. Regarding your army experience, what motivated you to want to expose the real nature of the work of this division of the army?

E.S. The mission of Politics and Beliefs is no secret. They blatantly say they don't want "unbelievers" in the Iranian army. I wanted to bring this example to show a general tendency in the Iranian youth. They are less ideological these days and therefore many of them do not want to enter these kinds of institutions. One important thing I learned during my five months in this section of the Army was that there were some really good people in that section who believed in the theocratic government; they were honest, poor, and trustworthy. This taught me not to judge too soon.

D.R.H. Was it a personal experience that led you to protest your Army's assignment?

E.S. I did not favor working there. They said serving in this section would guarantee my safety and working there was very comfortable for a soldier. I was healthy, and I had no reason to seek comfort.

D.R.H. Regarding the participation in the demonstration rally, how did you feel about the girls participating with you in the rally?

E.S. You have lived in Iran and you know Iranian women enjoy some privileges (in addition to some limitations) compared to other countries. Resisting what women ask you to do in my country is considered rude behavior. After the girls insisted, I agreed to take them. In my culture protecting women is every man's duty. That is why I ran back to help them. It was a spontaneous reaction. The images on the TV which showed the *Basijis* and the police beating the women really incensed Iranians. Even Ahmadinejad's supporters called this a shameful behavior.

D.R.H. The girls said they wanted to participate for women's voices to be heard. Why is that particularly important in Iran?

E.S. Women are very active in cyberspace, but their presence on street rallies sends important messages to other people in the country and around the world. Their participation shows their numbers and their commitment.

D.R.H. Regarding the confrontation about the media, why does it appear that the authorities in Iran are predisposed to blaming foreign media for fomenting protests rather than accepting the fact that there may be genuine disagreement with the government about what they are doing?

E.S. They do not want to admit that there is a problem inside the country. The theocratic government must be the best in the world. Only the devil challenges the reign of God. However, calling Iranians demonic is a clear provocation. Therefore, they try to demonize foreign sources.

D.R.H. What in Iran's history or culture legitimizes or explains this behavior?

E.S. Iranians are a highly nationalist people and do not tolerate foreign intervention. The neutral policy of the Obama government at the time of the protests defeated the strategy of the Iranian authorities in connecting the Green Movement to the United States. Moreover, the Green Movement fired back by accusing the authorities of becoming the puppet of Russia and China.

D.R.H. How did you choose the discursive strategy you used with the member of the *Basij* militia?

E.S. Thanks to my experience in discourse analysis, I turned to what is known as "change footing." But, even the people who are not formally educated use these kinds of strategies, although they may not know the theories behind them. In Iran you should think twice before you speak truth to power. It may cost you your life.

D.R.H. What historical, cultural, or personal characteristic is being demonstrated in each of these instances that help us to understand the nature of the Iranian approach to speaking truth to power?

E.S. All three aspects, historical, cultural, and personal, play a role in the dialectical political processes in Iran. In speaking up, you should employ subtle methods to convince your audiences, implying your impartiality and, more importantly, avoiding direct confrontation. But at the appropriate moment, one must show courage and challenge power directly. I know this is a paradox, but there is a fine line between avoiding and taking on direct confrontations. The girls in the demonstrations chose direct confrontation, and they were right. Nonviolent methods are the most effective because they are the most difficult for the power to confront and, therefore, the government seems more interested in violent demonstrations. But, the presence of women is a big hindrance to the government. Sometimes protesters capture an antiriot guard, and when women come to save the policeman, the angry men cannot hurt him.

D. Ray Heisey's Response to Ehsan Shaghasemi's Questions

E.S. Why did you join a church that condemns war? Does your church condemn every kind of war, even in defense of your country?

D.R.H. I made a conscious decision to adopt a nonviolent approach to solving international conflict. I accept the principle taught by Jesus that we should love our enemies and bless those who curse us. How can one love his enemy and at the same time want to kill him in a war that is usually fought for the interests of the military-industrial complex that President Eisenhower warned against? In my view, the principle of nonviolence does not make an exception for defending one's country. Participating with those who take up arms is identifying with killing. It is the wrong way to solve problems. This church today allows people to hold a variety of views, including the right to defend one's country. But as a matter of principle, I still believe that it is morally wrong for me to support the military in armed conflict. I respect the right of others to hold opposing views, but taking this stand places me on the side of those who emphasize love and reconciliation, not hate and killing.

E.S. In the Kent State University shootings crisis, you were on the side of students. Did authorities threaten you to give up? Do American people think National Guard members opened fire on their own or do they think they had orders?

D.R.H. There are many opinions in the United States as to why the Kent State University incident happened. This is an oversimplification, but it may be generational; the younger people generally took the side of the students, and the older people sided with the National Guard and with the Nixon Administration. Some suggest that the students were protesting illegally, threatening the soldiers, and others think that the soldiers were unjustified in firing into the crowd of students who were exercising their right of free speech on their own campus.

The facts show that students were not physically close enough to hurt the soldiers, so the soldiers' fear for their safety was unjustified. Besides, one of the students killed was not even involved in the protests but was on her way to class. The facts also show that due to poor communication, the students had not been adequately informed that the rally had been banned, and those who knew about it considered the banning a violation of their right of free speech. For the governor to send in the National Guard troops to take control of the campus was considered by the faculty as a political action that resulted in an assault on the integrity and independence of the academic community. The President's Commission on Campus Unrest, called the Scranton Commission that investigated the Kent State shootings, concluded that the shootings were "unnecessary, unwarranted, and inexcusable" (Axelrod and Phillips 321).

Conclusion

Our two narratives present rhetorical strategies from two different cultures on speaking truth to power, which is an intellectual praxis. They show that it is possible to voice one's values and take a stand for freedom of speech in three ways:

First, these experiences demonstrate how speaking truth to power embodies personal and cultural values. Studies often neglect subjective accounts of events in order to remain "objective." Second, these experiences demonstrate how speaking truth to power integrates the cognitive and affective domains of a person's psyche in confronting the issue at hand. Intellectuals, like nonintellectuals in their society, have experiences that come from a life of discovering and interpreting events. But, intellectuals are more skillful in constructing discourses in an articulate manner that, in turn, may influence others to act as well. Third, these experiences demonstrate how speaking truth to power exposes perceived wrongdoing on the part of authorities who cannot continue in exercising their power unjustly because they are exposed.

Notes

1. Persia and Iran are terms referring to the same nation. But as the term Persian has more historic, linguistic, and cultural connotations, it is more often used when referring to cultural affairs of the Iranian people.
2. After the revolution of 1979, this section was added to the secular army of the Shah of Iran to allegedly keep the army "clean" of corrupt ideas.
3. *Basij* in Persian means "mobilization" and consists of ordinary people who are organized only in critical situations.
4. This is an annual commemoration of the killing of three students at a protest at the University of Tehran on Dec. 7, 1953, in the aftermath of a coup in which Mohammad Mosadeq, the democratically elected Prime Minister, was overthrown.

Works Cited

Axelrod, Alan, and Charles Phillips. *What Every American Should Know about American History: 225 Events that Shaped the Nation*. Avon, MA: Adams Media, 2008.

Eszterhas, Joe and Michael Roberts. "James Michener's Kent State: A Study in Distortion," *The Progressive* September 1971: 35–40.

Heisey, D. Ray, Calkins, Ken, and Jones, Daniel. "Excerpts from the Analysis of the Ohio Grand Jury Report." *No Heroes, No Villains: New Perspectives on Kent State and Jackson State*. Ed. Robert M. O'Neil, John P. Morris, and Raymond Mack. San Francisco: Jossey-Bass Inc., 1972. 139–144.

Karimi-Hakkak, Ahmad. "Protest and Perish: A History of the Writers' Association of Iran." *Iranian Studies*. 18.4 (1985): 189–229.

Michener, James A. *Kent State; What Happened and Why*. New York: Random House, 1971.

Moore, Carl M. and Heisey, D. Ray. "Not a Great Deal of Error...?" Unpublished paper. Copy in the Kent State University Special Collections and Archives, 1972.

O'Neil, Robert M, John P. Morris, and Raymond W. Mack. *No Heroes, No Villains New Perspectives on Kent State and Jackson State*. San Francisco: Jossey-Bass Inc., 1972.

Shamisa, Sirous. *Negahi Tazeh be Badi* (in Persian). Tehran: Mitra, 2008.

CHAPTER 13

IMAGINED COMMUNITY SERVICE:
QUEERING NARRATIVES OF PLACE
AND TIME IN SERVICE LEARNING

Amin Emika

> And they live for the most part in hope; for hope is for the future, and memory is of what has gone by, but for the young the future is long and the past short; for in the dawn of life nothing can be remembered, and everything [can be] hoped for.
>
> Aristotle, *On Rhetoric: A Theory of Civic Discourse*
>
> We can begin with endings.
>
> Thomas Newkirk, *The Performance of Self in Student Writing*

Globalization has made conceptual models that view the planet as a spaceship or village increasingly relevant for understanding how environmental degradation, technological innovation, and global capitalism have altered our understanding of space and time; however, these metaphors are incongruent with how most people understand and perform community in their everyday lives. As a result, one collateral impact of globalization may be increased anxiety over the language and practices that define community in an otherwise shrinking world. Many scholars, less reticent when drawing this connection, posit that we are currently facing a crisis of community. Adam Renner is one service-learning proponent who forwards this argument; however, since a crisis implicitly posits a previous period of stability, Renner is quick to question if a stable sense of community has ever truly existed (59). That he does not pursue this question further is not surprising since it would inevitably highlight the chimeric nature of community.

As Benedict Anderson has noted, *all* communities are imagined (6). For service-learning practitioners such an admission necessarily creates a degree of cognitive dissonance. This is because the overwhelming tendency is to privilege spaces outside the university as somehow authentic, real, and everyday. While this framework grants service learning a certain legitimacy, the benefit of recognizing communities as imagined is twofold; it positions service-learning practitioners as always, already involved with these communities, and—as Anderson notes—it highlights the importance of analyzing *how* these communities are imagined (6). Overstating this claim would fail to account for our inevitable engagement with *real* individuals and *real* issues; however, ignoring the ways that communities are imagined conveniently avoids considering how we participate in their construction. In the case of service-learning scholars and practitioners, a consideration of the dialogic relationship between narrative and action is also avoided.

Within our academic community, we burden scholarship with the responsibility of maintaining a critical, coherent sense of exactly what we are talking about when we talk about service learning. It is primarily moments like this—the simultaneous *now* of reading and writing—that elide differences in space and time, thereby substantiating our limited sense of fraternity. So much of who *we* are depends upon the page, and yet the boundaries between our service narratives and the history of service learning collapse in upon one another as both manipulate and are manipulated by the author. Paul Ricoeur explains this process—how history and narrative are mutually definable—by pointing out that a single event is not historic; rather, an event is defined through "its contribution to the development of a plot" (106). It is the organization of events that gives them meaning. The location of each event defines and is defined by the location and importance of all other events. This spatial understanding of how history and narrative develop is fitting since service learning is, fundamentally, a critique of the spatial politics that exist physically, culturally, and intellectually within and around universities.

In this chapter, I will briefly explore the spaces and events that service learning tends to privilege, the stories we are told by students about service, and the stories we tell ourselves. Integrating queer theory provides one way of disrupting these narratives and reimagining community work. After a critical appraisal of service learning in theory and practice, the final sections will begin to demonstrate the benefits of queer service learning. At its core, this chapter is about the connection between identity, narrative, and service; it is about troubling service as we work toward community and locating service learning in a queer time and place.[1]

Troubling Locations of Service Learning

While scholars such as Brooke Hessler have called attention to the power dynamics underlying how we choose to label community-based projects, service learning currently remains the best choice when speaking across contexts, projects, and disciplines. At the same time, service learning posits that education and community engagement happen concurrently. This limits what can be said about service learning without first locating the discussion within a particular field. As I am an instructor of Composition and Rhetoric, the chapter will approach service learning from a vantage point that is necessarily limited by my own disciplinary background and teaching experiences. Nonetheless, the academic discussions and classroom situations should be familiar across a variety of disciplines, and therefore the arguments derived from them should have an equally broad application. If an interdisciplinary audience is considered, the history of service learning might appear to offer a common foundation, but these narratives become continually more diverse and complex as our understanding of service learning matures.

It is generally accepted that our contemporary understanding of service learning originated during the mid-1980s. At this time service learning "was an innovation lingering on the periphery of the academy" (Harkavy and Hartley 418). With that in mind, it is not surprising that many articles written during the 1990s began by locating the field as new, marginal, and undertheorized. This framework allowed scholars to write themselves as pioneers into larger narratives of discovery. However, by the end of the 1990s, these writings were increasingly seen as ahistorical, and scholars responded by uncovering historic and theoretical precursors for service learning. Taken in conversation with one another, the current body of scholarship on service learning highlights the narrative function of history and the impossibility of meta-narratives. These histories present a sea of influences that encompasses Aristotle, Franklin, and Dewey, and a constellation of origins that chart connections from the founding of land-grant universities to the Tennessee Valley Authority and the Civil Rights

Movement (Rocheleau, Harkavy, and Hartley, Stanton, Giles, and Cruz). These works highlight that service learning must be understood as having multiple, simultaneously occurring histories. Without undercutting the importance of this line of scholarship, there are limits on how valuable these histories are for understanding contemporary service learning. To the extent that practitioners in the early 1990s understood themselves as pioneers and were only later informed of these complex roots, it is equally important to consider the impact and recurrence of the discovery narrative in service-learning scholarship.

Like the spatial metaphors used by writing instructors—most notably Mina Shaughnessy—early service-learning scholarship mediated the increased stress and time commitments of service learning through a variety of expansionist narratives. These writings encouraged community engagement by privileging spaces outside of the university as *real* locations where *real* work takes place. Contemporary scholarship continues to claim that service learning increases the space of the classroom, improves the civic character of students, and adds value to assignments by providing real contexts and audiences for student work. As Nedra Reynolds notes in *Geographies of Writing,* the way a discipline conceives itself spatially—for example, through spatial metaphors—is important because these spatial relationships become conceptual foundations that have epistemological, pedagogical, and social consequences (27). For service learning, spatial metaphors help us recognize gaps to bridge and spaces to transverse, both in the community and in the curriculum. This can lead to meaningful connections between coursework and community issues and between two imagined communities, the university and the surrounding community. At the same time, frontier imagery can also lead to imperialist encounters. For example, unequal power relations between teachers, students, service providers, and community members can become explicit when resolving cultural conflicts or constructing project goals and timelines. The origin of service learning within academic institutions means that where these fault lines appear, they will tend to underline—rather than undermine—preexisting systems of privilege. The inherent difficulty in creating equitable service-learning projects is textually represented in the space allocated to various stakeholders within most articles on service learning. Each article reflects the real struggle to balance institutional, professional, student, and community needs within a single course, and decisions about which voices to include and what to frame as important often demonstrate the unequal power dynamic mentioned above.

One troublesome metaphor that works as a conceptual foundation for service learning is the university as ivory tower. While the ivory tower is occasionally referenced explicitly, the spatial and power implications of the metaphor are implicit throughout the writing on service learning. This metaphor can be a useful because it highlights the decussating cracks within the idealized notion of the university and marks the spots of its faltering structural integrity. It represents not only a perceived distance from real-world events but also a bourgeois elevation above them. The cream color continues to highlight the exclusion and marginalization of people of color and issues of race within the academy, while the phallic structure points to the continued masculine nature of academia: subtly representing its able-bodied, heteronormative character through a virile penetration of the skyline. However, when called upon uncritically, service learning only draws upon the spatial implications and power dynamics between abstract universities and imagined communities. At the same time, these works advocate for greater participation in community-based projects that require an understanding of all the realities listed above. What is most troubling is how the spatial logic of service learning reinforces the very binary it attempts to undermine. Locating the university at a distance, arguing that service learning "seemingly breaches the bifurcation of lofty academics with the lived reality of everyday life," misses the university's position within the culture as a whole (Butin vii). To imagine only one setting as real dismisses the question: how larger social issues adapt to and are prevalent in every setting even if their presence is an absence.

Concerning Student Narratives about Service Learning

Even a limited overview of how we position ourselves in relation to community projects should prompt further consideration of how and why we implement service-learning courses. The common justifications idealize external environments as intrinsically educational and do not adequately complicate the space of the classroom. A failure to integrate both environments encourages students to treat the course just like any other, with an added volunteer component. For many students, their understanding of volunteerism is likely to originate in a middle-class value system that uses community service to alleviate social anxieties by reifying notions of community and individual identity. In this context, even when community service is recognized as self-serving, it is typically viewed as the character defect of a particular individual rather than something that is endemic to the system as a whole. This bolsters the notion that community service is a fundamentally altruistic endeavor, and this outlook encourages community projects that are overly simplistic, impatient, and insensitive. Service-learning instructors face the difficult task of promoting civic engagement at the same time that they undermine many of the narrative features that encourage participation. A failure to do this—the unreflective implementation of student-centered service learning—reinforces preexisting cultural logics that maintain inequality and use that inequality to reestablish particular class-based notions of community and identity. To the extent that we can counteract this, service learning must operate from a more complex dialogue where all participants interrogate the underlying factors that create and sustain the need for service.

As instructors, we need to seriously question our own motivations before requiring students to engage in community-based projects. The writing on service learning, however, continues the larger pedagogical trend where administrative issues and logistical concerns overshadow these considerations. In her article, "Difficult Stories: Service-Learning, Race, Class, and Whiteness," Ann Green captures the current trend in scholarship and the need to move beyond pragmatics when she states:

> As service-learning scholarship enters its second generation, the writing on service-learning must begin to reflect our own—and our institutions'—complex relationship to "doing good." Since service-learning is a widely accepted part of many college curriculums, those who write about service-learning must go beyond the pragmatics of when and how to integrate service into composition courses and begin to theorize who participates in service-learning programs and why they do so.
>
> (276)

Service-learning scholars, perhaps more than others, must be prepared to present complex justifications that genuinely explore concepts like civic engagement and social justice. Neil Postman has recognized that if we want to promote, complicate, and adequately address student questions we must first be willing to discover and discuss our work in terms that are "metaphysical in nature, not technical" (27). For service learning, moving scholarship in this direction will give educators the language necessary to cocreate and meaningfully discuss our community projects.

One reason that these discussions are necessary is the ideological perspectives and past community service experiences students bring with them into service-learning courses. While David Bartholomae has detailed the process where students "invent the university" in their writing, community service is an increasingly problematic subject for student writing precisely because of its familiarity. While Green alluded to the increasing likelihood that students will experience service learning through many disciplinary perspectives within the university, they are also increasingly encouraged to see community service as a prerequisite for college admission. For first-year writing instructors, disrupting student preconceptions about service and their narratives must be seen as a primary focus of the course. As Alan France has noted, introductory writing courses are "crucially implicated in the process of cultural reproduction" (593). One reason is that these courses require students to write on topics and in settings and genres that are more intimate than many other introductory courses. This claim becomes more universal when service learning is integrated into coursework, and instructors across the disciplines should recognize that service narratives are—or at least should be—intensely personal. Therefore, we should remember that an invitation to write about service experiences, just like writing about other significant life events, "is hardly the open and innocent invitation that it appears to be—for we as teachers have criteria, often unstated, for the kind of subjectivity that we will take seriously" (Newkirk 11). The result of service-learning courses is that at the same time that students are inventing the university they are also inventing themselves and the world around them.

The reality that many students are underprepared for community-based work can be seen in the variety of problem narratives that are presented in service-learning scholarship. For example, Wendi Maloney provides a service narrative that demonstrates how dramatic student preconceptions can be about unfamiliar communities. She begins by outlining how a service project took place in a low-income, predominantly African American neighborhood in St. Louis. After the project was completed, students were asked to reflect on the experience. These reflections indicated how "working with the residents changed the negative preconceptions" that students previously held about the space; however, one student stated "that he had never been scared because he brought a knife" (Maloney 41). This student, originally from a Chicago suburb, likely saw the service project as a mandate to enter a space he perceived as hostile. While the decision to bring a weapon and the male posturing inherent in this comment both indicate the need to complicate gender within service-learning classrooms, it is also important to interrogate how the location was prefigured as dangerous through a complex "sociospatial construction of difference" (Reynolds 109). This student's reaction must be considered within a complex matrix of influences including the spatial resonance of *city* having grown up *outside* Chicago, conscious and subconscious triggers and reactions to racial difference and class stratification, and the larger student discourses on campus about this particular space.

Queering Service-Learning Narratives

There is a certain formula that is used when introducing queer theory. Most texts begin by working to disambiguate the theoretical use of the term queer from its increasingly historic use as a pejorative. This decision is interesting inasmuch as it creates a subtle tension in the opening of many queer texts. After demarcating what queer theory is not, scholars tend to either bask or struggle in the relative ambiguity that remains. For many, "part of queer's semantic clout, part of its political efficacy depends on its resistance to definition" (Jagose 1). Historically, scholars such as David Halperin and Michael Warner have forwarded arguments of this type; however, it becomes increasingly difficult to ignore the extent to which queer theory has been institutionally situated, claimed, and contained. To the extent that certain disciplines have integrated queer theory into upper-level special topics and survey courses, it continues "to resist closure and remain in the process of ambiguous (un)becoming" (Sullivan v). This is, in part, because academic discourse promotes a degree of inconsistency when it comes to definitions. That a leading queer theorist can begin a book-length work on the subject by requesting that expectations for a comprehensive understanding be lowered should highlight the limitations of providing a genuinely useful introduction within the limited space of this project (*Queer Theories* 1). Nonetheless, understanding the benefit of queer theory for service learning requires certain boundaries be drawn.

As Lisa Duggan has noted, the term "queer" often functions as "a synonym for lesbian or gay" (157). While this understanding is theoretically limiting, it is important to recognize the origins of queer theory. At the outset of *In a Queer Time and Place,* Judith Halberstam states that "queer time" and "queer space" develop from an "opposition to the institutions of family, heterosexuality, and reproduction" (Halberstam 1). While these categories are meant very literally, they also represent space, identity, and time more broadly. As our histories connect service learning to analytic philosophers and pragmatists, we must also embrace that we are creating service-learning courses within a postmodern landscape. Queer theories offer service learning an understanding of time, space, and identity that is intimately mapped on bodies through discursive practices. For example, queer time provides service-learning practitioners with a framework for understanding a ruptured form of service that is less intimately tied to "our foundational faith in the reproduction of futurity" (Edelman 16–17). The underlying optimism of service learning can stand in opposition to the more nihilistic drives of some queer theorists, but there is a need to break from progress narratives mapped across linear time. The academic time of students and instructors, for example, is already fragmented in ways that are atypical and problematic for community projects. While student assignments must be completed in order to assign grades, these projects connect to larger social issues. In order to maintain responsible community projects we must fight against the "seemingly inexorable march of narrative time" and imagine queer locations for service.

The university represents one queer location for reimagining service learning. For example, introductory writing courses are a contested location primarily because of our preconceptions of where service can occur and what constitutes service projects. Ellen Cushman presents a common argument against service learning in the first-year classroom. She argues that first-year students should not have the stress of adjusting to college "compounded by first-year writing courses requiring service" ("Sustainable" 49). Even if we ignore how this claim problematically imagines students in first-year courses as sharing homogeneous educational and life narratives, this argument clearly understands the labor and location of service beyond the classroom. In combination this spatial configuration of service and outlook on first-year courses have unintended consequences. As Bruce Herzberg notes, logistical discussions on implementing service learning should recognize the danger of "presuming that there is a serving class and a served class," and the scholarship on service learning needs to remain mindful of a readership that extends beyond tenure faculty at research universities (555). Absent from Cushman's argument is any consideration of how her position could impact students at two-year colleges or graduate instructors and contingent faculty, many of whom never leave the first-year classroom.

Linda Alder-Kassner and Katherine Stavrianopoulos represent two proponents of a more immediate integration of service learning. Recognizing the potential benefits for first-year or underprepared students, their articles argue that service learning can curb student attrition, introduce and connect them to the surrounding community, and provide a subject matter that may be easier for students to translate into academic writing. However, integrating outreach initiatives requires careful consideration of the needs and capabilities of student writers and an understanding of the services that are needed within particular communities. These questions require highly contextualized answers, and so it is unlikely that an argument favoring or opposing service learning in the first-year classrooms could ever be universally appropriate. Recognizing the merit in both positions, and the troubles facing service-learning courses generally, a third option is to create first-year courses that are community oriented. Given that students increasingly enter first-year classrooms with past service experience, a community-oriented classroom encourages students to consider and question the foundational concepts of service learning, to critically reflect on past service narratives, and to learn about local issues and service providers.

A community-oriented classroom acknowledges that first-year writing instructors are limited in their ability to actualize Cushman's call for "sustainable service-learning programs" because many inhabit a tenuous relationship to the university and/or the larger community. Beyond framing service so that every instructor is invited into the discussion, these primarily conceptual courses could distribute the overwhelming demand of most service-learning courses to make projects relevant and encourage complex considerations of community issues simultaneously. The fact that even in the best contexts, "service experiences are more likely to transform and enlighten the student than the community" highlights the need not only for sustained participation, but for vertical integration of place-based, service-oriented curriculum (Hessler 36). An early emphasis on exploring student identities and identity categories more broadly can help offset the problematic ways that many students conceptualize and execute community projects.

Broader definitions of queerness highlight identity as fluid and better able to inhabit multiple, contradictory understandings of self (Duggan 157). For service learning, queer theory can help expose students to the contradictions in their own identities and to dwell in those contradictions long enough to understand how identity is socially constructed. The benefit of community-oriented courses is the reflective space they create for both instructors and students. The process of meaningfully deconstructing identity is necessarily one of discovery that requires time and space. Instructors must also have the space to begin these discussions at locations that seem wholly removed from the larger aims, but that meet students in safe locations where they are prepared to participate. In my own courses, I begin with discussions of the self-censorship and selection that occur in routine writing. Appropriately framed, discussions as mundane as e-mail etiquette allow students to explore how "all forms of 'self-expression,' all of our ways of 'being personal' are forms of performance" (Newkirk 3). This allows us to discuss how these performances work through "their selectivity; [where] every act of self-presentation involves the withholding of information that might undermine the idealized impression the performer wants to convey" (Newkirk 3). As these textual discussions transition into discussions of identity more broadly, students can begin to interrogate how categories such as race and gender are formed through the repetition of various behaviors until they are ultimately perceived as inherent.

One way to approach this task is to begin with exercises that ask students to focus on important moments in their development from childhood into adulthood since "development can be read only as normalization" (Butler 36). Students can then share these stories and construct lists of gender-specific and gender-ambiguous behaviors, those that are encouraged and those that are viewed suspiciously. In the past, these examples have prompted students to interrogate the societal function of phrases such as "becoming a man" or "act like a man," and have helped students see how identity is "produced through the compulsory ordering" of these life events into coherent narratives (Butler 32). In his article "Transgender Rhetorics: (Re)Composing Narratives of the Gendered Body," Jonathan Alexander approaches gender construction using transgender texts. He found that using a transgender narrative (female to male) helped students question gender as natural because when "given such a description, such self-narration about a highly conscious and purposeful self-fashioning, students felt compelled to accept that [the author] is indeed a man" (46). At the same time, that students generally valued this narrative highlights their own resistance to view their identity as compulsory. While this is understandable, underlying all of these discussions a tension has been planted between students' desire to retain agency and the development of identity as a collaboratively written text.

Students are then prepared to critically consider preconceived notions of community, community need, and volunteerism through the same constructivist lens. In the past, local agencies have sent a representative to provide students with information on current needs, how to volunteer, the issues they address, and the communities they serve. The larger social issues that local agencies bring into the classroom helps to disrupt the "illusion of self-sufficiency and ... the trap (and tedium) of self-referentiality" that can develop as students deconstruct previous notions of identity (Hall 42). Drawing from earlier discussions, as students question what makes a community, they are quick to recognize multiple communities and to question who determines and defines those communities. This approach lead one group researching homelessness to discover discrepancies in how various agencies defined homeless, to question how these definitions were created, and to explore their impact on multiple stakeholders. Then, during peer review, students look for connections between their own issues and those selected by other students in an attempt to find connections between what they often perceive as disparate issues. The course's larger process of discovery can be exciting, but it is also demanding and exhausting. This course structure and subject matter requires additional work and a greater personal investment from students and instructors in order to be successful. To sustain this classroom requires that students and teachers cocreate idealistic narratives about the future and connect classroom work to those narratives.

QUEERING FUTURES

While utopian thinking can be a powerful tool within a service-learning pedagogy, I recognize, where it can become dangerous both theoretically and practically. For example, in his book *Teaching Student Writing: Confessions, Meditations, and Rants,* Lad Tobin dismisses what he calls the "grandiose fantasy" that teachers can have a dramatic impact on every student, arguing that this fantasy leads to every teacherly ill imaginable (91). In discussing this fantasy Tobin calls upon that ultimate creator of national fantasy: movies. What I am interested in, which I feel he overlooks, is the fact that all of these fantasies point to failure, often multiple and successive failures. In fact, while it is not their focus, failure typically outweighs success. Considering all the inconsistencies within these movies, including that most protagonists teach only one class, I would argue that the only truly defeating fantasy, the only one that may in fact lead to exactly the resentment and burnout that Tobin warns of, is the illusion of an ending and the idea that such an ending is soon approaching and so universally recognized that we will receive something as overblown as an auditorium full of cheering fans, or at the very least a standing ovation from students atop their desks.

However, a fair bit of the literature advocating service learning attempts to renew just such a fantasy. Unsurprisingly, when classroom practice is included along with theory, there is often a sense of disappointment in how the class concludes. It is not surprising then that all too frequently agencies are suspicious of service-learning courses simply because of the rate at which such programs and community ties are created and then, at the semester's conclusion, abandoned ("Sustainable" 40-1). I would also argue that students enter service in a very similar mindset to that of Tobin's teacher: "I will build this house and end homelessness," or, "I will plant this tree and end global warming." In my experience, on a fundamental level, this is the mentality that most students have toward service, and I believe a large reason they find service to be disappointing and why, in many instances, they are not particularly good at providing it.

Therefore, unlike Tobin, I would argue that some version of fantasy must be kept alive, especially in a service-learning course where the goals of the classroom intersect such incredibly ambitious goals for substantive social change. However, in order to keep such utopian fantasies from creating exactly the negative outcomes Tobin posits as inevitable requires humility and the ability to recognize that if the outcome is truly utopian, then it is always mutating upon the horizon of possibility.[2] Therefore, rather than find some faulty compromise with our desire for stasis and finality, our nebulous, elusive ideals should, continue to drive us to repeatedly stand in the face of sleepy, disengaged freshman and attempt to facilitate and support meaningful dialogue. This is not because we have submitted to the fantasy that we will succeed, but rather because we recognize that whatever we deliver to our students, and they to us will and should be as much a failure as a success. Similarly, students should not be shunned for the goals that motivate their service but challenged to conceptualize even more radical goals, while at the same time being provided with a fuller understanding of the complex, interconnected nature of the issues addressed through the course. They should be motivated to see the ways in which they are always already a part of those issues they "reach out" to address.

While the essay fails to illuminate all of the possible points at which students can be challenged to reinterpret cultural texts—for instance, discussion of class, race, sexuality, or national identity could not be included for lack of space—I hope that from the brief look at some of my classroom practices analyzing the construction of gender that it is possible to see how each form of identity is vulnerable and infinitely approachable within a queered context. Implemented at the outset, these tactics develop a way to counter the dominant modes of thinking about community service as well as, in my case, writing and thinking about writing. The nation's mentality toward outreach is often demeaning in the way it is implemented and frequently calls upon conceptions of charity, while it reifies white, middle-class values. This allows those who engage in service to not only feel good about "helping," but it also validates their own social position as correct without ever questioning the ways in which that social position (and the privileges it confers) are part of what creates the needs they are variously attempting to combat. Thus, as students begin to address the complex nature of their own social positions, they may be more likely to locate agency within the communities they attempt to serve. They may then recognize those communities as consisting of individuals who may not subscribe to the student's notions of community, but may still be trapped by the student's mode of viewing them, the dominant discourse concerning what "their problem" is, and trapped by how we script "humane" discourse and how institutions script services. Hopefully, after such a course students will question how providing service impacts not only those they serve in a conventional sense, but also the many complex ways it impacts personhood, in terms of both the person seeking service and the person providing it. The deconstruction of any stable sense of community may then help students understand that there is a genuine need for service. When we lay down our scripts we become more aware that everyone's hand is extended.

NOTES

1. While indebted to the work of Judith Halberstam, this chapter will draw a broader definition of the term in relation to time and space.
2. This conception of utopian thinking originates in the work of queer theorists José E. Muñoz and Donald Hall.

WORKS CITED

Adler-Kassner, Linda. "Digging a Groundwork for Writing: Underprepared Students and Community Service Courses." *College Composition and Communication* 46.4 (1995): 552–55.

Alexander, Jonathan. "Transgender Rhetorics: (Re)Composing Narratives of the Gendered Body." *College Composition and Communication* 57.1 (2005): 45–82.

Anderson, Benedict. *Imagined Communities: Reflections on the Origin and Spread of Nationalism*. New York: Verso, 2006.

Aristotle. *On Rhetoric: A Theory of Civic Discourse*. Trans. George A. Kennedy. New York: Oxford UP, 1991.

Bartholomae, David. "Inventing the University." *Literacy: A Critical Sourcebook*. Ed. Ellen Cushman, Eugene R. Kintgen, Barry M. Kroll, and Mike Rose. Boston: St. Martin's Press, 2001. 511–24.

Bauer, Dale M. "Indecent Proposals: Teachers in the Movies." *College English* 60.3 (1998): 301–17.

Butin, Dan W. *Service-Learning in Higher Education: Critical Issues and Directions.* New York: Palgrave MacMillan, 2005.
Butler, Judith. *Gender Trouble: Feminism and the Subversion of Identity.* London: Routledge, 1999.
Cushman, Ellen. "Sustainable Service Learning Programs." *College Composition and Communication* 54.1 (2002): 40–65.
Duggan, Lisa. "Making It Perfectly Queer." *Sex Wars: Sexual Dissent and Political Culture.* 10th ed. Ed. Lisa Duggan and Nan D. Hunter. London: Routledge, 2006. 149–63.
Edelman, Lee. *No Future: Queer Theory and the Death Drive.* Durham, NC: Duke UP Books, November 15, 2004.
France, Alan W. "Assigning Places: The Function of Introductory Composition as a Cultural Discourse." *College English* 55.6 (1993): 593–609.
Green, Ann E. "Difficult Stories: Service-Learning, Race, Class, and Whiteness." *College Composition and Communication* 55.2 (2003): 276–301.
Halberstam, Judith. *In a Queer Time and Place: Transgender Bodies, Subcultural Lives.* New York: New York UP, 2005.
Hall, Donald E. *Reading Sexualities: Hermeneutic Theory and the Future of Queer Studies.* London: Routledge, 2009.
——. *Queer Theories.* New York: Palgrave MacMillan, 2003.
Harkavy, Ira and Matthew Hartley. "Pursuing Franklin's Dream: Philosophical and Historical Roots of Service-Learning." *American Journal of Community Psychology* 46.3/4 (2010): 418–27.
Herzberg, Bruce. "Community Service and Critical Teaching." *College Composition and Communication* 45.3 (1994): 307–19.
Hessler, Brooke. "Composing and Institutional Identity: The Terms of Community Service in Higher Education." *Language and Learning across the Disciplines* 4.3 (2000): 27–42.
Jagose, Annamarie. *Queer Theory: An Introduction.* New York: New York UP, 1996.
Maloney, Wendi A. "The Community as a Classroom." *Academe* 86.4 (2000): 38–42.
Newkirk, Thomas. "Finding a Language for Difficulty: Silences in Our Teaching Stories." *Holding on to Good Ideas in a Time of Bad Ones: Six Literacy Principles Worth Fighting For.* Portsmouth, NH: Heinemann, 2009. 157–74.
——. *The Performance of Self in Student Writing.* Portsmouth, NH: Heinemann, 1997.
Renner, Adam. "Teaching Community, Praxis, and Courage: A Foundations Pedagogy of Hope and Humanization." *Educational Studies* 45.1 (2009): 59–79.
Reynolds, Nedra. *Geographies of Writing: Inhabiting Places and Encountering Difference.* Carbondale, IL: Southern Illinois UP, 2004.
Rocheleau, Jordy. "Theoretical Roots of Service-Learning: Progressive Education and the Development of Citizenship." *Service Learning: History,*

Theory, and Issues. Ed. Bruce W. Speck and Sherry L. Hoppe. Westport, CT: Praeger, 2004. 3–23.

Stanton, Timothy K., Dwight E. Giles Jr, and Nadinne I. Cruz. *Service-Learning: A Movement's Pioneers Reflect on Its Origins, Practice, and Future.* San Francisco: Jossey-Bass Inc., 1999.

Stavrinanopoulos, Katherine. "Service Learning within the Freshman Year Experience." *College Student Journal* 42.2 (2008): 703–12.

Sullivan, Nikki. *A Critical Introduction to Queer Theory.* New York: New York UP, 2003.

Tobin, Lad. *Reading Student Writing: Confessions, Meditations, and Rants.* Portsmouth, NH: Heineman, 2004.

GPSR Compliance

The European Union's (EU) General Product Safety Regulation (GPSR) is a set of rules that requires consumer products to be safe and our obligations to ensure this.

If you have any concerns about our products, you can contact us on

ProductSafety@springernature.com

In case Publisher is established outside the EU, the EU authorized representative is:

Springer Nature Customer Service Center GmbH
Europaplatz 3
69115 Heidelberg, Germany

www.ingramcontent.com/pod-product-compliance
Lightning Source LLC
LaVergne TN
LVHW011817060526
838200LV00053B/3812